Protecting the Displaced

Protecting the Displaced

Deepening the Responsibility to Protect

Edited by

Sara E. Davies and Luke Glanville

MARTINUS NIJHOFF PUBLISHERS

LEIDEN • BOSTON
2010

Also partly published as Volume 2, issue 1-2 (2010) of Brill's journal *Global Responsibility to Protect.*

This book is printed on acid-free paper.

Library of Congress Cataloging-in-Publication Data

Protecting the displaced : deepening the responsibility to protect / edited by Sara E. Davies and Luke Glanville.
p. cm.
Includes index.
ISBN 978-90-04-18403-9 (pbk. : alk. paper) 1. Refugees--Legal status, laws, etc.--United States. 2. Internally displaced persons--Legal status, laws, etc.--United States. I. Davies, Sara Ellen. II. Glanville, Luke.

KF4836.P76 2010
342.7308'3--dc22

2010011395

ISBN 978 90 04 184 039

PRINTED IN THE NETHERLANDS

Contents

List of Contributors

Alex J. Bellamy is Professor of International Relations and Executive Director of the Asia-Pacific Centre for the Responsibility at the University of Queensland, Australia. His recent books include 'The Responsibility to Protect: The Global Effort to End Mass Atrocities (Polity, 2009) and (with Paul D. Williams), 'Understanding Peacekeeping' (2nd edition, Polity, 2010). Alex is also co-Editor-in-Chief of Global Responsibility to Protect.

Roberta Cohen co-founded the Brookings Institution Project on Internal Displacement and co-directed it from 1997-2007. She also served for more than a decade as principal senior adviser to the Representative of the United Nations Secretary-General on Internally Displaced Persons and the Representative of the Secretary-General on the Human Rights of Internally Displaced Persons. Today, she is a Non-Resident Senior Fellow in Foreign Policy Studies at the Brookings Institution, Senior Advisor to the Brookings-Bern Project on Internal Displacement, and Senior Associate at Georgetown University's Institute for the Study of International Migration. She remains Senior Adviser to the Representative of the UN Secretary-General. For her publications on internal displacement, she won (together with Francis Deng) the 2005 Grawemeyer Award for Ideas Improving World Order.

Sara E. Davies is an Australian Research Council Postdoctoral Fellow at the Griffith Asia Institute and Centre for Governance and Public Policy, Griffith University. Dr Davies is author of *Legitimising Rejection: International Refugee Law in Southeast Asia* (Martinus Nijhoff, 2007) and has published a number of articles concerning international refugee law and refugee policy in Southeast Asia. She is author of *The Global Politics of Health* (Polity Press, forthcoming 2010) and co-Editor-in-Chief of Global Responsibility to Protect.

Luke Glanville is a Research Fellow in the Griffith Asia Institute and Centre for Governance and Public Policy, Griffith University, Australia. He recently submitted his PhD thesis at the University of Queensland. He has articles published or forthcoming in European Journal of International Relations and Journal of Genocide Research. Luke is co-Editor-in-Chief of Global Responsibility to Protect.

Emma Haddad's interests and expertise span the policy and academic worlds. Emma has a Ph.D. from the London School of Economics and Political Science for which she was awarded the 2004 British International Studies Association prize for the best thesis in International Studies. Recent publications include The Refugee in International Society: Between Sovereigns (Cambridge University Press: 2008) and contributions to Government and Opposition (2008) and Borderscapes: Hidden Geographies and Politics at Territory's Edge (Minnesota: 2007). Emma is currently Director of International Policy in the UK Border Agency. She has worked in a number of policy advisor roles, including in DG Justice, Freedom and Security at the European Commission where she specialised in the external relations of immigration and asylum.

Susan F. Martin holds the Donald G. Herzberg Chair in International Migration and serves as the Director of the Institute for the Study of International Migration in the School of Foreign Service at Georgetown University. Her recent publications include Women, Migration and Conflict: Breaking a Deadly Cycle (ed.); Mexico-U.S. Migration Management: A Binational Approach (ed.); Managing Migration: The Promise of Cooperation; Beyond the Gateway: Immigrants in a Changing America (ed.); The Uprooted: Improving Humanitarian Responses to Forced Migration; and Refugee Women. Dr. Martin earned her MA and Ph.D. in American Studies from the University of Pennsylvania and her BA in History from Douglass College, Rutgers University.

Erin Mooney has been engaged, both as a researcher and practitioner, in the issue of protection for internally displaced persons (IDPs) since 1992. She has worked extensively throughout Africa, the Balkans and the Caucasus as well as in Asia and the Americas. From 1995-2006, she served with the United Nations Representative of the Secretary-General on IDPs, from 2001 as Senior Adviser. She was Deputy Director of the Brookings Institution project on Internal Displacement (2001-2006) and served with the UN High Commissioner for Human Rights (1995-2001), responsible for UN mandates on IDPs and on Human Rights and Mass Exoduses. From 2006-2009, she was Senior Protection Officer with ProCap, a small cadre of senior experts deployed to strengthen the UN's protection response in humanitarian crises; recent postings include Bosnia-Herzegovina, Chad, Georgia and Somalia. She has authored over 40 peer-reviewed publications on internal displacement as well as numerous international policy and guidance documents in use by the UN, regional organizations, Governments, and civil society, including *Policy* *for the Protection of Internally Displaced Persons* (Inter-Agency Standing Committee, 1999), *Addressing Internal Displacement: A Framework for National Responsibility* (Brookings, 2005) published in over 12 languages; and as primary co-author of the *Handbook for the Protection of Internally Displaced Persons* (UN, 2007 and 2010). Currently, she is a Visiting Lecturer in International Relations at the University of Toronto and a consultant on IDP issues to: the Government of Georgia (for USAID), the UN Special Representative of the Secretary-General on Children and Armed Conflict, and the Brookings Institution (on the interface between national responsibility for IDPs and the Responsibility to Protect - R2P).

Phil Orchard is a Lecturer in Peace and Conflict Studies and International Relations at the University of Queensland. He received his PhD from the University of British Columbia and is a former Canadian Department of National Defence Security and Defence Forum Post-Doctoral Fellow. He has also served as the Assistant to the Representative of the UN Secretary-General for Internally Displaced Persons. His research focuses on the origins and evolution of state policy towards protecting the displaced.

Paul D. Williams is Associate Professor in the Elliott School of International Affairs at The George Washington University, USA. He is author of *British Foreign Policy under New Labour, 1997–2005* (Palgrave-Macmillan, 2005); coauthor of *Understanding Peacekeeping* (Polity, 2nd edn, 2010); editor of *Security Studies: An Introduction* (Routledge, 2008); and co-editor of *The International Politics of Mass Atrocities: The Case of Darfur* (Routledge, 2010). His primary research interests are in contemporary peace operations and Africa's international relations.

Protecting the Displaced: Introduction

Sara E. Davies and Luke Glanville

The concept of the 'responsibility to protect' was recently invoked in the landmark African Union Convention for the Protection and Assistance of Internally Displaced Persons in Africa. This Convention, for the first time, calls upon states to recognise the rights of internally displaced persons (IDPs) to humanitarian assistance, and defines the obligations of states and armed groups to protect uprooted citizens. The Convention not only applies to those forced into displacement by conflict, but also natural disasters. As the UN High Commissioner for Refugees, António Guterres, said after the African Union adopted the Convention on 23 October 2009: 'this represents the concept of "responsibility to protect" in action. It demonstrates that national sovereignty is fully compatible with the responsibility to protect'.[1] This Convention will come into force when, and if, it is ratified by 15 African Union member states. Surprisingly, this is the first time that international law has been created to try and address the lack of protection that IDPs have within their home country. Though this Convention is not yet in force and only applies to the African continent, it is significant that the African Union – the first region to adopt the responsibility to protect – has also been the first to codify the humanitarian and protection needs of those displaced within their home country. The UNHCR reported 42 million forcibly displaced people worldwide at the end of 2008 – this includes 15.2 million refugees, 827,000 asylum-seekers (pending cases) and 26 million IDPs.[2] Whose responsibility is it to protect people when their home country no longer wishes to? How can the international community step in to assure such persons protection when the home country is unwilling? The African Union adoption of the Convention is significant for advancing the principle of sovereignty as responsibility into policy, but is it

[1] Melissa Flemming and Yusuf Hassan, 'African Union adopts major convention to protect and assist the internally displaced', *Reuters AlertNet*, 23 October 2009. http://www.alertnet.org/thenews/newsdesk/UNHCR/9ae65e392e513d8aee119d50b88ebfd5.htm Accessed 30 October 2009.

[2] UNHCR, *UNHCR – 2008 Global Trends: Refugees, Asylum-seekers, Returnees, Internally Displaced and Stateless Persons*. http://www.unhcr.org/4a375c426.html Accessed 30 October 2009.

premature for High Commissioner Guterres to label this document as the responsibility to protect in action? These are some of the questions that this volume seeks to answer.

As those who have followed the responsibility to protect debate are intimately aware, member states at the United Nations 2005 World Summit agreed that the 'responsibility to protect' (R2P) principle imposed upon each individual state a primary responsibility to protect its population from genocide, war crimes, ethnic cleansing and crimes against humanity. When the state is unable to uphold their responsibility, the international community is to assist states to exercise their responsibility. The significance of R2P for refugees and IDPs is that these are often the persons at most risk from genocide and mass atrocities. When a state commits to protect IDPs and refugees, they are exercising their responsibility to protect. However, as has been noted by those concerned with the protection of refugees and displaced persons, there has been relatively little debate about how the R2P principle – in practice - enhances the work of those who have long advocated a link between the protection of IDPs and refugees with the principle of sovereignty as responsibility.[3] Furthermore, it is unclear to what extent R2P protects people in situations of displacement due to natural disaster, severe economic crises, food shortages and disease outbreaks? Opinion is divided between those calling for the application of R2P when states fail to protect persons in such instances,[4] and those who demand that R2P remain restricted to the duty to protect under the remit of paragraphs 138 and 139 in the World Summit document.[5]

Erika Feller from UNHCR argued in 2006 that the responsibility to protect 'should imply that affected states, donor governments, and partner agencies alike make all efforts to bring sovereignty, political will, mandates and resources into alignment with better protection'.[6] Yet prior to the recent African Union Convention for IDPs, we have seen little policy elaboration from states or international organisations on how such an alignment between R2P and displaced persons may apply in the day to day protection needs of IDPs and refugees, or to what extent the responsibility to protect should be broadened to accommodate instances where people need protection, and not only from genocide and mass atrocities. As such, the purpose of this book is to invite

[3] Brian Barbour and Brian Gorlick, 'Embracing the "Responsibility to Protect": A Repertoire of Measures Including Asylum for Potential Victims', *International Journal of Refugee Law*, 20/4: 533-66 (2008).

[4] Lloyd Axworthy and Allan Rock, 'R2P: An Unfinished Agenda', *Global Responsibility to Protect*, 1/1: 54-69 (2009).

[5] Eli Stamnes, '"Speaking R2P" and the Prevention of Mass Atrocities', *Global Responsibility to Protect*, 1/1: 70-89 (2009).

[6] Quoted in Barbour and Gorlick, 'Embracing the "Responsibility to Protect"', p. 566.

some of the leading thinkers and practitioners on displacement to elaborate on the conceptual and practical challenges that face the international community in attempting to align R2P with the protection of persons.

In 2009, there were two important advances made in the promotion of the R2P principle from 'words into deeds'. The first was the UN Secretary General Ban Ki-moon's report on *Implementing the Responsibility to Protect*, released in January.[7] The second advancement was the General Assembly's (GA) formal plenary debate of the Secretary-General's report on 23, 24 and 28 July. Of significance, at the GA, a large number of countries expressed their support for the R2P principle and for the Secretary-General's recommendations in his report. The debate was one of the largest plenary debates of the 63rd Session of the GA, with 108 member states' views represented. On 7 October 2009, Resolution 308 was adopted by the 63rd Session, which reaffirmed Member States' commitment to R2P.[8]

The significance of the Secretary-General's report was that it sought to advance a framework for states and international organisations to use in aligning R2P with their protection responsibilities. State support for the report was widespread. Its key architect – Edward Luck, Special Advisor to the Secretary General – observed that the level of positive engagement by states in the July General Assembly debate was 'historic and positive in moving things forward' as no state recanted their support for R2P.[9] Now that states have reaffirmed their support and commitment to R2P, the next task for states and the broader international community is to think about how those most vulnerable can be protected by R2P. For refugees and IDPs, the question is how useful a concept is R2P for advancing their protection? For those seeking to prevent R2P situations in the first place, how far back do we need to go in promoting R2P aligned initiatives that may or may not contribute to genocide and mass atrocities? For example, should every state with a high infant-mortality rate be considered as a potential R2P case given that high infant mortality is one precondition for genocide and mass atrocities?[10]

---

[7] United Nations General Assembly, *Implementing the responsibility to protect*, Report of the Secretary-General, Sixty-Third Session, A/63/677, 12 January 2009.

[8] United Nations General Assembly, *The Responsibility to Protect*, A/RES/63/308, 7 October 2009.

[9] Asia Pacific Centre for the Responsibility to Protect, *Implementing the Responsibility to Protect at the United Nations: Presentation by Edward Luck, Special Advisor to the United Nations Secretary- General*, 3 August 2009, University of Queensland, p. 16. http://www.r2pasiapacific .org/documents/presentation_summary.pdf Accessed: 4 November 2009.

[10] Jack A. Goldstone, Robert H. Bates, Ted Robert Gurr, Michael Lustik, Monty G. Marshall, Jay Ulfelder, and Mark Woodward, *A Global Forecasting Model of Political Instability*. (Washington D.C. 2005), p. 26. We thank Stephen McLoughlin for this point.

In his report, the Secretary-General recalled the principle's origins as developing from the concept of 'sovereignty as responsibility' developed by the UN's Special Representative on Internally Displaced Persons (IDPs), Francis Deng, and Roberta Cohen, a Senior Fellow at the Brookings Institution, in the 1990s.[11] Their principal challenge was to persuade governments to improve protection for IDPs. Their exhaustive study of the human rights situation of IDPs across all the conflict ridden corners of the world led to the publication of *Masses in Flight: the Global Crisis of International Displacement* and *Forsaken People: Case Studies of the Internally Displaced* in 1998. In the same year, Deng presented to the Human Rights Commission a 'Compilation and Analysis of the Legal Norms' of IDPs, which led to the Commission recommending that he draft Guiding Principles on Internal Displacement. The Guiding Principles were then acknowledged by the Commission in 1999.[12] The concept's starting point was recognition that the primary responsibility for protecting and assisting IDPs lay with the host government.[13] No legitimate state, they argued, could quarrel with the claim that they were responsible for the well-being of their citizens and in practice no governments did in fact quarrel with this proposition. Where a state was unable to fulfil its responsibilities, it should invite and welcome international assistance.[14] During major crises, troubled states faced a choice: they could work with international organisations and other interested outsiders to realise their sovereign responsibilities or obstruct those efforts and sacrifice their good standing and sovereign legitimacy.[15] As such, sovereignty as responsibility focused on the responsibilities of host governments and maintained that effective and legitimate states were the best way to protect vulnerable populations.

Fast forward to the Secretary-General's report, and we see great progress in how the 2005 World Summit Outcome made a positive contribution to strengthening global humanitarianism – affirming both the Guiding Principles for the protection of IDPs and sovereignty as responsibility through the paragraphs concerning R2P. The responsibility to protect, 192 states decided,

[11] Francis M. Deng, Sadikiel Kimaro, Terrence Lyons, Donald Rothchild and I. William Zartman, *Sovereignty as Responsibility: Conflict Management in Africa* (Washington: The Brookings Institution, 1996); Roberta Cohen and Francis M. Deng, *Masses in Flight: The Global Crisis of Internal Displacement* (Washington, D.C.: The Brookings Institution, 1998).

[12] Francis M. Deng, 'Impact of State Failure on Migration', *Mediterranean Quarterly*, 15/4 (2004), p. 20.

[13] Cohen and Deng, *Masses in Flight*, p. 275.

[14] Deng, 'Impact of State Failure on Migration', p. 20.

[15] Deng et al, *Sovereignty as Responsibility*, p. 28.

applies to genocide, war crimes, ethnic cleansing and crimes against humanity. In July 2009, this definition of R2P was again accepted unanimously by the General Assembly. In November 2009, the UN Security Council again reaffirmed their commitment to R2P, noting that it had a direct relationship to the protection of civilians at risk in conflict, especially vulnerable groups such as refugees and internally displaced persons.[16]

Because the vast majority of the world's refugees are fleeing persecution, R2P's normative underpinnings speaks to the protection 'gap' that faces refugees and IDPs – when neither the state they come from nor the state they are seeking asylum in is providing protection from harm. In line with the Guiding Principles doctrine put forth by Deng and Cohen, the principle of R2P asserts that all states have a primary responsibility to their own populations. All other states have a responsibility to assist their peers in fulfilling this primary responsibility. Should a state manifestly fail in its responsibility, the various bodies of the UN in partnership with relevant regional arrangements (and consistent with the UN Charter) have a responsibility to use whatever means it determines as necessary and appropriate to restore protection of affected persons. Furthermore, this responsibility is enduring - a state's responsibility does not appear and evaporate; nor does the world's responsibility or the Security Council's. In other words, it is not the nature of the responsibility that changes, but the most appropriate means of preventing genocide, war crimes, crimes against humanity and ethnic cleansing, and protecting vulnerable populations in any given situation. This enduring responsibility shares much in common with the ethos presented by Deng and Cohen in their work on mass displacement.

The Secretary-General's report presented the R2P as embodying three equal, and non-sequential, pillars that go to the heart of its framework. First, every state has the primary responsibility to protect its population from genocide, ethnic cleansing, war crimes and crimes against humanity; second, the international community has a responsibility to assist states in fulfilling its protection role; and the third pillar entails the responsibility of the international community to take timely and decisive action if the state has failed to fulfil its responsibility to protect its population. Such action may require peaceful diplomatic and humanitarian means, or if that fails, forceful means consistent with Chapters VI, VII and VIII of the UN Charter. The report then sought to

[16] United Nations Security Council, Resolution 1894 (2009), *S/RES/1894*, 11 November 2009, pp. 1-2.

link existing cases that embody examples of pillar one, two and three to highlight the cause for the international community to progress R2P from a concept into policy.[17]

The Secretary General notes numerous times in his report that R2P is closely related to refugee and IDP populations – as these are the populations most often seeking protection from the one or more of the R2P crimes. States, the report argues, have an obligation to sign on to international refugee law and humanitarian law, while international organisations such as the Office of the United Nations High Commissioner for Refugees (UNHCR) have an obligation to ensure that these populations are protected from R2P crimes.[18] Furthermore, the Secretary-General points out that the efforts of the UNHCR 'in obtaining grants of asylum and protecting refugees has served numerous potential victims of crimes and violations relating to the responsibility to protect' and those efforts have been (erroneously) less recognised as R2P in practice.[19] Questions therefore arise: Why has the role played by UNHCR in protecting vulnerable persons not been identified as R2P in practice? What are the dangers in linking R2P with the protection role played by host states and international organisations such as UNHCR? However, the Secretary General is also at pains to point out that R2P is limited in its application. It cannot be drawn into other political concerns that require sovereigns to also take responsibility for their commitments in areas such as prevention and treatment of HIV/AIDS, climate change, natural disasters.[20]

The July 2009 endorsement by UN member states of this report in the GA indicates acceptance of the natural link between R2P and protection of vulnerable persons fleeing the four key crimes. But ensuring that the link between R2P and the protection needs of refugees and IDPs becomes enduring requires institutional and political efforts to promote the natural link between sovereignty as responsibility and the protection of displaced persons and refugees. One reason for past failure to recognise the protection of refugees and IDPs as R2P in action has perhaps been a reluctance to demarcate responsibility. For example, promotion and acceptance of such a link means that host states as much as states of origin all have a responsibility to ensure the safety of persons

[17] Asia Pacific Centre for the Responsibility to Protect, *Implementing the Responsibility to Protect: Asia-Pacific in the 2009 General Assembly Dialogue* (Brisbane: Asia Pacific Centre for the Responsibility to Protect, 2009). http://www.r2pasiapacific.org/index.php?option=com_content&task=view&id=126&Itemid=6 Accessed 6 November 2009.

[18] A/63/677, pp. 5, 11, 12, 15, 23, 29.

[19] A/63/677, p. 17.

[20] A/63/677, p. 8.

at risk of the four R2P crimes – whether it is through ensuring the safe delivery of humanitarian assistance or providing resettlement. Consider that UN member states committed in 2009 to this responsibility as being enduring, but as of yet, have failed to fulfil or realise their promise to Afghan, Iraqi and Somali refugees awaiting return or resettlement, or ensure that the Darfuri, Somali, Congolese and Sri Lankan IDPs are able to safely return home. Sorting out who bears the responsibilities to resolve situations such as these, and where these responsibilities begin and end, is thus the next task that faces those who wish to implement Secretary-General's report.

This edited collection has sought contributions from some of the foremost scholars of refugee and IDP studies to engage with the conceptual and practical difficulties entailed in realising how the R2P can be fulfilled by states and the international community to protect vulnerable persons. The collection also includes authors who have been asked to consider how we go about implementing R2P to protect such persons and whether a broader application of R2P is desirable. Some of the contributors to this edited volume also contributed to a Special Issue of *Global Responsibility to Protect* on the theme of protecting refugees and IDPs through R2P.

Contributors to this book were given one theme: to consider, based on their experience and knowledge, how R2P may be aligned with the protection of the displaced. Importantly, pieces that both supported and criticised the principle and utility of Responsibility to Protect were encouraged and received. Some contributors sought to explore the history and progress so far in aligning R2P with IDPs and refugees while others discussed the practical ramifications that arise when attempting to expand R2P from words into deeds.[21]

Susan Martin asks us, in the first chapter, to reflect on the history of protection and to consider how R2P may introduce yet a further expansion of who sovereigns are responsible to protect. Martin persuasively argues that before we start aligning R2P with the protection of persons we need to first ask who should fall under the framework of protection? We have seen the creation and expansion of international refugee law in the twentieth century. In the twenty first century, we are hopefully witnessing the beginning of the inclusion of IDP into protection frameworks – as most recently illustrated by the African Union's groundbreaking Convention for the Protection and Assistance of IDPs. With the knowledge that cause for mass displacement will only increase with the projected outcomes of climate warming, Martin considers

[21] Alex J. Bellamy and Sara E. Davies, 'Introduction', *Global Responsibility to Protect*, 1/1 (2009), p. 6.

how wide the umbrella of protection should extend and, with this widening, what responsibilities upon sovereigns and international organisations such as UNHCR will it entail.

Roberta Cohen then argues that progress in the relationship between R2P and the protection of IDPs has been largely hampered due to three challenges. First, to what extent does the R2P definition as agreed to in the 2005 World Summit apply to refugees and IDPs? Second, can R2P's traditional focus on intervention be broadened to protection and humanitarian assistance, including cases of natural disasters (which will significantly increase this century due to global warming)? Third, will progress by UNHCR in promoting the Guiding Principles on Internal Displacement be lost if they align themselves to a principle (R2P) that has, wrongly, been aligned with coercive intervention? Cohen responds to these three challenges by examining the recent case of post election violence in Kenya, which has been described by Kofi Annan as a case which proved that the responsibility to protect can work in practice.[22] She argues that there is potential to reconcile R2P with the protection of IDPs, and proceeds to outline twelve specific strategies that seek to overcome the three broad challenges outlined above. Such strategies include the creation of an IDP protection office within the UN, inclusion of IDP protection into the prevention, capacity building and protection efforts of R2P, and formalisation of the Guiding Principles into international law. The realisation of these strategies, Cohen argues, would represent a significant step towards ensuring that R2P benefits those who states claim it protects – individuals at risk of genocide, crimes against humanity, war crimes and ethnic cleansing.

The final chapter to examine the conceptual dilemmas in linking R2P to IDP and refugee protection framework is provided by Erin Mooney. Mooney likens those proposing a 'natural union' between R2P and protection of the displaced to that of a marriage of convenience and inconvenience. R2P and the protection of the displaced bring their own frameworks to the 'marriage' and the shared normative roots provide great potential for policy advancement. However, Mooney also warns that the marriage may be at risk of promising too much. R2P relies upon states and the international community accepting their responsibility to protect, but we see a long history where this promise has not been fulfilled. The protection of persons requires real progress

[22] Kofi Annan, *Kofi Annan's Remarks to the International Rescue Committee*, Kofi Annan Foundation, 12 November 2008. http://kofiannanfoundation.org/newsroom/speeches/2009/07/kofi-annans-remarks-international-rescue-committee Accessed 4 November 2009.

in international law for IDPs, but also most crucially – for states to commit to the protection and humanitarian assistance obligations that they already have committed to for their populations. The risk is that R2P may promise too much and be unable to deliver real progress to those whose lives literally depend on the three pillars that the Secretary-General outlined in his report on implementing R2P.

The next two chapters by Emma Haddad and Phil Orchard focus on the term 'responsibility' to see how it compels actors in their cases (Haddad examines the European Union (EU), and Orchard the Security Council) to act on behalf of those in need of protection. Haddad examines to what extent states' collective acceptance of the terms 'responsibility' and 'protection' requires them to ensure the protection of displaced persons. If states fully engage with the Secretary-General's conception of R2P as representing three equal pillars of state responsibility, international community responsibility to assist, and the international community's responsibility to act in response to the failure of states to protect, what role should refugee receiving states play in linking R2P to their refugee/migration policies? Haddad explores this complicated question through examining what 'responsibilities' EU member states have to share asylum quotas (i.e. to what extent should the resettlement wishes of the asylum seeker factor against the states?), and to what extent should the EU be intervening to ensure that people are adequately protected in their country of origin (thus pre-empting the need to migrate). Furthermore, the nature of 'mixed migration' (people fleeing due to political *and* financial causes) affects the appreciations of EU member states about when their responsibility to protect must apply to asylum policy. This chapter examines a pertinent question which has not been adequately explored to date – what responsibilities do receiving states have for those fleeing R2P situations? Do states have a responsibility to receive these persons? Do they have a responsibility to ensure that they can return to their country of origin? Given the increased flow of asylum seekers from Afghanistan and Sri Lanka in 2009, the chapter provides an important guide on how to approach these questions.

Orchard considers the responsibility of the UN Security Council – to assist and encourage states to discharge their responsibility to protect and also to assume this responsibility when the state fails to protect – in the case of regime induced displacement. If regimes deliberately expel populations due to their political or ethnic affiliations – causing widespread displacement and humanitarian emergency – what obligation does the highest international institutional authority – the Security Council – have to act in reminding states of their responsibility to these populations? Furthermore, what protection role does the Security Council itself have with respect to these populations? Orchard examines the present crisis of regime induced displacement in the Sudanese province of Darfur, by reflecting on how the Security Council has sought to protect displaced persons in the past cases of northern Iraq in 1991 and Kosovo in 1999. Orchard reveals that these past cases herald little optimism for how the Security Council will seek to protect displaced Darfurians. The international community struggles to adequately respond to cases of regime induced displacement due to two conditionalities: sovereign consent and political will. When any of the Permanent Five members of the Council resist efforts to intervene to protect displaced persons, the Security Council will be deadlocked. Key Council members have historically been reluctant to adopt resolutions authorising Chapter VII interventions unless the host state has granted its consent, yet regimes actively engaging the displacement of their citizens will invariably refuse to give such consent. When such intransigence occurs – combined with the lack of political will amongst other states to either push harder for resolutions in the Council or to act outside of the Council – persons will remain unprotected. Orchard reveals that the nature of regime induced displacement thus poses a great dilemma for those who hope that R2P will galvanise the Security Council into acting on behalf of those being forcibly displaced from their country of origin.

Alex Bellamy and Paul Williams' chapter, following on from Phil Orchard's chapter, examines the questions of who, what, where and when does the responsibility to protect exist. Their chapter examines the conditions that lead to states being unable and unwilling to protect their citizens. Bellamy and Williams go into great detail examining the conditions that are required for a state to fulfil its responsibility to protect – from the social to economic preconditions required for the protection of citizens. They then go on to examine what precise state, regional and international level contributions are required to assist states in protecting their citizens. The call here is not for more intervention, but more prevention. The goal is for the protection of persons to become a task that states universally accept and practice – not through arm-twisting sanctions or threat of force but because states recognise that this is their responsibility and there are great benefits to the sovereign that can look after its citizens.

In the penultimate chapter, Sara Davies considers whether the responsibility to protect should be broadened to encompass situations when those affected and displaced by natural and man-made disasters are not provided with adequate care and relief from their state. Examining the International Law Commission's (ILC) study on the protection of persons in the event of a disaster, Davies examines whether the Special Rapporteur for this study was right to separate the protection of persons agenda from the responsibility to protect principle. Davies examines how both agendas share normative roots in the notion of sovereignty as responsibility, and from this history it would appear at first glance that there is reason to link the legal the protection of persons in the event of disasters to the R2P. However, Davies argues that while the protection of persons in the event of a disaster is closely linked to the normative agenda of sovereignty as responsibility, the Special Rapporteur has been right not to include R2P in the draft articles being framed on the protection of persons. Both agendas are best served by being kept separate from one another.

Luke Glanville's chapter asks what is next for those seeking to advance R2P into practical deeds, by examining the particular notion that the international community bears not merely a discretionary right but a responsibility to protect populations when states fail to do so. As Glanville notes, this idea has received little attention in comparison to the earlier and more established (though still controversial) notion of the right to intervene, yet it has seemingly extraordinary implications, not least for the protection of the displaced. Therefore, he seeks to consider how this notion that the international community bears a responsibility to protect might be fruitfully understood by considering what kind of responsibility it is – perhaps moral, legal, or political? – and who in particular bears the responsibility – perhaps international institutions such as the Security Council, regional organisations, or particular states? Glanville argues that if the international community is to effectively work towards protecting the displaced, as has been the focus of contributors to this book, we need to examine questions about which particular agents bear duties, and what these duties entail, in instances where states are failing to protect their own people.

This has been the goal of this edited collection – to understand the conditions required to protect persons rendered vulnerable by the very institution that is meant to protect them – the state. As Glanville notes, even Thomas Hobbes, a theorist of absolute sovereignty, argued that the state must protect the safety of the people if it is to claim legitimate sovereign authority. Unfortunately, the twentieth century saw too much of the opposite – states strengthened their power often by wreaking havoc and fear amongst their populations. This led to mass flight and displacement, and greater insecurity for the populations stranded across borders or trapped within their states. The purpose of the responsibility to protect is not to impose a legal doctrine or even to justify a right to intervene, but to commit states to no longer pursue internal power and authority through practices of violence and exclusion. The objective is to align sovereign statehood with awesome responsibility to safeguard the rights and needs of all citizens. The 2005 World Summit Outcome document was an attempt to start this century by remembering and declaring that the state should be a place of safety and security for those within its borders. This book is a small attempt at articulating how this goal may be achieved.

The contributors have revealed that we face a great number of conceptual and policy dilemmas if we are to fold the protection of persons and refugees under the R2P umbrella. First, should refugees and displaced persons both be seen as products of R2P crimes? If sovereignty as responsibility resides over both displaced persons and refugees how do we go about seeking protection solutions? Should we demand the safe return for displaced persons – as well as refugees? Does this mean asylum becomes a temporary solution rather than a permanent one as we had in the twentieth century? Should R2P broaden its parameters to include displaced persons due to natural disasters or should its protection framework remain exclusively adhered to those forced to flee due to suffering one or more of the four crimes? This book starts to seek answers to these questions, yet the challenge that remains for states, regional organisations and international organisations is to consider the practical dilemmas and advantages that will come in seeking to advance the notion that sovereignty entails a responsibility to protect the displaced – in law and in policy. While both concepts share a common history and purpose – to protect the most vulnerable – there is the risk of promising too much and delivering too little, unless states and organisations alike are forced to answer the hard questions and deliver on implementation.

Chapter One

Forced Migration, the Refugee Regime and the Responsibility to Protect

Susan Martin

Introduction

According to the UN High Commissioner for Refugees (UNHCR), about 42 million migrants are living outside of their home communities, forced to flee to obtain some measure of safety and security from conflict and repression.[1] The full extent of forced migration is much larger, however. Forced migration has many causes and takes many forms. People leave because of persecution, human rights violations, repression, conflict, natural and human-made disasters, and environmental hazards. Many depart on their own initiative to escape life-threatening situations although in a growing number of cases, people are driven from their homes by governments and insurgent groups intent on depopulating or shifting the ethnic, religious, or other composition of an area. Forced migrants include persons who cross international borders in search of refuge as well as those who are internally displaced. Also of concern are stateless persons, populations affected by natural disasters, those living in areas that are or will be affected by climate change, and those involuntarily resettled as a result of development projects.

Through most of the 20th century, international protection was focused—if at all—on persons who had crossed international borders in seek of refuge from war and persecution. Particularly during the Cold War, little international attention was paid to persons still within their own countries who faced

[1] UNHCR reported an estimated 16 million refugees and asylum seekers and 26 million internally displaced persons in its 2008 statistical report. In addition, there are about 4.7 million Palestinian refugees who are outside of UNHCR's mandate. See UNHCR, *2008 Global Trends: Refugees, Asylum-seekers, Returnees, Internally Displaced and Stateless Persons* (Geneva: UNHCR, 2009) and Internal Displacement Monitoring Centre, *Internal Displacement: Global Overview of Trends and Developments in 2008* (Geneva: IDMC, 2009).

similar dangers to those experienced by international refugees. Notions of sovereignty largely precluded intervention on behalf of internally displaced persons (IDPs). Moreover, many were displaced by Cold War proxy conflicts in which the United States and the Soviet Union supported different sides. It would have been difficult, if not impossible, to negotiate a Security Council resolution in support of intervention on behalf of IDPs in such conflicts. And, intervention without a resolution would have been exceedingly dangerous, potentially bringing the superpowers to direct confrontation.

With the end of the Cold War came changing concepts regarding the responsibility to assist and protect the internally displaced. During the past two decades, classic notions of sovereignty have been placed under considerable pressure when they are used to prevent humanitarian assistance and protection from reaching populations in acute need of aid. International human rights and humanitarian law have growing salience in defining sovereignty to include responsibility for the welfare of the residents of one's territory. To quote Francis Deng, the former Representative of the UN Secretary General on Internally Displaced Persons, and his colleague Roberta Cohen, in arguing for greater international attention to internally displaced persons,

> Since there is no adequate replacement in sight for the system of state sovereignty, primary responsibility for promoting the security, welfare and liberty of populations must remain with the state. At the same time, no state claiming legitimacy can justifiably quarrel with the commitment to protect all its citizens against human rights abuse.... Sovereignty cannot be used as justification for the mistreatment of populations.[2]

The concluding document of the landmark 2005 World Summit established the responsibility to protect in cases of genocide, war crimes, ethnic cleansing and crimes against humanity, even if it means intervention in the internal affairs of a member State:

> In this context, we are prepared to take collective action, in a timely and decisive manner, through the Security Council, in accordance with the Charter, including Chapter VII, on a case-by-case basis and in cooperation with relevant regional organizations as appropriate, should peaceful means be inadequate and national authorities manifestly fail to protect their populations from genocide, war crimes, ethnic cleansing and crimes against humanity.[3]

---

[2] Roberta Cohen and Francis Deng, *Masses in Flight: The Global Crisis of International Displacement* (Washington: The Brookings Institution, 1998), pp. 275-76.

[3] '2005 World Summit Outcome', Resolution adopted by the General Assembly, A/RES/60/1, 24 October 2005, Paragraph 139.

This emerging redefinition of sovereignty has also led the United Nations to think anew about its role in protecting those who are displaced by such events. As Kofi Annan, the UN Secretary General, describes:

> The United Nations is increasingly called upon to adopt a comprehensive approach aimed not only at keeping the peace but also at protecting civilian populations, monitoring human rights violations, facilitating delivery of needed humanitarian assistance, and promoting lasting solutions that include reintegration, development, and transitions to democracy.[4]

Reflecting the new role of the United Nations in addressing the situation of the internally displaced, the caseload of the UNHCR has shifted considerably. Although the number of refugees, asylum seekers and refugee returnees under UNHCR's mandate is about the same as it was a decade ago (about 16 million in 1997), the total number of concern to UNHCR has grown. As of the end of 2008, UNHCR assumed responsibility for about 34.4 million persons.[5] Of this number, 10.5 million were refugees and 14.4 million were internally displaced persons. The remainder was refugees and IDPs who had repatriated or returned home and stateless persons.

To date, much of the expansion in UNHCR's responsibilities has pertained to conflict-induced displacement. This process was aided by the promulgation of the Guiding Principles on Internal Displacement, which are based on binding international law although they are not themselves binding law. The Guiding Principles have been applied most often to those who were internally displaced for reasons that would have categorised them as refugees had they crossed an international border—that is, those displaced by persecution and conflict. The category is broader, however, leading to some developments regarding those displaced by other causes. For example, operational guidelines have been developed based on the Principles for protecting persons affected by natural disasters, including those who are internally displaced.[6]

Trailing these developments has been a similar understanding of the rights of those who are forcibly displaced by development projects, climate change or other environmental hazards that affect their habitat and livelihood. The World Bank and the regional development banks have established

---

[4] Kofi Annan, 'Preface,' in Cohen and Deng, *Masses in Flight*, p. xx.

[5] By contrast, in 1998, there were 22.4 million under UNHCR's responsibility, with only 4.6 million being IDPs. UNHCR, *2008 Global Trends: Refugees, Asylum-seekers, Returnees, Internally Displaced and Stateless Persons* (Geneva: UNHCR, 2009).

[6] Brookings-Bern Project on Internal Displacement, *Human Rights and Natural Disasters: Operational Guidelines and Field Manual on Human Rights Protection in Situations of Natural Disaster* (Washington: Brookings Institution, 2008) at http://www.brookings.edu/reports/2008/spring_natural_disasters.aspx

guidelines on involuntary resettlement from development projects, but these guidelines do not have the force of international law. Even less developed are international standards that define the rights of those who are internationally displaced as a result of natural disasters, environmental hazards, climate change or other potentially life-threatening events. Decisions on admission or deportation rest fully with sovereign States, which may or may not use their discretion to permit people exposed to such risks to remain in safety.

Antonio Guterres, the UN High Commissioner for Refugees, noted in a recent Foreign Affairs article that 'attempts by the international community to devise policies to preempt, govern, or direct these movements in a rational manner have been erratic.'[7] He acknowledged that 'new patterns of movement, including forms of forced displacement not envisaged by the Refugee Convention, have emerged.'[8] Guterres called for a global compact to tackle mass displacement, but he did not specify the nature of the international regime that might result from such a commitment on the part of States. Most specifically, he did not elaborate the role of UNHCR, or the broader refugee regime, in protecting those who have been displaced by these unenvisioned forms of displacement.

This article asks if the responsibility to protect concept—applied heretofore to persons displaced by conflict and repression—could usefully provide a framework for determining who among the broader category of forced migrants should be of concern to the international community. I begin with a discussion of the various categories of forced migrants, elaborating on three dimensions: where they are displaced, for what reasons and during what phase of displacement. The article thereafter discusses the evolution of the international community's involvement with the forcibly displaced, beginning with the League of Nations and its successes and failures, proceeding through the establishment of UNHCR and the entry into force of the UN Convention Relating to the Status of Refugees, and then discussing UNHCR's expanding role in using its good offices to provide assistance and protection to a widening range of forced migrants. The final section presents a framework for determining under what circumstances UNHCR should extend its good offices to the newly emerging categories of forced migrants, including those who may be displaced by the effects of climate change. I will argue that these decisions should be based on the principles underlying the responsibility to protect—that is, protection of persons whose own governments are unwilling to provide such protection.

---

[7] Antonio Guterres, 'Millions Uprooted: Saving Refugees and the Displaced,' *Foreign Affairs*, 87/5: 90–99 (2008), p. 90.

[8] Guterres, 'Millions Uprooted'.

Categorisation of Forced Migrants

Policy makers within and outside of the United Nations have used a classification system that places forced migrants into specific boxes, with the assumption that standards, mandates and programs will follow the designated classification. These categories reflect three dimensions. First, forced migrants are designated by where the displacement takes place. Those who cross international borders are designated as 'refugees' or 'international migrants' whereas those who remain within their national borders are 'internally displaced persons' or 'internal migrants.' Depending on whether they have received permission to enter another country, they may also be designated 'undocumented, unauthorised or illegal' migrants.

Individuals are also designated by the causes of the forced movements. The UN Convention Relating to the Status of Refugees gives specific recognition to persons who flee a well founded fear of persecution. If they cross an international boundary, they are 'refugees.' Persons fleeing conflict may also be specially designated, either by Convention (i.e., the OAU Refugee Convention) or because the UN High Commissioner for Refugees uses his good offices to recognise them as refugees. By contrast, there is no international legal framework for addressing cross-border movements caused by natural disasters, development projects, environmental degradation or climate change. The Guiding Principles on Internal Displacement uses a broad description that encompasses all of these causes in defining who is covered by the principles. Unlike refugee law, however, the Guiding Principles are not legally binding international law although based on binding human rights and humanitarian instruments. A number of governments have adopted the Guiding Principles into national law and in October 2009, 17 governments signed the newly adopted African Union Convention on the Protection and Assistance of Internally Displaced Persons in Africa, which is broadly based on the Guiding Principles.

The third dimension relates to time. Forced migration is addressed through different mechanisms depending on the phase of displacement. Emergency movements often require specialised assistance and protection due to the instability of the situation. Most refugees and displaced persons are in protracted situations, however, with the average period of displacement equaling 17 years or longer.[9] Although these situations are often treated as protracted crises, the needs, challenges and opportunities differ in many ways from the

[9] See UNHCR, *The State of the World's Refugees 2006: Human Displacement in the New Millennium* (Oxford: Oxford University Press, 2006), p. 109.

emergency phase. Camps often become settlements, sometimes approaching the size of cities, with an economic life that may remain dependent on international assistance but includes employment and entrepreneurial activity. New protection issues arise over time, sometimes shifting from outside threats to internal ones as domestic and other violence erupts in response to continuing displacement. When there is a resolution to the crisis, new challenges appear and the forced migrants may be re-designated as 'returnees' or 'resettled' persons. These formulations have arisen in the context of conflict-induced displacement, but they often apply in other situations. Those forced to migrate because of development projects (for example, dams) or the effects of climate change, for example, may remain displaced for protracted periods, finding they are unable to return, perhaps permanently, to their homes and instead are treated as resettled populations.

To a large extent, categorising the displaced by geography, cause and time has succeeded in raising the visibility of groups of forced migrants who heretofore had been either ignored or fell between the cracks in the international system. It also allows targeted responses to address issues arising from the specific cause or phase of an emergency. Options for those driven from their homes by conflict are different in nature and scope to those applicable to persons driven from their homes by development projects or the effects of climate change. Nor does the same approach make sense in every stage of a crisis.

There are limits to the approach taken to date, however. The categories of forced migrants are not mutually exclusive. More often they are overlapping. The victims of humanitarian emergencies may belong to more than one group, either at the same time or in close sequence. For example, the victims of Cyclone Nargis were harmed not only by the natural disaster but also by the repressive policies of the Burmese government. In other situations, refugees repatriate, thereby earning the designation of 'returnees,' only to find themselves newly designated 'internally displaced persons' because they were unable to return to their home communities because of continued instability.

In many cases, drawing careful lines between categories of forced migrants hinders rather than facilitates the ability of national, intergovernmental and nongovernmental organisations to offer appropriate assistance and protection. Agencies may too easily avoid responsibility by citing an institutional mandate to serve a specific population. Alternatively, agencies interested in intervening on behalf of a particular group may be denied the opportunity because they have no explicit mandate to do so. In the meantime, the forced migrants—whether refugees or internally displaced, whether fleeing conflict, natural disasters or other causes—may face serious deprivation of their human rights. If the government of the territory in which they seek safety is unable or unwilling to provide protection of their rights, including access to needed assistance, the cause of their displacement and their geographic location may be irrelevant to their plight.

Evolution of the Refugee Regime

The complexity of forced migration, as described above, poses challenges to the international community, which is called upon to provide assistance and protection to those who are displaced by events beyond their control. This article seeks to provide guidance as to who among this complex array of displaced populations merit the attention of the refugee regime. Answering this question requires an understanding of the evolution of the regime to date. The refugee regime is a 20th century invention, initially devised as a way to address the mass displacement caused by World War I, the Bolshevik Revolution and the collapse of the Ottoman and Hapsburg empires. While having limited success in protecting those who were displaced by these events, it failed miserably in protecting the victims of Nazi persecution. With the allied victory in World War II, the modern regime was shaped to find solutions to the persecuted as well as those displaced by the conflict. The refugee regime has not been static in dealing with displacement. It has taken on new roles in dealing with displacements caused by the Cold War, decolonisation, civil conflicts, and surrogate super-power conflicts.

League of Nations

In 1921, the League of Nations established the first High Commission for Refugees, charged with assisting and protecting Russian, and later, other refugees. Headed by Fridjoft Nansen, the Norwegian explorer and statesman, the High Commissioner's mandate was to provide material assistance and legal and political protection.[10] Nansen was asked in 1920 to direct the repatriation of prisoners of war, and then in 1921, to direct relief efforts to respond to growing famine in Russia. Then, in 1922, he arranged an exchange of about 1.25 million Greeks living in Asia Minor and about 500,000 Turks living in Greece. In 1925, Nansen's office succeeded in constructing villages to house

[10] For fuller discussions of the inter-war refugee regime, see Gil Loescher, *Beyond Charity: International Cooperation and the Global Refugee Crisis* (Oxford: Oxford University Press, 1993) and Michael Marrus, *The Unwanted: European Refugees from the First World War Through the Cold War* (Philadelphia: Temple University Press, 2002)

upwards of 40,000 Armenians in Syria and Lebanon and the resettlement of another 10,000 in Erivan.

After Nansen's death in 1930, the office of the High Commissioner ceased to exist and instead, the Nansen International Office for Refugees, an autonomous body working under the authority of the League of Nations, was established. The office never had sufficient resources to function effectively, relying primarily on fees paid for Nansen passports, a substitute travel document issued to refugees who were unable to obtain documentation from their own governments, and private contributions. Nevertheless, the League office provided material, legal, and financial help to about 800,000 refugees.

During the 1930s, with fascism and Nazism producing massive new refugee flows, the League established a High Commissioner for Refugees from Germany, which also gained a mandate to assist and protect refugees from Austria and the Sudetenland. During the course of the 1930s, it became evident that few countries were willing to provide refuge to the German refugees, particularly those facing growing persecution because they were Jewish. In July 1938, an international conference attended by representatives from thirty-two nations convened in Evian to discuss the problem of Jewish refugees. The participants established an Intergovernmental Committee on Refugees, to be based in London, to facilitate the emigration and resettlement of German and Austrian refugees, and later, refugees from other countries. The Evian conference did not, however, lead to any real pledges for the resettlement of the Jewish refugees, with many countries expressing outright bias against admission of the refugees.

At the end of 1938, the Nansen Office and the High Commissioner for Refugees from Germany merged and moved their offices to London. The new organisation was known as the Office of the High Commissioner for All Refugees under League of Nations Protection. The new organisation had little success in assisting and protecting the vast majority of Jews and others facing Nazi persecution, but it continued to provide material assistance to those refugees it could reach throughout World War II.

The tragic ramifications of the failure of the international community to come to the aid of refugees became clear with the liberation of the concentration camps. The camp survivors joined millions of people uprooted by the conflict itself. During the 1940s, a number of distinct organisations were established to address the problem of refugees and displaced persons in Europe. The United Nations Relief and Rehabilitation Administration (UNRRA) was founded in 1943 to give aid to areas liberated from the Axis powers. The International Refugee Organization took over in 1946. Its main mission was to care for, repatriate or resettle those made homeless by the war. Also, in

1948, the UN Relief and Work Administration for Palestinian Refugees was established to provide assistance to Palestinians displaced from Israel. There was another system for dealing with refugees in Hong Kong.

One of the most important, but ambiguous developments in the refugee regime was the adoption of the 1948 Universal Declaration of Human Rights. Article 13 establishes the individual right to move and reside freely within one's own country. That article also declares the right to leave any country, including one's own, and to return to one's own country. Having established a right to leave one's own country, the committee then turned to the problem that to be able to leave one's own country, an individual must enter another one. Member states differed considerably on how to resolve this issue. Some supported a right to asylum, but others, including the United States delegation led by Eleanor Roosevelt, preferred to limit state obligations with regard to refugees. Article 14 affirms only a 'right to seek and to enjoy in other countries asylum from persecution.' In a very close vote, states rejected any obligation to grant asylum.

UNHCR and the UN Refugee Convention

Within just a few years, states addressed this issue again, but in a very different, European-focused context.[11] The 1951 UN Convention Regarding the Status of Refugees and its 1967 Protocol emerged in the early days of the Cold War, largely to resolve the situation of the millions of refugees who remained displaced by World War II and fascist/Nazi persecution. Defining refugees as persons who were unable or unwilling to avail themselves of the protection of their home countries because of a 'well-founded fear of persecution based on their race, religion, nationality, political opinion or membership in a particular social group,'[12] the 1951 Convention included geographic (Europe) and time limitations (persons displaced before 1951) that were lifted in the 1967 Protocol.[13] Since 1967, the Refugee Convention has been a universal instrument, applying to refugees worldwide.

At its core, the Refugee Convention substitutes the protection of the international community (in the form of a host government) for that of an unable

[11] For a fuller discussion of the early years of UNHCR, see UNHCR, *State of the World's Refugees: 50 Years of Humanitarian Action* (Oxford: Oxford University Press, 2000).

[12] UN Convention Relating to the Status of Refugees Adopted on 28 July 1951 by the United Nations Conference of Plenipotentiaries on the Status of Refugees and Stateless Persons convened under General Assembly Resolution 429 (V) of 14 December 1950.

[13] Protocol to the UN Convention Relating to the Status of Refugees, entered into force on 4 October 1967.

or unwilling sovereign. In effect, the agency was to provide alternative protection for those who had been persecuted by their own state, or who could not claim the protection of their state because of a well-founded fear of future persecution. This reasoning is based on the understanding that States produce refugees because they are unwilling or unable to protect their citizens from persecution. As Charles Keely explains, 'A state is not behaving as a state when people flee or are forced out because of racial, ethnic, religious or political reasons.' He argues that the international refugee regime is 'not based primarily on humanitarian feelings.' Rather, the refugee regime is designed to protect the 'international system of states that is threatened when states fail to fulfill their proper roles.' [14]

The Convention sets out the principal obligation of States—to refrain from forcibly returning (*refouling*) refugees to countries in which they would face persecution. States do not have the obligation to provide asylum or admit refugees for permanent settlement, and they may relocate refugees in safe third countries that are willing to accept them. The Convention has been interpreted to require States to undertake status determinations for asylum applicants at their frontiers or inside their territories in order to determine if they have valid claims to refugee protection. While the only obligation towards refugees is non-*refoulement*, in practice this has often meant admission and asylum in the host country.

The Convention sets out the rights of refugees who have been admitted unto the territory of another country. Fundamental human rights such as freedom of religion and access to courts are guaranteed to be at least those accorded to the citizens of the state hosting the refugee. Refugees lawfully residing in a host country are guaranteed public relief in this way as well. Rights regarding employment, property, elementary public education, and housing are accorded to refugees in a manner no less favorable than those accorded to citizens of other countries. In addition, the Convention cannot be applied in a discriminatory way regarding race, religion, and country of origin.

UNHCR was charged from the beginning to find solutions for refugees, generally in the form of voluntary repatriation when conditions permitted, integration into a country of asylum, or resettlement to a third country. These solutions reflected the aim of the refugee regime to restore the refugee to a sovereign authority that would provide protection. If conditions change and the refugee is willing and able to return, that is the best solution. Otherwise,

[14] Charles Keely, 'How Nation-States Create and Respond to Refugee Flows,' *International Migration Review*, 30/4: 1046-1066 (1996).

obtaining citizenship in another country would enable the refugee to enjoy State protection. Because those solutions were often not forthcoming, however, UNHCR's day-to-day activity was generally to provide assistance to those who were unable to return, integrate or resettle.

Good Offices of UNHCR

The first big expansion of UNHCR's role in dealing with refugee issues came in 1956 with the Hungarian Revolution and the flight of Hungarian refugees into Western Europe. Although its mandate limited UNHCR's responsibility to those displaced prior to 1951, the UNHCR offered its good services to find solutions for the Hungarian refugees, generally via resettlement to the traditional immigration countries – the United States, Canada, and Australia.

In the 1960s, a further expansion occurred as UNHCR was asked to assist and protect refugees in Africa and Asia who were displaced by various wars of liberation. As the numbers of refugees grew and solutions were elusive, more and more of the resources of a growing regime were spent on care and maintenance of large numbers of refugees who were forced out of their homes because of conflict, and were living in refugee camps with international assistance.

In recognition of the nature of the forced movements occurring regularly in Africa, the Organization of African Unity (OAU) adopted the Convention Governing the Specific Aspects of Refugee Problems in Africa in 1969. While acknowledging the UN Refugee Convention as the basic and universal instrument regarding the protection of refugees, the OAU Convention broadened the definition and set out other important protection provisions. The expanded definition includes those who, 'owing to external aggression, occupation, foreign domination or events seriously disturbing public order in either part or the whole of his country of origin or nationality, is compelled to leave his place of habitual residence in order to seek refuge in another place outside his country of origin or nationality.'[15]

The OAU explicitly forbids states from rejecting asylum seekers at the frontier. The grant of asylum is declared to be a peaceful and humanitarian act, not to be regarded as unfriendly by other states. The Convention also establishes the importance of settling refugees at a reasonable distance from the frontier of their country of origin for security reasons. This regional treaty also states

[15] Organization of African Unity Convention Governing the Specific Aspects of Refugee Problems in Africa Adopted by the Assembly of Heads of State and Government at its Sixth Ordinary Session, Addis-Ababa, 10 September 1969.

that no refugee shall be repatriated against his will. Most African states are parties to the OAU Convention.

In a similar vein, the Cartagena Declaration on Refugees expands the definition of protected refugees in the Latin American region. Like the OAU definition, it supports the 1951 Convention and adds protection to those who have fled their country 'because their lives, safety or freedom have been threatened by generalized violence, foreign aggression, internal conflicts, massive violation of human rights or other circumstances which have seriously disturbed public order.'[16] It emphasises that repatriation of refugees must be voluntary, and embodies principles for their protection, assistance and reintegration. Although a non-binding instrument, the Declaration has been endorsed by the General Assembly of the Organization of American States and some States in the region have incorporated this definition into their own national legislation.

The OAU/Cartagena definition increasingly characterised the population of concern to UNHCR wherever in the world they were located. UNHCR and most countries of asylum made no attempt to determine which among the large number of persons who fled conflict also had a well-founded fear of persecution, instead treating those escaping conflict as prima facie refugees. Large-scale refugee movements occurred from such places as Vietnam, Cambodia, Afghanistan, Ethiopia, Somalia, Sudan, Angola, Mozambique, Nicaragua, El Salvador, and Guatemala.

In 1990, with the collapse of communism and the end to many of the surrogate Cold War conflicts, there was a major rethinking within the international humanitarian regime of how to deal with refugee issues. No longer was there a strong foreign policy rationale for a refugee regime that would support the civilian families of those fighting Communist governments. As many of the conflicts of the 1970s and 1980s ended, refugees began returning to their home countries in record numbers. The UN High Commissioner for Refugees adapted, and in 1990, the then High Commissioner, Sadako Ogata, declared the 1990s to be the decade of repatriation.

At the same time, however, new refugee movements received international attention. They often occurred as the result of nationalist or ethnic conflicts, which were usually internal in nature and difficult for the Western powers to understand fully. Examples are Bosnia, Kosovo and Rwanda. Moreover, many of the peace agreements that ended the Cold War conflicts were very fragile,

---

[16] Cartagena Declaration on Refugees Adopted by the Colloquium on the International Protection of Refugees in Central America, Mexico and Panama, Cartagena de Indias, Colombia, 22 November 1984.

and they did not necessarily take into account the fact that there were deep seated internal problems that could lead to the resumption of fighting. Refugees who repatriated during the 1990s often returned home to high levels of insecurity. In some places, such as Afghanistan, conditions deteriorated back into complete civil war and the takeover by such repressive regimes as the Taliban.

Addressing Internal Displacement

From at least the 1970s, UNHCR has aided persons still within their home countries. Often, implementing programs for returning refugees prompted UNHCR to offer its good offices to the internally displaced as well. This was the case in southern Sudan in the early 1970s when UNHCR assisted about 180,000 returnees and about 500,000 internally displaced persons.[17] The UNHCR also assisted displaced people in Cyprus, in this case, acting as the Secretary General's Special Representative and Coordinator for United Nations Humanitarian Assistance for Cyprus.

Although UNHCR had exercised its mandate on behalf of the internally displaced, the agency had considerable discretion in determining if and when to do so unless specifically requested by the General Assembly. In March 2000, UNHCR issued a position paper clarifying its relationship to internally displaced persons. The agency made clear its interest in this population arises from its humanitarian mandate on behalf of persons displaced by persecution, situations of general violence, conflict or massive violations of human rights. This mandate places upon UNHCR 'a responsibility to advocate on behalf of the internally displaced; mobilize support for them; strengthen its capacity to respond to their problems; and take the lead to protect and assist them in certain situations.'[18] Stopping short of asserting an operational responsibility for all internally displaced persons, UNHCR set out six requirements for its involvement: 'a request or authorization from the Secretary General or a competent principal organ of the UN; consent of the state concerned, and where applicable, other entities in a conflict; access to the affected population; adequate security for staff of UNHCR and implementing partners; clear lines of responsibility and accountability with the ability to intervene directly on protection matters; and adequate resources and capacity.'[19]

---

[17] Louise Holborn, *Refugees: A Problem of Our Time* (Metuchen, NJ: Scarecrow Press, 1975).

[18] UNHCR, 'Internally Displaced Persons: The Role of the United Nations High Commissioner for Refugees', 2000.

[19] UNHCR, 'Internally Displaced Persons'.

The policy paper specified that UNHCR would be ready to take the lead where its protection and solutions expertise was particularly relevant, or where involvement with the internally displaced was closely linked to the voluntary repatriation and reintegration of refugees. Recognition was given that the linkages between refugees and the internally displaced could be complicated: 'Countries of asylum may be more inclined to maintain their asylum policies if something is done to alleviate the suffering of the internally displaced, reduce their compulsion to seek asylum and create conditions conducive to return. On the other hand, UNHCR's activities for the internally displaced may be (mis) interpreted as obviating the need for international protection and asylum.'[20]

Gaps continued to persist in establishing responsibility for internally displaced persons. After trying what it called a collaborative approach that failed to fill the gaps, the United Nations shifted to what it now calls the cluster leadership approach, in which a single UN agency is responsible for coordinating activities in a particular sector. UNHCR has taken on responsibility for the protection cluster (focusing on conflict-induced displacement) as well as the emergency shelter and camp management clusters.[21] The cluster approach is being pilot tested to determine if it is effective in improving responses to IDPs.

The Interagency Standing Committee (IASC) Guidance Note on Using the Cluster Approach explains:

> the role of sector leads at the country level is to facilitate a process aimed at ensuring well-coordinated and effective humanitarian responses in the sector or area of activity concerned. Sector leads themselves are not expected to carry out all the necessary activities within the sector or area of activity concerned. They are required, however, to commit to being the 'provider of last resort' where this is necessary and where access, security and availability of resources make this possible.[22]

The Note also recognises that 'The "provider of last resort" concept is critical to the cluster approach, and without it the element of predictability is lost.'[23] For agencies with technical leads (e.g., health, nutrition, water and sanitation), the ability of the lead agency to take on responsibility is straightforward.

---

[20] UNHCR, 'Internally Displaced Persons'.

[21] The International Organization for Migration has responsibility for camp management in the context of natural disasters.

[22] Inter-Agency Standing Committee (IASC), 'Guidance Note on Using the Cluster Approach to Strengthen Humanitarian Response', 24 November 2006 at http://www.humanitarianreform.org/humanitarianreform/Portals/1/Resources%20&%20tools/IASCGUIDANCENOTECLUSTERAPPROACH.pdf

[23] IASC, 'Guidance Note'.

However, the Note is more circumspect regarding the leadership for cross-cutting areas such as Protection, Early Recovery and Camp Coordination: 'The concept of "provider of last resort" will need to be applied in a differentiated manner. In all cases, however, sector leads are responsible for ensuring that wherever there are significant gaps in the humanitarian response they continue advocacy efforts and explain the constraints to stakeholders.'[24]

UNHCR's 2007 policy on internal displacement went significantly further than its 2000 policy in specifying the circumstances under which the agency would assume responsibility: 'UNHCR stands ready to contribute to the inter-agency response in situations of internal displacement in any conflict-affected country where the presence and programmes of the Office have the consent of the authorities, where the humanitarian activities of UNHCR and its partners are free from undue political or military interference, and where the security environment enables its personnel to function within acceptable levels of risk.'[25] Although still constrained in terms of sovereignty and security, and limited to conflict-affected countries, the 2007 policy represented a major shift from earlier policies that severely limited UNHCR's involvement with internally displaced persons. UNHCR reports in 2008 that 14 million of an estimated 25 million internally displaced from conflict fall under its mandate.[26]

Non-Conflict Displacement

During this period, UNHCR also began responding, albeit in an ad hoc way, to forced migration stemming from causes other than persecution or conflict. Although UNHCR has limited its cluster leadership to conflict-induced internal displacement, it has nevertheless been drawn into providing assistance during several notable natural disasters. In the *State of the World's Refugees*, UNHCR explained its involvement in tsunami relief: 'The sheer scale of the destruction and the fact that many of affected populations were of concern to the organisation prompted the move. Responding to requests from the UN Secretary-General and UN Country Teams, UNHCR concentrated on providing shelter and non-food relief. In Sri Lanka, UNHCR's presence in the country prior to the tsunami allowed for a comparatively swift and sustained

---

[24] IASC, 'Guidance Note'.

[25] UNHCR, 'Policy Framework and Corporate Strategy: UNHCR's Role in Support of an Enhanced Inter-Agency Response to the Protection of Internally Displaced Persons', January 2007 at http://www.unhcr.org/excom/EXCOM/45c1ab432.pdf

[26] UNHCR, *2007 Statistical Yearbook* (Geneva: UNHCR, 2008).

humanitarian intervention – including efforts focused on the protection of internally displaced persons.'[27] UNHCR also assisted tsunami victims in Somalia and Aceh, Indonesia, pointing out: 'The protection of displaced populations was especially urgent in areas of protracted conflict and internal displacement in Aceh, Somalia and Sri Lanka. Furthermore, there was concern for some affected populations whose governments declined offers of international aid, such as the Dalits (formerly known as untouchables) of India and Burmese migrant workers in Thailand; it was feared they might be discriminated against and their protection needs compromised.'[28] More recently, UNHCR has become involved in the international response to Cyclone Nargis in Burma and China's earthquake, providing shelter and supplies, but not protection.

The potential for mass displacement from climate change is an issue that has increasingly occupied the High Commissioner's attention. In several recent speeches, Mr. Guterres has given voice to his concerns: 'When we consider the different models for the impact of climate change, the picture is very worrying. The need for people to move will keep on growing. One need only look at East Africa and the Sahel region. All predictions are that desertification will expand steadily. For the population, this means decreasing livelihood prospects and increased migration. All of this is happening in the absence of international capacity and political will to respond.'[29] The Assistant High Commissioner for Protection, Erika Feller, summarised the dilemma before the Executive Committee: 'New terminology is entering the displacement lexicon with some speed. The talk is now of "ecological refugees", "climate change refugees", the "natural disaster displaced". This is all a serious context for UNHCR's efforts to fulfill its mandate for its core beneficiaries.... The mix of global challenges is explosive, and one with which we and our partners, government and non-government, must together strike the right balance.'[30] Thus far, however, there has been no inclination on the part of the Executive Committee for UNHCR to become involved with those who cross borders because of natural disasters or climate change.

Nor is there support for UNHCR's expanded operations when it comes to helping disaster IDPs. UNHCR has made clear to the Emergency Relief

[27] UNHCR, *State of the World's Refugees 2006*, p. 21.

[28] UNHCR, *State of the World's Refugees 2006*, p. 21.

[29] Keynote Speech by UN High Commissioner for Refugees, Mr. António Guterres, Third Symposium on Corporate Social Responsibility and Humanitarian Assistance, Tokyo, 26 November 2007, http://www.unhcr.org/admin/ADMIN/476132d911.html

[30] Statement by UNHCR Assistant High Commissioner for Protection, Ms. Erika Feller, at the 42nd Meeting of the Standing Committee, Agenda Item 3, 24 June 2008.

Coordinator that while it will lead the cluster on protection of conflict IDPs, it will not do the same for disaster IDPs. This cluster therefore has no leader since the two other potential candidates—UNICEF and the Office of the High Commissioner for Human Rights—do not have the requisite capacity.

There is also debate over the expansion of UNHCR's operations when it comes to conflict IDPs. Although generally, governments on the Executive Committee of the UNHCR have been supportive of the agency's initiatives on behalf of IDPs uprooted by conflict, they have also cautioned the High Commissioner that UNHCR was not the 'IDP agency.' A number of governments expressed concern in the 2007 Executive Committee session that 'UNHCR's work with IDPs should not come at the expense of its protection of refugees.'[31] The agency was also encouraged to develop exit strategies for internal displacement situations. Since then, UNHCR has incorporated 'When Displacement Ends: A Framework for Durable Solutions,'[32] developed by the Brookings-Bern Project on Internal Displacement and Georgetown University, into its Handbook on Internal Displacement.[33]

Within the academic community, the debate about the pre-occupation of the refugee regime with internally displaced persons has been particularly pointed. In a keynote speech to the International Association for the Study of Forced Migration, James Hathaway, who is a law professor at the University of Michigan, raised the alarm about a shift in focus from refugees to forced migrants. He argued that refugees have a special place in international law, whereas others who migrate or are displaced do not have an explicit status. Interestingly, Hathaway argues for the special treatment of refugees because they 'are seriously at risk because of who they are or what they believe.' Constructing a human rights argument, he argues that refugees are 'doubly-deserving' of international protection having fled 'profoundly serious' risks because of unchangeable and/or fundamental characteristics.[34]

Adelman and McGrath, in their responses to Hathaway, point out that most refugees under UNHCR's mandate are not covered under the Refugee

[31] UNHCR, 'Report of the fifty-eighth session of the Executive Committee of the High Commissioner's Programme', p. 21 at http://www.unhcr.org/excom/EXCOM/471615cb2.pdf

[32] Brookings Bern Project on Internal Displacement, 'When Displacement Ends: A Framework for Durable Solutions', June 2007. Online. UNHCR Refworld, available at: http://www.unhcr.org/refworld/docid/469f6bed2.html

[33] UNHCR, 'Handbook for the Protection of Internally Displaced Persons', Provisional Release 2007 at http://www.unhcr.org/protect/PROTECTION/4794b6e72.pdf

[34] James C. Hathaway, 'Forced Migration Studies: Could We Agree Just to "Date"?' *Journal of Refugee Studies* 20: 349-369 (2007).

Convention because they have fled conflict not persecution.[35] UNHCR's mandate had already evolved, as it used its good offices to provide assistance and protection to millions of refugees because of the humanitarian, not legal imperative to act. To the extent that internally displaced persons meet the same criteria, there would be no reason to treat them in an essentially different manner. Cohen argues further that widespread acceptance of the Guiding Principles on Internal Displacement, as well as the 'Responsibility to Protect' doctrine espoused at the 2005 World Summit, demonstrate a high degree of acceptance that there is an international responsibility to protect and assist internally displaced persons.[36]

Responsibility to Protect?

The debate about the scope of the refugee regime's responsibility to protect forced migrants has focused primarily on conflict-induced displacement, reflecting UNHCR's increasing involvement in providing assistance and protection to persons who would have been considered refugees had they crossed an international border. Despite UNHCR's occasional forays into providing assistance to victims of natural disasters, there has been relatively little policy or academic debate as to the extent to which the refugee regime should also take on a responsibility to protect those forcibly displaced for reasons other than conflict.[37] Yet, as High Commissioner Guterres' statements indicate, the number of those so displaced could easily surpass the numbers of conflict-induced refugees and internally displaced persons in the years ahead, particularly as the impact of climate change is manifest in increased displacement. In this context, UNHCR's recent note, 'Climate change, natural disasters and human displacement: a UNHCR perspective,' states that: 'it is legitimate to ask whether new legal protection instruments might be needed for cross-border movements that are induced by climate-related reasons. UNHCR is not seeking an extension of its mandate, but it is our duty to alert the international community to the protection gaps that are emerging.'[38]

---

[35] Howard Adelman and Susan McGrath, 'To Date or To Marry: That is the Question', *Journal of Refugee Studies,* 20: 376-380 (2007).

[36] Roberta Cohen, 'Response to Hathaway', *Journal of Refugee Studies,* 20: 370-376 (2007).

[37] As an exception, see Roberta Cohen, *For Disaster IDPs: An Institutional Gap* (Washington, DC: Brookings Institution, 2008).

[38] UNHCR, Climate change, natural disasters and human displacement: a UNHCR perspective, October 2008 at http://www.unhcr.org/protect/PROTECTION/4901e81a4.pdf

Regardless of its own concerns about mandate, UNHCR will no doubt be called upon to extend its good offices to these populations. The question is: By what criteria should UNHCR engage with those displaced by climate change, natural disasters, development projects and other similar causes? To answer this question, it is necessary to identify UNHCR's mandate and capabilities relative to the rest of the international community. I argue that UNHCR has evolved to protect persons whose own governments cannot or will not provide such protection. Other UN and international agencies, such as the International Organization for Migration, have a demonstrated capacity to provide assistance to persons displaced by natural disasters and environmental hazards, but only UNHCR has a history of providing protection to displaced populations.

Following this line of reason, one can divide forced migrants in three categories based on the extent to which their own governments are willing and able to protect them. In the first group are individuals whose governments are *willing and able* to provide protection. Those displaced by natural disasters and climate change in wealthy, democratic countries generally, though not always, fall into this category. There are examples of poorer and more authoritarian governments that also have good track records of demonstrating they are willing and able to protect their citizens affected by natural disasters and environmental hazards. Generally, displacements in these contexts are internal, not international, since the forced migrants are able to find assistance from their own governments and have few reasons to cross an international border. There is a limited role for the international community, although other governments and international organisations may offer assistance—for example, in the form of search and rescue teams, financial aid for rebuilding homes, health professionals, and other experts in disaster relief. There would be no role for the refugee regime to involve itself since there is no need for protection from the international community.

The second group includes forced migrants in situations in which governments are *willing but unable* to protect persons displaced by disaster or environmental hazards. Certainly, poor countries that do not have the financial capacity to provide assistance may fall into this category. They would like to protect their citizens from harm but do not have the capacity or resources to do so. If the affected population moves within the country of origin to find safety, a government may well attempt to fulfill its protection responsibilities by calling upon the international community to assist. There would be little reason for the refugee regime to involve itself because protection is not at stake, but the international community has an important role to play in ensuring that it buttresses the willing State's ability to provide protection by offering financial and other aid. Of course, UNHCR might be called upon for material goods and expertise, as has been the case in some of the massive displacements occurring from natural disasters, but this population would not otherwise fall within its mandate.

The third group includes displaced persons whose governments are *unwilling* to provide protection to their citizens, regardless of their ability to do so. This would include situations in which the government has the capacity to provide protection, but is unwilling to offer it to some or all of its citizens. For example, the government may not spend its resources on political opponents or ethnic or religious minority groups. Failed States would also fit into this category because they have neither the willingness nor the ability to protect their citizens.

These are the situations in which UNHCR can play a constructive role in promoting protection for persons whose rights have been violated by States that are unwilling and/or unable to ensure their safety. In cases of internal displacement, UNHCR would need to use the same criteria the agency uses in determining whether to intervene in conflict displacement situations. The form of intervention would differ depending on the circumstances. If the agency were able to reach the affected populations, UNHCR would have an obligation to offer both assistance and protection. If State sovereignty or security conditions precluded direct access, UNHCR could still play an important role as an advocate for unprotected persons, up to and including encouraging the Security Council to intervene.

Also complicated are cases in which large numbers move across borders because of the unwillingness of their own government to provide protection. In such situations, the need for international protection will be determined by the destination country's policies and the extent to which the displaced would be harmed if returned home. If the destination country is willing and able to provide assistance and protect the cross-border population, there would be little reason for the international community to become involved. On the other hand, if the destination country is unwilling or unable to assist and protect the forced migrants, or it attempts to return the forced migrants to the home country without adequate guarantees of their protection, the international community may well have a reason to offer its assistance and protection. The complication, of course, is the absence of international law defining the rights of persons with a well-founded fear of harm from natural disasters or environmental hazards and the responsibilities of States towards them. One can nevertheless posit that if the country of origin's ability to provide protection and assistance is buttressed by the international community and the cross-border migrant could return safely, the destination country would be well within its right to return the migrants without international intervention. On the other hand, if protection is unavailable in the home country, and returnees would be seriously harmed if they were to return, then the destination country as well as the international community has a greater responsibility to offer its protection. As in conflict-induced displacement, UNHCR could offer its assistance as a way to encourage the country of destination to permit the cross border migrants to remain until safe to return or other solutions are found for them.

Conclusions

The responsibility to protect is a relatively new concept that was conceived primarily to address situations of 'unavoidable catastrophe—from mass murder and rape, from starvation....'[39] The core principle enunciated by the International Commission on Intervention and State Sovereignty to guide intervention is 'where a population is suffering serious harm, as a result of internal war, insurgency, repression or state failure, and the state in question is unwilling or unable to halt or avert it, the principle of non-intervention yields to the international responsibility to protect.'[40] Among the situations listed by the Commission as fitting into this framework were 'overwhelming natural or environmental catastrophes, where the state concerned is either unwilling or unable to cope, or call for assistance, and significant loss of life is occurring or threatened.'[41] This failure of state protection, I would argue, provides an appropriate framework for determining when the refugee regime should become engaged in offering protection and assistance to those displaced by natural disasters or severe environmental harm.

Even before the responsibility to protect was elaborated and adopted by governments, protection was the hallmark of UNHCR's role in the international community. During the past century, the international refugee regime has evolved, as the international community learned from its mistakes and slowly expanded the mandate of its refugee agency to protect persons displaced by persecution and conflict. At first focused on specific nationalities and events, in the years after World War II and the advent of the Cold War, the refugee regime became more universal in its scope, protecting refugees

[39] Commission on Intervention and State Sovereignty, *The Responsibility to Protect* (Ottawa: International Development Research Centre, 2001), p. viii.

[40] Ibid., p. xi.

[41] Ibid., p. 33.

throughout the world. With the end of the Cold War and the increased ability to reach persons internally displaced by conflict and persecution, the refugee regime has expanded to assume a responsibility for the protection of persons still within their home countries, particularly if the events leading to their internal displacement were similar to those affecting refugee movements.

As new forms of forced migration loom on the horizon, the international community may well see itself challenged to intervene to assist and protect those displaced by climate change, environmental hazards and natural disasters. This article has attempted to set out criteria under which the refugee regime would appropriately be the mechanism through which the international community would respond to these new displacements. To the extent that States are unwilling to protect their own citizens who are displaced from these causes, UNCHR would legitimately have a role to play in advocating for and, when possible, assisting and protecting these forced migrants.

Chapter Two

Reconciling R2P with IDP Protection

Roberta Cohen

Introduction

The concept of the responsibility to protect (R2P) developed in large measure from efforts to design an international system to protect internally displaced persons (IDPs).

The explosion of civil wars emanating from and following the Cold War brought into view millions of persons inside their own countries who were uprooted from their homes and in need of international protection and assistance. Many had little or no access to food, medicine or shelter and were vulnerable to assault, sexual violence, and all manner of human rights abuse. When first counted in 1982, 1.2 million IDPs could be found in 11 countries; by 1995, the number had surged to 20 to 25 million.[1]

The international system, however, set up after the Second World War, focused almost exclusively on refugees – persons who fled *across* borders to escape persecution. The 1951 Refugee Convention and the UN High Commissioner for Refugees (UNHCR) provided international protection to people who were *outside* their countries of origin and deprived of the protection of their own governments. As UNICEF's Executive Director observed, 'The world has established a minimum safety net for refugees,' but 'This is not yet the case with respect to internally displaced populations.'[2]

In the displaced persons camps set up after the Second World War in Europe, the UN Relief and Rehabilitation Administration, a predecessor of UNHCR, protected *both* refugees and IDPs. But during the Cold War, borders

---

[1] Roberta Cohen and Francis M. Deng, *Masses in Flight: The Global Crisis of Internal Displacement* (Washington DC: Brookings Institution Press, 1998), p. 3.

[2] James P. Grant, 'Refugees, Internally Displaced and the Poor: An Evolving Ethos of Responsibility,' address at the Round Table on the Papal Document, UNICEF, 9 March 1993.

became sacrosanct and concepts of non-interference in internal affairs overrode most efforts to protect people inside their countries.[3] During the Biafra civil war in the 1960s, the High Commissioner for Refugees restricted help to IDPs with the explanation that: 'my Office is not in a position to deal with situations affecting nationals who find themselves within a territory of their country.'[4]

It was not until the 1990s that this gap in treatment was challenged and the international community began in a concerted way to try to assist and protect people uprooted inside their countries. UN Secretary-General Javier Perez de Cuellar pointed the way in 1991with these words: 'We are clearly witnessing what is probably an irresistible shift in public attitudes towards the belief that the defense of the oppressed in the name of morality should prevail over frontiers and legal documents.'[5] Concepts of human security, sovereignty as responsibility and the responsibility to protect developed in large measure in response to the need of IDPs and other affected civilians for protection from the gross violations of human rights perpetrated in civil wars and internal strife.

This chapter examines the origin of R2P from the perspective of IDP protection and identifies the problems that arise in applying the concept to displaced persons. It then offers suggestions for reconciling R2P with IDPs so that the concept may benefit displaced persons, as was intended.

International Protection for IDPs

A complex mix of motivations produced the broader international approach that seeks to protect and assist people uprooted within their own countries. The growing number of IDPs was a key consideration as was the risk that conflict and displacement in one country could spill over borders and disrupt regional and international stability. International preoccupation with preventing refugee flows also lent support to protecting people inside their countries.

---

[3] To be sure, the International Committee of the Red Cross had a special mandate to protect civilians in armed conflicts and beginning in the 1970s could explicitly act in non-international armed conflicts. But often it was denied entry and did not easily act in conflicts below the threshold of civil wars. UNHCR also began in the 1970s on a select basis to assist people displaced inside their own countries at the request of the General Assembly or Secretary-General. But by and large deference to traditional notions of sovereignty prohibited an international role with IDPs for much of the 20th century.

[4] Adam Lichtenheld, *From Exclusion to Expansion: Internally Displaced People and the Evolution of the International Refugee Rights Regime*, Spring 2008 (unpublished Senior Honors Thesis, University of Wisconsin, on file with author).

[5] Javier Perez de Cuellar, as quoted in Cohen and Deng, *Masses in Flight*, p. 1.

So too did the Cold War's end, which facilitated access and was accompanied by an erosion in traditional notions of sovereignty. From 1991 on, Security Council resolutions began to demand access to IDPs and other affected populations, and sometimes authorised the establishment of relief corridors and cross-border operations or the use of force to reach IDPs and others in need.[6]

The international response to IDP emergencies, however, initially focused on providing food, medicine and shelter to the displaced. In 1989, UN Resident Coordinators were assigned the task of coordinating 'assistance' to IDPs in the field. But with the displacement of Kurds, Bosnians and Somalis, it became clear that security was as overriding a priority as food. In the former Yugoslavia, IDPs told UNHCR,

> We do not need food, we are not starving to death. We are being persecuted and we prefer to be hungry for a week than not to sleep every night, in fear of being beaten, raped, or killed.[7]

IDPs began to look to the international community for protection when their states collapsed or when their governments proved unable or unwilling to provide them with elemental security.

The Refugee Policy Group (RPG), a small think tank in Washington DC, took the lead in pointing out that United Nations mechanisms to coordinate assistance to IDPs would prove ineffective unless there were comparable 'measures to protect the human rights of those displaced.'[8] The assumption that because IDPs were within the borders of their countries their governments would protect them was proving erroneous. Before a special meeting of delegates of the UN Commission on Human Rights in 1990, RPG argued that when governments do not have the willingness or ability to protect their displaced populations, international involvement becomes essential:

---

[6] For a discussion of the reasons why IDPs came onto the international agenda, see ibid, pp. 3-5.

[7] UNHCR, Information Notes on former Yugoslavia, 1/94, January 1994, p.ii, cited in Erin D. Mooney, 'Presence, ergo Protection? UNPROFOR, UNHCR and the ICRC in Croatia and Bosnia and Herzegovina,' *International Journal of Refugee Law* 7/3: 430 (1995).

[8] See Roberta Cohen, Refugee Policy Group, 'U.N. Human Rights Bodies Should Deal with the Internally Displaced,' Statement before delegates to the UN Commission on Human Rights, organised by the Quaker UN Office and the World Council of Churches, Geneva, 7 February 1990. See also Roberta Cohen and Jacques Cuenod, *Improving Institutional Arrangements for the Internally Displaced* (Washington DC: The Brookings Institution-Refugee Policy Group Project on Internal Displacement, October 1995), pp. 6–7; and Thomas Weiss and David A. Korn, *Internal Displacement: Conceptualization and its Consequences* (Abingdon and New York: Routledge, 2006), pp. 11-29.

> The fact that they are displaced internally does not mean that the international community does not have a major ***responsibility to protect*** them [emphasis added].[9]

In 1991, RPG convened the first international conference on human rights protection for internally displaced persons. Its letter of invitation affirmed, 'Although recently the United Nations has begun to address the relief needs of internally displaced people, the international community has been slow to recognize that they also need human rights protection.'[10] The meeting called for an international system to provide protection to the displaced when their governments were unwilling or unable to do so.[11]

The debates over whether the international community had a responsibility to protect people inside their countries originated in large measure from the gap in the international system that provided *international* protection primarily to refugees and left IDPs to the care of their own governments. The need of IDPs for protection when caught up in civil wars, forced relocations and serious human rights abuse precipitated the *breakdown* in traditional ways of thinking about sovereignty and humanitarian action. It also triggered operational changes in the field. Sadako Ogata, the High Commissioner of Refugees, wrote in her memoirs that she asked herself:

> Should we follow the legal dictate of not exercising our mandate inside the border and thereby refrain from helping those prevented from crossing or should we stand more on realistic humanitarian grounds and extend whatever support we could?[12]

Ogata chose the humanitarian course and UNHCR, despite its refugee mandate, began to protect displaced Kurds inside Iraq in the safe haven created by a US-led coalition, in the wake of the Gulf War; and in the former Yugoslavia UNHCR became the lead agency on the ground for refugees, IDPs and other affected populations.

Mrs. Ogata's decision was supported by many UNHCR staff who found it unconscionable not to provide some protection to IDPs. Sergio Vieira de Mello of UNHCR, for example, who went on to become the UN's Emergency Relief Coordinator called upon the Security Council 'to alleviate the suffering

---

[9] Cohen, ibid.

[10] Refugee Policy Group, Letter of Invitation, 15 March 1991.

[11] Roberta Cohen, 'Human Rights Protection for Internally Displaced Persons,' Refugee Policy Group, June, 1991; and Refugee Policy Group, 'Human Rights Protection for Internally Displaced Persons: An International Conference,' 24-25 June 1991.

[12] Sadako Ogata, *The Turbulent Decade* (New York: W.W. Norton & Company, 2005), p. 38.

of innocent people throughout the world irrespective of their location.'[13] Kamel Morjane, when he became Assistant High Commissioner, asserted that it was 'neither ethical nor practical to distinguish between human beings because of a border they may or may not have crossed.'[14] Others at UNHCR however feared that greater involvement with IDPs would threaten the institution of asylum, undermine refugee protection and lead the agency into too challenging a course in trying to protect people inside their countries.[15]

UNHCR and other humanitarian organisations called for a conceptual and legal foundation on which to base their growing involvement with IDPs. For refugee protection, UNHCR could rely on the Refugee Convention, but for IDPs no comparable document existed.

Sovereignty as Responsibility and the Guiding Principles on Internal Displacement

It fell to Francis M. Deng, who became Representative of the Secretary-General on IDPs in 1992, to undertake the work of developing the conceptual and legal framework for the international protection of IDPs. Deng put forward the concept of sovereignty as responsibility as the most appropriate protection framework for people displaced inside their countries. The concept arose from work he and other scholars had done on Africa at the Brookings Institution[16] and also from work done by RPG on the protection of IDPs.[17]

The concept posits primary responsibility for the welfare and safety of IDPs with their governments. However, when governments are unable to fulfill

---

[13] UN Office for the Coordination of Humanitarian Affairs, 'Briefing of the Security Council on emergency situations outside the Federal Republic of Yugoslavia by Under-Secretary-General Sergio Vieira de Mello,' 3 June 1999.

[14] Kamel Morjane, *ICVA Talk Back*, Vol. 7-2, Geneva, 30 March 2005.

[15] See 'Should UNHCR become a "displacement agency"'? *The State of the World's Refugees* (UNHCR: Oxford University Press, 2006), pp. 166-167.

[16] See Francis M. Deng, *Protecting the Dispossessed* (Washington DC: Brookings Institution), 1993, pp. 14-20; and Deng et al, *Sovereignty as Responsibility: Conflict Management in Africa* (Washington DC: Brookings Institution, 1996), pp. 2-19, 27-33.

[17] See Cohen, 'Human Rights Protection for Internally Displaced Persons,' pp. 16-19, which says that 'Sovereignty carries with it a responsibility on the part of governments to protect their citizens,' and discusses the human rights and humanitarian contributions to this concept; and Roberta Cohen, 'Statement to International Journalists Round Table on Human Rights and the United Nations,' United Nations, New York, 14-16 October 1991, which says that 'sovereignty implies humanitarian and human rights obligations by governments to the persons residing on their territories.'

their responsibilities, they should request and accept offers of aid from the international community. If they refuse or deliberately obstruct access and put large numbers at risk, the international community has a right and even a responsibility to take a series of calibrated actions. These range from 'diplomatic demarches to political pressures, sanctions, or, as a last resort, military intervention.' State failure to provide protection and life-supporting assistance 'legitimized the involvement of the international community.'[18]

The Guiding Principles on Internal Displacement, introduced by Deng into the UN in 1998,[19] are based on the concept of sovereignty as responsibility. They set forth the rights of IDPs and the responsibilities of governments and international organisations toward these populations. They affirm that primary responsibility for displaced populations rests with their governments (Principles 3, 25); but if governments are unable to provide life-supporting protection and assistance, they are expected to request assistance from the international community. In such cases, offers of aid shall not be regarded 'as an unfriendly act or an interference in a State's internal affairs' (Principle 25); nor shall offers of aid be 'arbitrarily withheld' when the authorities concerned are 'unable or unwilling' to provide the required assistance. The Principles do not *explicitly* state that international aid can be provided without the consent of the affected country but according to Deng and the author, the

> ...obligation imposed on states by humanitarian and human rights law to refrain from refusing reasonable offers of international assistance makes it difficult to dispute the existence of a duty to accept such offers.[20]

The Principles further emphasise that in providing assistance, international humanitarian organisations should pay attention to the 'protection needs and human rights' of IDPs and take 'measures' in this regard (Principle 27). IDPs therefore must have access not only to material assistance from the international community but also to protection from violence and abuse when governments fail to provide these to its citizens.

Challenges of R2P's Application to IDPs

When R2P was adopted by the UN General Assembly in 2005, it was generally expected that the concept would enhance security for IDPs since the

---

[18] Cohen and Deng, *Masses in Flight*, p. 7.

[19] UN Commission on Human Rights, The Guiding Principles on Internal Displacement, UN Doc. E/CN.4/1998/53/Add.2, 11 February 1998.

[20] Cohen and Deng, *Masses in Flight*, p. 277.

concept of sovereignty as responsibility was recognised as its antecedent,[21] and IDPs were so often the victims of R2P related crimes.

Like its antecedent, R2P places primary responsibility on the state to protect its population and calls on the international community to support states in discharging that responsibility. But if states fail in that obligation, responsibility shifts to the international community. There is an international responsibility to take 'collective action' when people are threatened by genocide, crimes against humanity, war crimes, and ethnic cleansing. Such action can include 'diplomatic, humanitarian, and other peaceful means,' to be followed if necessary by the use of force on a case by case basis under Chapter VII of the UN Charter.[22]

R2P's application to IDPs, however, has proved problematic. The reasons are varied:

Limited application. To begin with, many states are wary of invoking R2P. The result is that the concept has been applied to only *one* case since its adoption. In early 2008 UN Secretary-General Ban Ki-moon characterised the post-election ethnic clashes in Kenya as R2P and took diplomatic and political steps to address the violence. By the time he acted, however, not only had 1,500 people died but up to 600,000 had been forcibly displaced. The application of R2P did not thus succeed as a preventive measure. Nonetheless, Ban's linkage of R2P to the situation underscored that the violence and displacement were being viewed seriously. The Secretary-General warned Kenya's leaders that they 'could be held accountable for violations of international law committed at their instigation' and urged them 'to call publicly for an end to the violence and to statements inciting violence.'[23] Ban then sought to implement R2P by supporting Kofi Annan's political mediation, the involvement of the African Union and the use of political pressure by the US and other Western governments. These collective efforts ultimately led to a halt in the violence and forced displacement. According to Annan, his own success as a peace-broker in Kenya 'owed something to the existence of R2P as a moral instrument.'[24]

---

[21] See Gareth Evans, *The Responsibility to Protect: Ending Mass Atrocity Crimes Once and For All* (Washington DC: Brookings Institution Press, 2008), pp. 35-7.

[22] UN General Assembly, World Summit Outcome 2005, Resolution A/RES/60/1, 24 October 2005 available at http://www.unorg/summit2005/documents.html

[23] UN General Assembly, Report of the UN Secretary-General, *Implementing the responsibility to protect*, A/63/677, 12 January 2009, para. 55.

[24] 'An Idea whose Time has Come and Gone?' *The Economist*, 23 July 2009.

Yet R2P's effectiveness in Kenya can not easily be replicated. For one, the Kenyan authorities accepted, to some extent even welcomed, regional and international involvement so that the objection of intervention in internal affairs hardly arose. Second, R2P's application did not involve sanctions or military intervention which meant that the Secretary-General could invoke R2P 'without the explicit authorization of the Security Council.'[25] This bypassing of the Council ensured that members of the Permanent Five (P5) did not move to obstruct the application of R2P.[26]

Other situations have been more prohibitive. In the case of Burma, for example, in 2007, Western governments drew attention in the Security Council to the massive attacks by the military on civilians in ethnic minority areas in which systematic rape, abuse of prisoners and forced displacement were being carried out. However, both China and Russia made clear that they would oppose any collective action against the junta on the grounds that the situation did not constitute a threat to international peace and security.[27]

In the case of Darfur, China at the behest of Sudan blocked any reference to R2P in the Security Council Resolution authorising an African Union-UN force to protect IDPs and other civilians.[28] Although several hundred thousand Darfurians had died in 2003-4 and more than two million had been pushed into squalid IDP camps, the umbrella of R2P was denied them.

In his report to the General Assembly in 2009, the Secretary-General regretted the 'failure' of the international community to stem the massive violence and displacements in Darfur, the Democratic Republic of the Congo (DRC) and Somalia, pointing out that this 'has undermined public confidence in the United Nations and our collective espousal of the principles relating to the responsibility to protect.'[29]

In the case of Sri Lanka, neither the Secretary-General nor the Security Council invoked R2P when the Sri Lankan military cornered tens of thousands of Tamil IDPs in a no fire zone in 2009 and began shelling and bombarding

---

[25] Report of the UN Secretary-General, *Implementing the responsibility to protect*, para. 51.

[26] It was nonetheless difficult to achieve Council support for some of the steps taken, see Remarks of Susan E. Rice, US Ambassador to the UN, USUN Press Release #126, 15 June 2009.

[27] See Jurgen Haacke, 'Myanmar, the Responsibility to Protect, and the Need for Practical Assistance,' *Global Responsibility to Protect*, 1/2: 179-181 (2009).

[28] UN Security Council Resolution 1769, 31 July 2007 superseded Resolution 1706, 31 August 2006, which in preambular para. 2 did mention R2P when it authorised a Chapter VII force. See Roberta Cohen, 'Will Security Council Resolution 1769 Make a Difference in Darfur?' Brookings Institution, 9 August 2007.

[29] See Report of the UN Secretary-General, *Implementing the responsibility to protect*, para. 55.

them. UN officials predicted 'a bloodbath', but it was left to NGOs to remind the international community that the fight against 'terrorists', in this case the LTTE (Liberation Tigers of Tamil Eelam), did not 'absolve' states of their responsibility to protect their citizens or the international community of its responsibility to react.[30] It is conceivable that at an early stage R2P might have worked preventively and achieved some protection for civilians, but it was never applied in deference to the Sri Lankan government's 'war on terror'. Even in the post-conflict period, there was no reference to R2P when the Sri Lankan government interned hundreds of thousands of IDPs behind barbed wire in overcrowded camps and restricted access to them by humanitarian organisations.[31]

The failure to apply R2P to any situation other than Kenya has meant that IDPs at this point in time can not readily look to this new concept for protection.

Narrowness of Application. When R2P was applied to the crisis in Kenya, its focus was narrow, responding mainly to the emergency phase of halting mass displacement. Yet in the *aftermath* of the violence, displaced people also suffered heavily. By most accounts, the government arbitrarily closed the camps irrespective of whether or not areas of return were sufficiently secure. IDPs were just 'dumped', said one leading UN expert,[32] and even today thousands remain in temporary settlements and transit sites without proper shelter, medicine and food. There also was a lack of planning for those who did not wish to return, and inadequate compensation for destroyed homes and property.[33] Moreover, '...the causes of the displacement are yet to be addressed conclusively, and tensions between communities remain high in areas such as the Rift Valley.'[34]

---

[30] See Global Centre for the Responsibility to Protect, 'Open Letter to the Security Council on the situation in Sri Lanka,' 15 April 2009; James Traub, 'At Risk in Sri Lanka's War,' *Washington Post*, 22 April 2009; and 'Amnesty International Urges UN to Publicize Civilian Casualty Figures,' *Press Release*, 29 May 2009.

[31] See Amnesty International, ibid; Rhys Blakely, 'Death toll is 1,400 a week at IDPs camp in Sri Lanka,' *The Times*, London, 10 July 2009; and Lydia Polgreen, 'Displaced by War, Many Tamils Languish in Sri Lankan Camps,' *New York Times*, 13 July 2009.

[32] Interview of author, 2 June 2009.

[33] Jacqueline Klopp and Nuur Mohamud Sheekh, 'Can the Guiding Principles make a difference in Kenya?', *Forced Migration Review*, December 2008, pp. 19-20. See also Tom Odula, 'Official: Kenya's postelection aid program failed,' Washington Post, 7 December 2009; and IDP Action, Statement on World Refugee Day, 20 June 2009.

[34] Internal Displacement Monitoring Centre, *Global Overview of Trends and Developments in 2008*, April 2009, p. 43. See also Jeffrey Gettleman, 'Under Wraps, Kenya's Bill For Bloodshed Nears Payment,' *New York Times*, 16 July 2009.

Under R2P, the international community is supposed to help states 'build capacity to protect their populations.' The concept includes an international 'responsibility to rebuild.'[35] The UN Peacebuilding Commission to its credit did in 2008 fund a small community volunteer program in the Rift Valley to provide food, sanitation and medical essentials to IDPs and help prepare the groundwork for some returns.[36] But the application of R2P to Kenya did not appear to encompass an overall strategy for protecting IDPs after they were uprooted, so that safety and sustainability could be assured in all areas of return or integration. The Kenya National Commission for Human Rights has charged the government with violating the Guiding Principles on Internal Displacement, and the Commission of Inquiry into Post-Election Violence in Kenya has called for the adoption of a national IDP policy based on the Guiding Principles.[37]

The Sidelining of the Guiding Principles on Internal Displacement. The Secretary-General's report on implementing R2P makes no mention of the Guiding Principles even though in the one case where R2P was applied, civil society organisations and Kenya's national human rights commission called for the application of the Principles. The UN legal office reportedly removed the reference from the text on the grounds that the Principles are not 'hard law'. Not only is this shortsighted and a bad precedent for R2P, but it is at variance with the resolutions of the General Assembly, Commission on Human Rights and Human Rights Council. They all call for the promotion and implementation of the Principles and regularly refer to them as an 'important tool' and 'standard' for the protection of IDPs;[38] further, the World Summit Outcome document recognises the Principles as 'an important international framework for the protection of IDPs.'[39] At least 20 states have adopted laws or policies based on the Principles and they should be encouraged to implement their provisions. John Holmes, UN Under-Secretary-General for Humanitarian Affairs, provided just that in calling for the implementation of the Principles and affirming that 'the Guiding Principles have become the accepted international standard for IDPs' and 'a watershed

[35] International Commission on Intervention and State Sovereignty, *The Responsibility to Protect*, 2001, available at www.iciss-ciise.gc.ca

[36] UN Peacebuilding Fund, Bulletin No. 5, January 2009, p. 2.

[37] Klopp and Sheekh, 'Can the Guiding Principles make a difference in Kenya?'

[38] See for example General Assembly Resolution 56/154, 19 December 2001; UN Commission on Human Rights Resolution 2003/51, 23 April 2003; and General Assembly Resolution A/RES/62/153, 6 March 2008.

[39] UN General Assembly, World Summit Outcome 2005, para. 132.

event in protecting IDPs.'[40] When R2P is applied, the promotion of the Principles must be part and parcel of the protection of IDPs.

Exclusion of Disaster IDPs. In a speech in Berlin in 2008, the UN Secretary-General warned that 'Extending the principle [of R2P] to cover other calamities, such as HIV/AIDS, climate change, or response to natural disasters, would undermine the 2005 consensus and stretch the concept beyond recognition or operational utility.'[41] By the stroke of a pen the Secretary-General thus ruled out of R2P's potential protection the millions of persons expected to be uprooted by disasters and climate change. The exclusion is said to accord with the World Summit Outcome document which omits natural disasters from the R2P formulation even though the ICISS report upon which R2P was based recommended as a criteria for R2P's application,

> ...overwhelming natural or environmental catastrophes, ***where the state concerned is either unwilling or unable to cope, or call for assistance, and significant loss of life is occurring or threatened*** [emphasis added].[42]

The Secretary-General's Special Adviser Edward Luck reinforced this exclusion with the argument that R2P could only be triggered if 'murder or extermination committed as part of "a widespread or systematic attack" against the civilian population' were to take place.[43] However, if, in the context of a natural disaster, a government were to deliberately cause serious injury to the physical and mental health of massive numbers of the civilian population through blatant neglect, its action (or inaction) could well be said to constitute an attack on that population as postulated by Luck. Indeed, the Burmese government's 'reckless indifference' toward the victims of Cyclone Nargis in 2008 made it possible to argue that it was intentionally causing suffering on a massive scale and possibly crimes against humanity.[44] Former Canadian Foreign Minister

---

[40] John Holmes, 'Foreword,' *Forced Migration Review*, December 2008, p. 3.

[41] Ban Ki-moon, Address of the UN Secretary General at event on Responsible Sovereignty: International Cooperation for a Changed World, Berlin, 15 July 2008.

[42] ICISS, *The Responsibility to Protect*, p. 33.

[43] Edward C. Luck, Testimony before Subcommittee on International Development, Foreign Assistance, Economic Affairs and International Environmental Protection, Committee on Foreign Relations, U.S. Senate, 17 June 2008. Under the Rome Statute of the International Criminal Court, adopted in Rome, Italy on 27 July 1998 (entered into force 2 July 2002), inhumane acts 'intentionally causing great suffering, or serious injury to body or to mental or physical health' are included under crimes against humanity when committed as part of 'a widespread or systematic attack directed against any civilian population.'

[44] Gareth Evans, 'Facing Up to Our Responsibilities,' *The Guardian*, 12 May 2008. See also Roberta Cohen, 'The Burma Cyclone and the Responsibility to Protect,' *Global Responsibility to Protect*, 1/2: 253-257 (2009).

Lloyd Axworthy argued that Burma's 'actively impeding the timely arrival of assistance and medications to more than one million people' should have invoked R2P: 'What is the moral distinction between closing the door of rescuing people from death by machete and closing the door of life-saving aid?'[45]

When the definition of IDPs was first debated in the 1990s, similar controversies arose. Those opposed to the inclusion of disaster victims argued that this would broaden the concept and make it less meaningful. Disaster IDPs were said not to have the same protection needs as those uprooted by conflict. However, the majority pointed out that governments sometimes responded to disasters by persecuting or neglecting certain groups on political or ethnic grounds. In Ethiopia, in the mid 1980s, the Derg, under the pretext of responding to a natural disaster, forcibly and brutally relocated hundreds of thousands of highland Tigreans whom it considered political opponents into lowland malaria-infested areas; large numbers died as a result. In Sudan, the government refused to declare a state of emergency or request international aid during drought-related famines until it was forced to by the international community because of the widespread sickness and death.[46]

A number of scholars, moreover, have pointed out that the mere invoking of R2P can prove valuable to protecting those at risk. Its mention at the time of Cyclone Nargis reportedly made the Burmese government more responsive to the victims and the international community more actively engaged.[47]

Tensions between human rights and humanitarian protection of IDPs. R2P's emphasis on human rights protection has at times created tensions with humanitarian programs for IDPs. When French Foreign Minister Bernard Kouchner called for R2P's application during Cyclone Nargis, and French, British and US warships neared Burma's coast, UN Emergency Relief Coordinator Holmes strongly protested against any form of coercion to protect the IDPs as this could undermine international and regional efforts to bring in humanitarian aid. Military force, he did not believe 'would be helpful to the people we are actually trying to help.'[48] R2P was even opposed as an umbrella for the *non-military* actions taken by the Secretary-General, the UN

[45] Lloyd Axworthy and Allen Rock, 'Responsibility to Protect? Yes,' *Globe and Mail*, 9 May 2008.

[46] Cohen and Deng, *Masses in Flight*, p. 16.

[47] Haacke, 'Myanmar, the Responsibility to Protect, and the Need for Practical Assistance,' p. 169.

[48] World Federalist Movement Institute for Global Policy, 'The Responsibility to Protect and its Application,' 9 May 2009.

and the Association of Southeast Asian Nations (ASEAN). It was argued that negotiation and cooperation with the authorities without reference to R2P was the most effective means of gaining access to affected areas. Similarly, in Darfur, humanitarian aid workers have opposed coercive military action under the R2P label on the grounds that it could lead to the expulsion of their assistance programs for IDPs.[49]

For the Executive Director of Médecins Sans Frontières USA, Nicholas de Torrente, the integration of humanitarian aid into broader political and security frameworks risks politicising and jeopardising relief operations. It also identifies aid workers with one side of a conflict and can expose them to attacks.[50] Many humanitarian aid workers have expressed difficulty as well with the very concept of 'protection,' arguing that going beyond delivering food, medicine and shelter could lead to denial of access, the expulsion of staff and interfere with relationships with governments on humanitarian and development issues. Other aid workers, however, consider protection essential to their work, and argue that when genocide and atrocity crimes are being committed, neutrality is not an option.

The extent to which R2P will encourage humanitarian organisations to engage more actively in protecting the physical safety and human rights of IDPs caught up in humanitarian emergencies remains to be seen. Nor is it clear whether UN human rights bodies will move beyond monitoring to play more of an actual protection role in the field.

Another area of tension between human rights protection and humanitarian operations is in the pursuit of international criminal justice. The Secretary-General's 2009 report affirms that the International Criminal Court (ICC) and the United Nations-assisted tribunals 'have added an essential tool for implementing the responsibility to protect.'[51] Yet when the ICC issued an arrest warrant for Sudanese President Omar al-Bashir for having committed crimes against humanity against IDPs and other affected civilians in Darfur, the Sudanese government put more than one million IDPs at risk. It expelled from the IDP camps thirteen international humanitarian NGOs and closed three local NGOs, affecting vital humanitarian services for more than one million people. For humanitarian advocates in Darfur, the pursuit of justice could not have been more ill timed and some supported Security Council

[49] See Julie Flint, 'In Sudan, Help Comes From Above,' *New York Times*, 6 July 2007; and 'Aid Held Hostage,' MSF Foundation, October 2006.

[50] Statement of Nicholas de Torrente, Northwestern University Conference on Human Rights, 22 January 2009.

[51] Report of the UN Secretary-General, *Implementing the Responsibility to Protect*, para. 18.

deferral in exchange for the readmission of the humanitarian workers. For human rights advocates, however, the arrest warrant constituted the long awaited culmination of an investigation into international crimes in Darfur that had been authorised by the Security Council.[52] The clash demonstrates how ICC decisions implementing R2P could undermine humanitarian field operations in certain instances.

R2P's equation with military action. Although the Secretary-General regularly has repeated that R2P 'could involve any of the whole range of UN tools, whether pacific measures under Chapter VI of the Charter, coercive ones under Chapter VII, and/or collaboration with regional and sub-regional arrangements under Chapter VIII,' R2P is often equated by governments and the non-governmental community with military action. This misinterpretation of R2P can affect the protection of IDPs because it reinforces the view that efforts at protection really mean intervention under the cloak of humanitarian assistance. Such confounding of R2P with coercive action can be a setback to what has been achieved thus far for IDPs.[53] Indeed, it has taken more than a decade for governments and the international community to accept that they have responsibilities for the assistance and protection of IDPs and that national and international involvement does not constitute infringement of their sovereignty. From 1992 to 2004, Deng worked tirelessly to persuade governments that concern for IDPs was not a pretext for international political or military involvement. Indeed, the concept of 'sovereignty as responsibility' was intended to allay governmental fears about international programs for IDPs. Deng's 'farewell' letter to the Secretary-General underscored this:

---

[52] See Eric Reeves, 'Darfur, an ICC arrest warrant, and the humanitarian imperative,' *Boston Globe*, 13 March 2009; and Democracy Now, 'Human Rights Watch's Richard Dicker and Scholar, Mediator Alex de Waal, Debate International Criminal Court Indictment of Sudanese President for Mass Killings in Darfur,' http://www.democracynow.org/2009/3/6/hrws_richard_dicker_and_scholar_mediator. In Uganda, the initial reaction of the Lord's Resistance Army to ICC indictments in 2005 was to increase the intensity of its attacks on civilians and humanitarian workers, see Jacqueline Geis and Alex Mundt, 'When To Indict? The Impact of Timing of International Criminal Indictments on Peace Processes and Humanitarian Action,' Brookings-Bern-Project on Internal Displacement, February 2009, p. 7.

[53] See Erin D. Mooney, 'The Guiding Principles and the Responsibility to Protect,' *Forced Migration Review*, December 2008, pp. 11-13, which points out that while there is a compatibility and shared lineage between the two concepts, in certain circumstances, 'explicitly linking R2P to internal displacement and the [Guiding] Principles could risk confounding the latter with intervention in internal affairs and undermine the wide acceptance of the Principles that has been so carefully cultivated over the past decade.'

> The main principle that guided me in my work on the mandate has been to balance between allaying the fears of Governments about national sovereignty while impressing upon them the compelling humanitarian and human rights concerns of the international community with the plight of the internally displaced.[54]

Walter Kälin, the UN's current Representative of the Secretary-General on the Human Rights of IDPs, has carefully avoided linking internal displacement to military intervention when setting forth protection strategies for IDPs so as not to compound humanitarian and human rights crises.

Limited confidence in military action. Although R2P may often be equated with military action, the results of such action for IDPs have been limited. Security Council resolutions have increasingly authorised UN peacekeepers to assume protection responsibilities for IDPs and other affected populations in internal conflict situations. The responsibilities have ranged from ensuring humanitarian access, protecting IDPs in and around camps, deterring sexual violence, ensuring the protection of humanitarian staff, creating conditions for safe and dignified returns, and accompanying IDPs home. Whether in the Balkans, Rwanda, the DRC, Darfur, Sierra Leone or a host of other countries, peacekeepers have been charged with providing protection to displaced persons and in many instances they have enhanced security for them.[55] But peacekeeping missions have also proved a great disappointment to those in need of protection. Missions have often been thwarted by host country interference with their operations, insufficient numbers of troops and equipment, insufficiently trained forces, and ambiguous mandates that do not fully allow for robust protection. In some cases, peacekeepers even have become involved in abusing IDP populations, especially women and girls they are expected to protect. As a result, IDP advocates have become more cautious about looking to peacekeeping missions as a panacea for protection.

Even where robust military force has been applied, as in Kosovo when NATO took unilateral action, the intervention was not able to prevent mass killings, rapes and deportations. Preoccupation with preventing NATO casualties resulted in no ground troops being introduced and reliance on air strikes from 15,000 feet, which at times hit caravans and trains carrying IDPs. To be

---

[54] Letter from Francis M. Deng to Kofi Annan, 10 November 2004, quoted in Weiss and Korn, *Internal Displacement: Conceptualization and its consequences*, p. 50.

[55] See William G. O'Neill, *A New Challenge for Peacekeepers: The Internally Displaced*, Brookings-SAIS Project on Internal Displacement, April 2004, pp. 6-7, 8-9, 24-39; and William G. O'Neill and Violette Cassis, *Protecting Two Million Internally Displaced: The Successes and Shortcomings of the African Union in Darfur*, Brookings-Bern Project on Internal Displacement, November 2005.

sure, all Serb forces were eventually forced to withdraw, but the military strategy failed to prevent many of the immediate atrocities against IDPs and other civilians.[56]

International interventions have also been slow in coming. Because the UN has not yet developed the rapid response military capacity needed to protect IDPs and other civilians in unfolding emergencies, it must start from scratch each time. In Darfur, after more than two years the UN has still not been able to deploy 26,000 troops and police while needed equipment like helicopters is still lacking. In the DRC, it took more than a month for the UN to authorise 3,000 additional troops to deal with accelerated violence in North Kivu and many more months to actually deploy the force. The mandate and conduct of the UN Mission in the DRC (MONUC) are also questionable when it comes to IDP protection. MONUC has been authorised to assist the government to create a safe environment, but government troops have been responsible for much of the displacement and sexual violence affecting IDPs and other civilians.[57]

The Way Forward

There are a number of steps that can be taken to better reconcile the protection needs of IDPs with R2P. Before identifying them, however, it is important to reiterate that the concept may in fact be applied in very few cases because there is little or no consensus on how to operationalise R2P. Nonetheless, an in-depth study of the Kenya case would be helpful to evaluate the factors that contributed to the positive results as well as to identify what failed to be achieved. IDP concerns for example were not taken into account as fully as they should have been. Indeed, strategies can be gleaned from the Kenya experience that better reconcile R2P with IDP protection.

First, when R2P is applied, the special protection needs of IDPs should be made an integral part of the strategy. Displaced people after all are often among the principal victims of crimes against humanity, ethnic cleansing and war crimes. In most emergencies they are found to suffer higher mortality rates than the general population and are more vulnerable to physical attack, disease, sexual

---

[56] Roberta Cohen and David A. Korn, 'Failing the Internally Displaced,' *Forced Migration Review*, August 1999, pp. 12-13.

[57] Mary Beth Sheridan, 'Clinton to Visit E. Congo,' and Stephanie McCrummen, 'Congo Women Treated as Spoils of War,' *Washington Post*, 11 August 2009.

assault and abduction.[58] The Office of the Secretary-General should consult with international and non-governmental organisations engaged in IDP protection to ensure that any application of R2P incorporates the full range of their needs.

Second, the meaning of IDP protection should be made clear when R2P is applied. In the absence of an international treaty or dedicated agency like UNHCR to define protection for IDPs, the UN's Inter-Agency Standing Committee (IASC), composed of the major international humanitarian, human rights and development organisations, assumed the task in 1999. The IASC protection policy for IDPs, based on the Guiding Principles, defines protection as encompassing 'all activities aimed at obtaining full respect for the rights of the individual in accordance with the letter and spirit of the relevant bodies of law (human rights, humanitarian and refugee law).'[59] More simply put, IDP protection is interpreted as defending the physical security of IDPs, providing them with the basic necessities of life and promoting the enjoyment of their fundamental economic, social cultural, civil and political rights.[60] The policy calls for international monitoring and reporting of protection problems, assertive advocacy for the rights of IDPs and efforts to strengthen community initiatives. Any application of R2P should be guided by this policy and the documents developed for its implementation.[61]

Third, applying R2P to IDPs must go beyond the emergency phase and encompass prevention, protection and capacity building. The IDP protection policy encompasses preventive actions to diminish the risk of displacement, measures to assure protection and assistance during displacement, and the integration of protection concerns into return or resettlement programs. In Kenya, preventive efforts might have served to save lives and head off mass displacement. The intense ethnic tensions preceding the 2007 election should have acted as an alert to the international community to plan for possible involvement. Once the violence and displacement occurred, the scope of involvement should have gone beyond emergency needs and encompassed safe and

[58] Erin D. Mooney, 'The Concept of Internal Displacement and the Case for Internally Displaced Persons as A Category of Concern,' *Refugee Survey Quarterly*, 24/3: 15-18 (2005).

[59] Inter-Agency Standing Committee, Protection of Internally Displaced Persons, Policy Paper no. 2, Geneva, October 2000, p. 4.

[60] See UN Economic and Social Council, Commission on Human Rights, 'Report of the Representative of the Secretary-General on the human rights of internally displaced persons,' Walter Kälin, E/CN.4/2005/84, 12 December 2004, para. 42.

[61] See Roberta Cohen and Francis M. Deng, 'Mass displacement caused by conflict and one-sided violence: national and international responses,' *SIPRI Yearbook 2009* (New York: Oxford University Press, 2009), pp. 28-9.

sustainable solutions. As Kälin has repeatedly reminded the international community, 'Forced displacement is not a passing event in peoples' lives. It is a devastating transformation.'[62] Between half and three-quarters of all major refugee and IDP situations last five years or more, whether in camps or urban centers, and the need of the displaced for international attention after the emergency is over often remains acute.[63]

Fourth, any application of R2P must include reinforcement of the national responsibility to protect IDPs. A report defining the benchmarks of national responsibility was presented by Kälin to the UN in 2005.[64] These include: 1) preventive steps, in particular early-warning and rapid response mechanisms to protect populations under threat; 2) campaigns that build national solidarity around the displaced so as to counteract the ethnic, racial and ideological stigmas to which IDPs are often subject; 3) the adoption of national laws and policies to uphold the rights of the displaced based on the Guiding Principles on Internal Displacement; 4) the designation of state offices to carry out the laws and policies; 5) the allocation of adequate national resources; 6) the finding of solutions for the displaced that include safe and sustainable returns, integration where they currently reside or relocation in another part of the country; 7) assistance with property restitution or compensation and the establishment of mechanisms to settle disputes; and 8) the introduction of reconciliation measures to bring rival ethnic groups together.

Fifth, the promotion of the Guiding Principles on Internal Displacement must be a part of an R2P strategy. The Secretary-General and the entire UN system need to stand behind and promote the implementation of the Principles in R2P situations. To help states shape laws and policies based on the Principles, Kälin has developed a manual for law and policy makers,[65] which should be disseminated by the UN. A focus on the Principles will help reinforce the efforts of IDP associations and civil society organisations to hold their

---

[62] Walter Kälin, 'Strengthening the rights of internally displaced persons,' Statement at Conference on Ten Years of Guiding Principles on Internal Displacement, Achievements and Future Challenges, Oslo, 16 October 2008.

[63] Elizabeth Ferris, 'Durable solutions for IDPs in protracted situations: a work in progress,' 1 June 2007, Background paper prepared for the Expert Seminar on Protracted IDP Situations, UNHCR and Brookings-Bern Project on Internal Displacement, Geneva, 21-22 June 2007, p. 25.

[64] Brookings-Bern Project on Internal Displacement, *Addressing Internal Displacement: A Framework for National Responsibility*, April 2005 (the Foreword acknowledges Erin Mooney as author), available at http://www.brookings.edu/projects/idp/20050401_nrframework.aspx

[65] Brookings-Bern Project on Internal Displacement, *Protecting Internally Displaced Persons: A Manual for Law and Policymakers*, October 2008, available at http://www.brookings.edu/papers/2008/1016_internal_displacement.aspx

governments accountable to these standards. Support also should be given to regional organisations that develop normative frameworks based on the Principles. The African Union, for example, has adopted a legally binding convention on internal displacement while the Great Lakes region of Africa already has a legally binding protocol on IDPs requiring states to make the Guiding Principles part of their domestic law.[66] In R2P situations, regional bodies should be expected to promote national efforts in line with the Principles.

Sixth, the UN Peacebuilding Commission should ensure that IDP needs are integrated into recovery plans when R2P is applied. The Commission's program in Kenya in the Rift Valley is to be commended but it is too small an effort and does not extensively encompass the sustainability of IDP returns or the grievances of the different ethnic groups, in particular their disputes over property, land and power sharing, which lie at the root of the conflict and displacement. The Commission's 2009 'strategic framework' for the Central African Republic is more instructive. It recognises that post-conflict recovery should include the reintegration of displaced people and calls for 'a strategy for internal displacement,' covering all phases of displacement – prevention, protection and sustainable solutions.[67] This strategic framework should be applied more regularly, especially in R2P situations when large numbers of IDPs and returning refugees are involved.[68]

Seventh, flexibility must be shown in applying R2P when it comes to natural disasters. Cyclone Nargis could well have been a case for applying R2P, although most observers concluded from hindsight that R2P would not have produced the access and cooperation that was achieved with the Burmese government. Nonetheless, it would be a mistake to make this cyclone the litmus test of response to all future situations where crimes against humanity might be committed within the context of a disaster. The peremptory exclusion of *all* disaster survivors from the umbrella of R2P protection may need to be revisited in

---

[66] For AU Convention for the Protection and Assistance of IDPs in Africa, 22 October 2009, see www.africa-union.org/root/ar/index/AU-IDP%20Convention%20Assembly%20-%20Final%20-%2010.23%20pm%2023%20Oct.doc; for Great Lakes Protocol on the Protection and Assistance to Internally Displaced Persons, 30 November 2006, see http://www.brookings.edu/projects/idp/Laws-and-Policies/~/media/Files/Projects/IDP/Laws%20and%20Policies/Great%20Lakes/GreatLakes_IDPprotocol_2006.pdf

[67] UN General Assembly/Security Council, Draft Strategic Framework for Peacebuilding in the Central African Republic 2009-2011, PBC/3/CAF/L.1, 23 March 2009 (limited distribution)

[68] See Walter Kälin, 'Durable Solutions for internally displaced persons: an essential dimension of peace-building,' Statement before the UN Peacebuilding Commission, Working Group on Lessons Learned, 13 March 2008.

cases where governments refuse to assume their protection responsibilities and commit mass atrocities against the survivors.

Eighth, addressing IDP protection effectively will require strengthened international and regional institutions that can be relied upon when R2P is applied. Although institutional arrangements for IDPs have improved over the past decade, many weaknesses persist. In the area of advocacy and policy, the UN basically relies on the Representative of the UN Secretary-General for the Human Rights of IDPs, a single individual, to raise awareness to the problem globally and promote adherence to the Guiding Principles. Although Kälin's efforts have been unremitting, he is an unpaid part-time volunteer who has to set aside time from his teaching and also find the resources for his activities. The Office of the UN High Commissioner for Human Rights (OHCHR) to which his mandate is officially tied provides only minimal support. In fact its approach is a model of mindless bureaucracy: it treats the IDP mandate the same way it does all other *rapporteurs* who report to the Human Rights Council. Yet many of the others prepare studies of single countries' human rights records or report on thematic issues like counterterrorism, whereas the Representative of the Secretary-General has to respond to the needs of more than 25 million persons throughout the world uprooted from their homes in destitute, life threatening conditions and mobilise national, regional and international efforts to protect them. Commenting on this inexplicable inadequacy, two leading experts wrote, 'Even for a seasoned UN observer, it is hard to understand how this theater has lasted so long.'[69] The need for a full-time Representative with sufficient staff and resources is long overdue.

In the field, institutional arrangements must also be strengthened. In 2005, the UN Office for the Coordination of Humanitarian Affairs (OCHA) signed an agreement with the different UN agencies to divide up responsibilities for IDPs. In the area of protection, UNHCR assumed the lead coordinating role. However, its in-house capacity to deal with IDPs is weak. To be sure, it increased the number of IDPs its overall programs reached, but it has yet to set up a corps of IDP protection officers, to expand its presence in the field where IDPs are in danger, and to undertake proactive advocacy with governments and non-state actors on behalf of IDP security.[70] Resources are insufficient for IDP protection and agency staff is divided over extensively altering the nature of the agency. Some prefer to make IDPs an 'add-on' to the work of a refugee

[69] Weiss and Korn, *Internal Displacement: Conceptualization and its consequences,* p. 123.

[70] See Cohen and Deng, 'Mass displacement caused by conflicts and one-sided violence,' pp. 29-30, 35.

agency rather than an integral part of its protection programs. However, if the gap between refugee and IDP protection persists, the UN may have to consider other options, including the creation of a new office more willing and able to extend protection to IDPs.

At the regional level, strengthened institutional capacity will also be needed so that organisations like the African Union, the South African Development Community, the Organization of American States and the Organization for Security and Cooperation in Europe can effectively contribute to the international protection of displaced populations.[71]

Ninth, in applying R2P, greater efforts will need to be made to reconcile human rights with humanitarian objectives. Consulting with IDPs should be an essential part of this process, given the impact of both human rights and humanitarian objectives on their lives. In Sudan, for example, IDPs and refugees interviewed were reported to be in favor of the ICC indictment of Bashir, the humanitarian cost notwithstanding.[72] At the same time, better planning and timing of potentially conflicting human rights and humanitarian programs has been recommended to reduce the tension,[73] as has stronger UN leadership. A 2004 UN evaluation urged senior officials to give greater support to personnel in the field who raised protection concerns and called for a more 'principled approach,' with better 'coordination, planning and strategizing'among UN offices where protection is concerned.[74]

Tenth, dialogue with insurgent groups should be encouraged as a form of protection for IDPs. Large numbers of IDPs and other civilians are often under insurgent control.[75] While the Secretary-General's report calls for military assistance to help states deal with armed insurgencies, it does not suggest direct measures for dealing with the insurgents themselves. For Jan Egeland, the former UN Under-Secretary-General for Humanitarian

---

[71] See Statement of the Representative of the Secretary-General on the Human Rights of Internally Displaced Persons, Dr. Walter Kälin, 39th Ordinary Session of the African Commission on Human and Peoples' Rights, Banjul, 12 May 2006, available at www.brookings.edu/fp/projects/idp/RSG_stmt_ACHPR_052006.pdf

[72] See 'The Reaction to the Arrest Warrant against Sudanese President Al-Bashir,' *Refugee Rights News*, 5/2 (April 2009); Nicholas D. Kristof, 'Watching Darfuris Die,' *New York Times*, 7 March 2009; and Eric Reeves, 'Darfur and International Justice,' *Dissent*, Summer 2009, p. 17.

[73] See Geis and Mundt, 'When to Indict?' pp. 13-18.

[74] Simon Bagshaw and Diane Paul, *Protect or Neglect: Toward a More Effective United Nations Approach to the Protection of Internally Displaced Persons*, UN Office for the Coordination of Humanitarian Affairs and Brookings-SAIS Project on Internal Displacement, 2004, pp. 5-7.

[75] See Greta Zeender, 'Engaging Armed Non-State Actors on Internally Displaced Persons Protection,' *Refugee Survey Quarterly*, 24/3: 96-111 (2005).

Affairs, negotiations with non-state actors are 'a humanitarian necessity' that can bring relief aid to beleaguered communities, lessen abuse of civilians and maintain ceasefires.[76]

Eleventh, efforts should be made to dispel the notion that human rights protection through R2P means first and foremost military intervention. Prevention, the weakest link in protecting civilians, should be strengthened by building state capacity to withstand internal crises and avert displacement as well by engaging UN offices, governments and regional bodies to take concerted action, ranging from diplomacy to preventive deployment.[77] Applying R2P regularly to situations where military intervention is *not* involved, as was the case in Kenya, could also help to demonstrate the broad range of measures R2P encompasses. Some have called this 'R2P-Plus' and contend that the focus on 'humanitarian assistance and conflict prevention without any semblance of armed intervention' could 'augur well for the advancement of R2P.'[78]

Finally, an effective international protection capacity should be developed when strong measures are called for. The creation of an international protection capacity able to rapidly deploy well-trained military and police forces with clear and strong mandates, adequate numbers and sufficient equipment has thus far eluded the international community. Yet when military or police action is called for, IDP protection will depend upon those elements being in place. Military operations, moreover, will not be meaningful for IDPs if these operations themselves produce widespread rape, displacement and abuse. 'Peacekeeping plus' or peacekeeping that effectively protects civilians is what is required.[79]

---

[76] See Gerard McHugh and Manuel Bessler, *Humanitarian Negotiations with Armed Groups; A Manual for Practitioners* (New York: UN Office for the Coordination of Humanitarian Affairs, January 2006); and Jan Egeland, *A Billion Lives: An Eyewitness Report from the Frontlines of Humanity* (New York: Simon & Schuster, 2008), pp. 57-8, 203, 209, 214.

[77] See, for example, Gayle E. Smith et al, *The Price of Prevention: Getting Ahead of Global Crises* (Center for American Progress and Enough, Washington, DC, November 2008); and David Hamburg, *Preventing Genocide: Practical Steps Toward Early Detection and Effective Action* (Paradigm: Boulder, Co, 2008), pp. 98-262.

[78] Mely Caballero-Anthony and Belinda Chng, 'Cyclones and Humanitarian Crises; Pushing the Limits of R2P in Southeast Asia,' *Global Responsibility to Protect*, 1/2: 135-155 (2009), p. 145; see also Brian Barbour and Brian Gorlick, 'Embracing the "Responsibility to Protect": A Repertoire of Measures Including Asylum for Potential Victims,' *International Journal of Refugee Law*, 20/4: 533-566 (2008).

[79] Evans, *The Responsibility to Protect*, pp. 120-125, 214.

Conclusion

The historically close relationship between providing protection to IDPs and the concept of R2P has created the expectation that R2P by definition will prove beneficial to IDPs. However, it can not be assumed that R2P will automatically provide greater protection for IDPs. There may be situations where R2P's application compounds their problems, creates more displacement and falls short of helping them. It is therefore essential to continue to explore the relationship between R2P and IDP protection and make sure that R2P strategies are carefully designed to fit the needs of IDPs. R2P after all is a new concept that needs to be tried out and carefully tailored to IDP concerns so as to ensure that genuine protection is provided.

Chapter Three

Something Old, Something New, Something Borrowed ... Something Blue? The Protection Potential of a Marriage of Concepts between R2P and IDP Protection[1]

Erin D. Mooney

Introduction

Around the world, across more than 50 countries, there are an estimated 26 million people who have been forced to flee their homes and communities due to conflict, violence, or massive violations of human rights, but who remain within their own country as 'internally displaced persons' (IDPs).[2] When natural disasters and development projects are taken into account, the number of IDPs swells by many tens of millions more.[3] Unlike refugees, who

---

[1] A draft of this paper was presented by the author at Protecting People in Conflict and Crisis: Responding to the Challenges of a Changing World, University of Oxford, 22-24 September 2009.

[2] Internal Displacement Monitoring Centre (IDMC), *Internal Displacement: Global Overview of Trends and Developments in 2008* (Geneva: IDMC, 2009), p. 8.

[3] In 2008 alone, compared with 4.6 million persons being newly internally displaced due to conflict and violence, at least 36 million people were displaced by sudden-onset natural disasters occurring that year, often as a result of climate change. Slow-onset disasters, such as drought and sea-level changes, are considered likely to have displaced many millions more people. *Monitoring Disaster Displacement in the Context of Climate Change* (Geneva: United Nations Office for the Coordination of Humanitarian Affairs and IDMC, September 2009), p. 3. As regards development-induced displacement, reference generally is made to statistics compiled by the World Bank's Environment Department, according to which approximately 10 million people are displaced worldwide each year due to dam construction, urban development, and transportation and infrastructure programs. However, the magnitude of development-induced displacement is thought to be much greater given that available figures typically only count persons compelled to leave legally acquired land as part of the process directly related to the planned project, while 'ignoring those living in the vicinity of, or downstream from, projects whose livelihoods and socio-cultural milieu might be adversely affected by the project.' Moreover, the World Bank

by definition are outside of their country of nationality, unable to access its protection and therefore require international protection, for IDPs and other populations still within their own country, responsibility for their protection and assistance lies, first and foremost, with the authorities of the country concerned; the international community has only an auxiliary role. However, countries often lack the capacity or even the political will to fulfill this responsibility; the authorities themselves may be complicit in creating or condoning the conditions causing displacement, in some cases even in deliberately displacing populations.

The plight of IDPs typically is highly precarious.[4] To begin with, the very fact of being displaced can constitute an abuse of rights. For instance, IDPs may be the victims of a strategy of deliberate displacement, typically carried out through extremely brutal terror tactics. When this occurs along ethnic or religious lines, it constitutes what has come to be known as 'ethnic cleansing'. Once it occurs, displacement, whatever its cause, inherently exposes those affected to a range of risks and vulnerabilities. Forced from their homes and often left exposed to the elements, compelled to leave most possessions behind, and cut off from their land and habitual livelihood, IDPs suddenly find themselves stripped of their habitual means of protection and survival. Moreover, in the chaos of flight, families often become separated, thereby breaking up the most fundamental unit of protection, especially for children, older persons and persons with disabilities. Compounding their situation, IDPs frequently are stigmatised and viewed with hostility and suspicion in the localities in which they sought safety. Many remain at risk of ongoing acts of violence, including sexual and gender-based violence, and abuse such as arbitrary arrest and forced military recruitment. IDPs often remain trapped in areas of conflict, to which humanitarian access may be constrained due to insecurity or other restrictions. The International Committee of the Red Cross (ICRC) points out that while IDPs have the same need for legal protection as other civilians during conflict 'it goes without saying that, deprived of shelter and their habitual sources of food, water, medicine and money, they have different, and often more urgent material needs.'[5] In fact, some of the highest rates of

figures do not take into account displacement due to other types of development projects, such as for natural resource extraction. See Jason Stanley, 'Development-induced Displacement and Resettlement', *Forced Migration Online Research Guide* (2004), http://www.forcedmigration.org/guides/fmo022/, accessed 28 October 2009.

[4] Erin Mooney, 'The Concept of Internal Displacement and the Case for Internally Displaced Persons as a Category of Concern', *Refugee Survey Quarterly*, 24/3: 9-26 (2005).

[5] Jean-Daniel Tauxe, 'We Should Have Access to Displaced Civilians', *International Herald Tribune*, 1 March 2009, p. 10. The author of this article at the time was the Director of Operations for the ICRC.

mortality and malnutrition recorded in humanitarian emergencies have been among IDPs.[6] Moreover, the specific vulnerabilities associated with displacement do not necessarily diminish with time. Worldwide, most IDPs are in a protracted situation of displacement, waiting years or even decades for a solution to their plight.[7]

International concern about the global crisis of internal displacement, in particular its protection dimensions, was placed indelibly on the international agenda by the UN Commission on Human Rights (CHR) in the early 1990s.[8] Since that time, international developments have crystallised in a number of areas. First, awareness of the problem has been raised and broad-based concern mobilised through advocacy and research; in the early years, this was carried out almost entirely by the UN Secretary-General's Representative on Internally Displaced Persons (RSG on IDPs) in collaboration with the Brookings Institution Project on Internal Displacement. Second, the normative framework for the protection of IDPs has been clarified with the Guiding Principles on Internal Displacement,[9] which enjoy broad international acceptance as well as significant traction at the national and regional levels. Third, international humanitarian and development agencies, which historically were averse to addressing IDP protection, have become progressively more engaged in rights issues and have collectively organised themselves towards promoting greater predictability and accountability in the international response.[10] Indeed, discussions about the protection concerns of IDPs have

---

[6] Peter Salama, Paul Spiegel and Richard Brennan, 'No Less Vulnerable: The Internally Displaced in Humanitarian Emergencies', *The Lancet*, 357/9266: 1430-31 (5 May 2001). A major factor leading to these high mortality rates has been that IDPs often lack access to vaccination for entirely preventable diseases such as measles, whereas for refugees '[m]ajor outbreaks of vaccine-preventable diseases such as measles have been uncommon in refugee camps since the late 1980s' owing to the high priority placed on vaccination campaigns in refugee camps. A study in 2003 by *Médecins Sans Frontières* (MSF) found IDPs in northern Uganda suffered mortality rates five to ten times higher than expected in Uganda, owing to the rate of violence as well as to measles outbreaks due to lack of vaccination. N. Nathan, M. Tatay, P. Piola, S. Lake and V. Brown, 'High Mortality in Displaced Populations of Northern Uganda', *The Lancet*, 363/9418: 1402 (24 April 2004).

[7] IDMC, *Internal Displacement*, p. 14. See also *Forced Migration Review*, Issue 33 (September 2009) dedicated to protracted displacement.

[8] See Thomas G. Weiss and David A. Korn, *Internal Displacement: Conceptualization and its Consequences* (London and New York: Routledge, 2006), pp. 11-29.

[9] *Guiding Principles on Internal Displacement*, Report of the Representative of the Secretary-General on Internally Displaced Persons, Mr. Francis Deng, E/CN.4/1998/53/Add.2, 11 February 1998.

[10] See Roberta Cohen and Francis M. Deng, *Masses in Flight: The Global Crisis of Internal Displacement* (Washington, D.C.: Brookings Institution, 1998); Erin D. Mooney, 'Towards a

expanded beyond the UN human rights forum to now be a central issue in humanitarian discourse and one featuring regularly in UN Security Council deliberations. Fourth, operational response capacities, strategies and coordination mechanisms have begun to be enhanced with a view to securing protection for IDPs in practice. The international community is now better equipped than ever before to respond to the global crisis of internal displacement. Nonetheless, and as any number of situations around the world epitomise, these developments have yet to amount to a comprehensive and effective international protection regime to which IDPs can turn when their own governments fail them.

In a more recent development, the 'responsibility to protect' (R2P) doctrine endorsed by states at the 2005 World Summit[11] is being promoted as holding the potential to unlock and unblock persistent gaps in the protection of IDPs.[12] There generally is 'an expectation among refugee and IDP advocates that R2P will be beneficial, even revolutionary' in enhancing the protection of people who are forcibly displaced.[13] This article explores what an association

---

Protection Regime for Internally Displaced Persons', in Edward Newman and Joanne van Selm (eds.), *Refugees and Forced Displacement: International Security, Human Vulnerability, and the State* (Tokyo, New York and Paris: United Nations University Press, 2003), pp. 159-80; Roberta Cohen, 'Developing an International System for Internally Displaced Persons', *International Studies Perspectives*, 7/2: 87-101 (2006).

[11] '2005 World Summit Outcome', UNGA Res. 60/1, 16 September 2005, (paras. 138-139).

[12] United Nations High Commissioner for Refugees (UNHCR), Erika Feller, Assistant High Commissioner for Refugees – Protection, at 'Towards a Culture of Protection', 8th Annual Forum on Human Rights, Dublin, Ireland: Global Human Rights Protection – The Way Forward, 30 June 2006, http://www.unhcr.org/refworld/docid/44aba8d54.html, accessed 29 October 2009 (describing R2P as 'a valuable framework for addressing prevailing human rights deficits' which would 'enable UNHCR to open up more protection possibilities for persons of concern, particularly in areas where there are currently real gaps', of which 'an obvious one has been protection of internally displaced persons.'); Brian Barbour and Brian Gorlick, 'Embracing the "Responsibility to Protect": A Repertoire of Measures Including Asylum for Potential Victims', *International Journal of Refugee Law*, 20/4: 533-566; António Guterres, 'Millions Uprooted: Saving Refugees and the Displaced', *Foreign Affairs*, 87/5: 90-100 (September/October 2008), pp. 92-93; and Corien W.A. Jonker, Chair of the Parliamentary Assembly of the Council of Europe (PACE) Committee on Migration, Refugee and Population, 'Future Directions for the Protection of IDPs through Domestic Law and Legally-binding Regional and Sub-Regional Instruments' at Ten Years of the Guiding Principles on Internal Displacement: Achievements and Future Challenges, Oslo, Norway, 16-17 October 2008, http://assembly.coe.int/ASP/APFeaturesManager/defaultArtSiteView.asp?ID=813, accessed 29 October 2009.

[13] Susan Harris-Rimmer, 'Refugees, IDPs and the R2P Doctrine', paper presented at Protecting People in Conflict and Crisis conference, University of Oxford, 22-24 September 2009.

with R2P might bring to existing approaches to the protection of IDPs. It sketches a portrait of a marriage between these two concepts, assessing their compatibility and considering what this suggests about the potential protection dividends that this match might engender. In contemplating this question, the core argument and conclusions of this essay call to mind an Anglo-American custom at marriage ceremonies captured in the rhyme: 'something old, something new, something borrowed, something blue'. According to this tradition, each item represents a good-luck token, usually worn by the bride; if she carries all of them on her wedding day, the marriage will be a happy and successful one.[14]

Something Old

The significance in the wedding custom of the element of 'something old' is straightforward, symbolising continuity with the past. Indeed, while 'R2P' as a catch-phrase is a recent addition to the international lexicon, in terms of international law, it is neither novel nor radical. Rather, its normative roots run deep. As UN Secretary-General Ban Ki-Moon has underscored, the formulation of R2P that was endorsed by the 2005 World Summit – that is, concerned with protecting populations from genocide, war crimes, ethnic cleansing and crimes against humanity – is 'firmly anchored in well-established principles of international law.'[15] For at least 60 years now, genocide, war crimes and crimes against humanity have been recognised as international crimes entailing responsibilities, under both treaty and customary international law, for states to prevent and punish their occurrence. This is set out, in particular, in the 1948 Convention on the Prevention and Punishment of the Crime of Genocide, the Geneva Conventions of 1949 and their 1977 Protocols, and more recently reaffirmed in the 1998 Rome Statute of the International Criminal Court.[16]

---

[14] On the particular meaning of each of these items, which will be explained in the main sections of this paper, see: Helen Bradley Foster and Donald Clay Johnson (eds.), *Wedding Dress Across Cultures* (New York: Berg, 2003), p. 143; and http://wiki.answers.com/Q/Where_did_the_wedding_custom_of_something_old_something_new_something_borrowed_something_blue_come_from&src=ansTT, accessed 29 October 2009.

[15] UN, *Implementing the Responsibility to Protect,* Report of the Secretary-General, A/63/677, 12 January 2009, (para. 3).

[16] 'Rome Statute of the International Criminal Court', A/CONF.183/9, 17 July 1998, entered into force 1 July 2002.

Ethnic cleansing does not have the same status of being a recognised international crime in its own right. R2P advocates suggest that it nonetheless constitutes a criminal act under international law in that it can be subsumed within the scope of the recognised crimes of genocide, war crimes and crimes against humanity.[17] More specifically, the ICRC, which serves as the custodian of international humanitarian law, considers ethnic cleansing to be a 'composite war crime' as it consists of a number of war crimes under the Geneva Conventions, their Protocols and customary law.[18] These include the 'unlawful deportation or transfer' of parts of the civilian population of an occupied territory or, in a situation of non-international armed conflict, 'ordering the displacement of the civilian population, in whole or in part, for reasons related to the conflict, unless the security of the civilians involved or imperative military reasons so demand.'[19] Crimes against humanity, which can occur in all circumstances and consist of specified acts committed as part of a widespread or systematic attack directed against a civilian population, include apartheid, the persecution of an identifiable group and the 'deportation or forcible transfer of population', meaning the 'forced displacement of the persons concerned by expulsion or other coercive acts from the area in which they are lawfully present, without grounds permitted under international law.'[20] Moreover, intrinsic to ethnic cleansing is racial discrimination, which is prohibited under both treaty and customary law and, as *jus cogens,* is a peremptory and non-derogable norm.[21] Further, the principle of non-discrimination is a cornerstone of the UN Charter.

Situations of genocide, war crimes, crimes against humanity and ethnic cleansing almost invariably will result in mass displacement; with ethnic cleansing this is the very aim. It should therefore come as no surprise that all four of these trigger scenarios for R2P are expressly addressed in the international standards for protecting IDPs articulated in the 1998 Guiding Principles

---

[17] Gareth Evans, *The Responsibility to Protect: Ending Mass Atrocity Crimes Once and for All,* (Washington, D.C.: Brookings Institution, 2008), pp. 12-13; Edward C. Luck, 'The United Nations and the Responsibility to Protect', *Policy Analysis Brief* (Stanley Foundation, August 2008), p. 4.

[18] Jean-Marie Henckaerts and Louise Doswald-Beck (eds.), *Customary International Humanitarian Law. Volume I: Rules* (International Committee of the Red Cross and Cambridge University Press, 2005), p. 603.

[19] *Ibid.*, pp. 457-474.

[20] 'Rome Statute', Article 7.

[21] Ian Brownlie, *Principles of Public International Law,* 4th ed. (Oxford: Oxford University Press, 1990), pp. 598-600 and 512-513.

on Internal Displacement. The Guiding Principles, which reflect and are consistent with international human rights law, international humanitarian law and international criminal law,[22] reaffirm the rights of IDPs and restate the responsibilities of states and other authorities, namely non-state actors, towards them. The Principles cover all phases of displacement: prevention of arbitrary displacement, protection and assistance during displacement, and securing voluntary, safe, and durable solutions to displacement.

The Guiding Principles explicitly and implicitly prohibit the four crimes with which R2P is concerned. From the outset, Principle 1 states that the Guiding Principles 'are without prejudice to individual criminal responsibility under international law, in particular relating to genocide, crimes against humanity and war crimes.'[23] Principle 6 prohibits arbitrary displacement, defining this as including situations when displacement 'is based on policies of apartheid, "ethnic cleansing" or similar practices aimed at/or resulting in altering the ethnic, religious or racial composition of the affected population'; and, as per the above-mentioned prohibitions articulated in international humanitarian law, when it occurs 'in situations of armed conflict unless the security of civilians involved or imperative military reasons so demand'.[24] Addressing abuses to which IDPs often run the risk of being subjected, Principles 10-13 expressly restate international prohibitions of various acts, which when committed in the context of armed conflict, can constitute war crimes and, when carried out as part of a widespread or systematic attack against a civilian population also are punishable as crimes against humanity. These include: murder; enforced disappearances; starvation as a method of combat; torture; rape; enforced prostitution; slavery or any contemporary form of slavery; and the conscription of children or using them to take part in hostilities.[25] Principle 14, recalling the right to liberty of movement and freedom to choose one's residence, specifies that for IDPs this means that they 'have the right to move freely in and out of camps or other settlements.' Article 7 of the Rome Statute states that the 'severe deprivation of physical liberty in violation of fundamental rules of law', when committed 'as part of a widespread or systematic

[22] See Walter Kälin, *Guiding Principles on Internal Displacement: Annotations,* Revised Edition (Washington, D.C.: American Society of International Law and the Brookings Institution, 2008).

[23] This means that 'persons suspected of having committed these crimes cannot avoid prosecution and punishment under international law simply on account of being internally displaced or invoking the Guiding Principles.' *Ibid.,* pp. 13-14.

[24] *Ibid.,* pp. 26-32.

[25] *Ibid.,* pp. 45-65.

attack directed against any civilian population,' constitutes a crime against humanity.

While R2P and the Guiding Principles therefore enjoy considerable degrees of overlap, there also exist important differences. Each framework is both narrower and broader in scope than the other. The scope of R2P is strictly limited by the World Summit Outcome document to the four specified crimes, but covers all populations at risk of these crimes. The Guiding Principles, by contrast, focus specifically on IDPs (while often restating general norms, applicable to 'every person') but cover a broader range of situations and protection concerns than R2P. The Principles address all causes of internal displacement, encompassing not only the four trigger scenarios of R2P, but also displacement caused by, or in order to avoid, violence or violations of human rights falling below the threshold of these crimes, as well as displacement due to natural or human-made disasters and due to development projects.[26] Moreover, the Principles define the protection responsibilities of states, other authorities and all other actors working with IDPs in relation to the whole panoply of rights – civil, political, economic, social and cultural – which IDPs, like other human beings, are entitled to enjoy without discrimination. For instance, the responsibilities of states that the Principles reaffirm and spell out include: replacing IDPs' lost personal documentation; ensuring that IDPs have access to essential medical services and sanitation; reuniting families separated by displacement as quickly as possible; ensuring that IDP children, whether or not they are in camps, have access to free primary education; and assisting IDPs to recover or receive compensation for property of which they were dispossessed as a result of displacement. That states have a wide range of responsibilities to protect the safety, welfare and dignity of persons under their territorial jurisdiction is hardly a new concept; it is central to international human rights law[27] and also is reflected in the obligations of states and non-state actors articulated by international humanitarian law. Louise Arbour, then UN High Commissioner for Human Rights has explained:

> Whether we call it responsibility to protect or anything else, States do have a responsibility under existing international law *vis-à-vis* the people on their territory, to extent [sic] protection equally against genocide, as against famine, disease,

[26] *Guiding Principles on Internal Displacement,* (Introduction, para. 2 and Principle 6.2(c)).

[27] James Nickel, 'How Human Rights Generate Duties to Protect and Provide', *Human Rights Quarterly,* 15/1: 77-86 (1993).

> ignorance, deprivation of the basic necessities of life, discrimination and the lack of freedom.[28]

Conceptually and in terms of international law, there exists a notion of a 'responsibility to protect' that is much broader than the officially endorsed R2P doctrine; it is this broader concept which finds reflection in the Guiding Principles.

Indeed, the Guiding Principles have as their stated purpose to provide specific legal guidance – to the RSG on IDPs, states, other authorities, and inter-governmental and non-governmental organisations – on the rights of IDPs and the corresponding responsibilities of States and other authorities towards them.[29] The Principles bring together in one document the many norms relevant to the protection of IDPs which previously were diffused in numerous different international legal instruments and therefore not easily accessible or understood to the non-specialist, including to humanitarian personnel on the frontline of protection efforts in the field who needed quick and clear guidance.[30] Tellingly, with the ink barely dry on the Principles and even before their presentation to the CHR, the Inter-Agency Standing Committee (IASC), which is comprised of all the UN and other major international humanitarian, human rights and development agencies, unanimously welcomed the Guiding Principles, encouraging its members to share them with their executive boards and their staff, especially those in the field, and to apply them in their activities on behalf of IDPs.[31] Moreover, governments in a number of countries have utilised the Principles as an authoritative reference on the basis of which to review and revise national legislation or to develop new legislation and policies for addressing internal displacement. This trend is evident also at the regional and sub-regional level, most notably with the recent adoption by the African Union of the world's first continent-wide legally binding instrument for protecting and assisting IDPs.[32]

Given the above-mentioned areas of overlap between the Guiding Principles and R2P, these developments in applying the Guiding Principles also serve to

---

[28] Louise Arbour, 'The Responsibility to Protect as a Duty of Care in International Law and Practice', *Review of International Studies*, 34/3: 445-458 (2008), p. 458.

[29] *Guiding Principles on Internal Displacement,* ('Introduction: Scope and Purpose', para. 3).

[30] Erin D. Mooney, 'Principles of Protection for Internally Displaced Persons', *International Migration,* 38/6: 81-101 (2001).

[31] See E/CN.4/1999/79, 25 January 1999, (para. 13).

[32] African Union, *Convention for the Protection and Assistance of Internally Displaced Persons in Africa (Kampala Convention),* 23 October 2009, http://www.africa-union.org, accessed 31 October 2009.

reinforce, by extension, the norms encapsulated by R2P. For example, in heralding the recent adoption of the African Union IDP Convention, UN High Commissioner for Refugees António Guterres expressly proclaimed that it 'represents the concept of "responsibility to protect" in action.'[33]

In terms of normative content, both R2P and the Guiding Principles are part of a larger continuum. They reflect and restate pre-existing protection responsibilities enshrined in international human rights law, international humanitarian law and international criminal law. While R2P and the Guiding Principles are not binding on states, in a strict legal sense, they are based on existing law that is binding. That they both articulate pre-existing norms in no way diminishes their normative value. To the contrary, it is one of their strengths; the experience in promoting the Guiding Principles attests that this can be tremendously useful towards securing states' acceptance and, ultimately, application of these standards. As Walter Kälin, who chaired the committee that drafted the Guiding Principles, has pointed out, it is the fact that their content was 'solidly grounded in existing international law' already agreed to by governments that has assured the Principles' 'authoritative character'.[34] The Guiding Principles and R2P also shared an historic moment: it was with the adoption of the 2005 World Summit Outcome document that 190 states not only endorsed the R2P doctrine but also, just a few paragraphs earlier, recognised the Guiding Principles 'as an important international framework for the protection of internally displaced persons.'[35]

Something New

According to the wedding custom, 'something new' symbolises optimism and hope for good fortune and success.

For IDPs, the main protection gaps are due to a lack not of legal standards but of their implementation; the fact that R2P does not create new legal obligations therefore is not problematic. The significance of R2P, rather, lies in that it 'offers an opportunity to improve the implementation of existing legal obligations to protect populations from genocide, war crimes, crimes against

[33] Melissa Fleming and Yusuf Hassan, 'African Union Adopts Major Convention to Protect and Assist the Internally Displaced', http://www.unhcr.org/4ae1e09d9.html, accessed 23 October 2009.

[34] Walter Kälin, 'The Future of the Guiding Principles on Internal Displacement', *Forced Migration Review*, Special Issue: 5-6 (2006), p. 5.

[35] '2005 World Summit Outcome, (para. 132).

humanity and ethnic cleansing.'[36] The R2P doctrine breathes new life into these long-standing obligations by bolstering accountability among states, both individually and collectively, to fulfil their commitments to protect populations from these serious crimes. R2P thereby raises expectations that these protection responsibilities will be realised in practice.

In addition, R2P ushered in a breakthrough in the debate over humanitarian intervention by reframing this to no longer speak of a 'right' of outsiders to 'intervene' but rather a 'responsibility', first and foremost of the State concerned, 'to protect' its own population.[37] In so doing, R2P contributed to mollifying in some measure the increasingly hardened attitudes and heightened sensitivities of states as a result of events of the 1990s, towards any discussion of international efforts to secure protection for populations at grave risk, including IDPs.

From the outset, international efforts for the protection of IDPs at every turn had to confront and ultimately overcome deep-seated concerns among states that these efforts were tantamount to external interference in what was, by definition, an internal matter. Cognisant of this political minefield, when the UN first began to tackle the issue in 1990, it did so with the equivalent of kid gloves, beginning cautiously with two successive studies of the global problem of internal displacement. Seeking to strengthen the focus on protection issues, Austria then introduced a draft resolution at the CHR in 1992 requesting the appointment of an independent expert to study the human rights issues related to IDPs. However, as an observer of events in the CHR noted at the time, the robust collective military action initiated in 1991 to protect Kurd IDPs in northern Iraq, based on UN Security Council Resolution 688 (1991), gave some states pause:

> This is one expert that was not meant to be. India, Bangladesh and a number of other countries in the South all expressed deep reservations.
>
> [...]
>
> International assistance to and protection of persons displaced within their own countries have always been problematic. This year, however, delegates had the benefit of hindsight, if not vision, having witnessed in the meantime the full effects of international action on behalf of displaced persons in Iraq. States continued to be preoccupied with their sovereignty, and were clearly reluctant to

---

[36] Ekkehard Strauss, 'A Bird in Hand is Worth Two in the Bush – On the Assumed Legal Nature of the Responsibility to Protect', *Global Responsibility to Protect,* 1/3: 291-323 (2009), p. 291.

[37] International Commission on Intervention and State Sovereignty (ICISS), *The Responsibility to Protect* (Ottawa: International Development Research Centre, 2001), p. vii.

appoint an independent expert with a broad mandate. This is likely to remain the position of the majority for some time.[38]

The compromise, which in the end proved to be a blessing in disguise, was not to appoint a *special rapporteur* – the usual title given to an independent human rights expert of the CHR – but rather to request the Secretary-General to appoint for one year a representative on the issue of IDPs. This distinction in title was significant. From the perspective of states, it sent a clear signal of the need for a different, more diplomatic, approach to the issue than the close scrutiny and finger-pointing of human rights violations which was the perception of the work of *special rapporteurs*. In reality, though not understood at the time, this decision would have the opposite effect; giving a higher profile to international efforts to advance the issue of IDP protection.[39]

The RSG on IDPs initially was assigned a mandate that included 'to seek again views and information from all governments on the human rights issues' and to undertake 'a comprehensive study identifying existing laws and mechanisms for the protection of the internally displaced, possible additional measures to strengthen implementation of these laws and mechanisms and alternatives for addressing protection needs not adequately covered by existing instruments.'[40] Beginning with his first report, RSG on IDPs Francis Deng emphasised the importance of 'making contacts with Governments and other pertinent actors to play a more delicate diplomatic function of facilitating dialogue and otherwise seeking ways of ameliorating the suffering of the displaced masses.'[41] By the end of the decade, several years of deft diplomacy on his part had gone a long way to significantly assuaging states' initial suspicions and strong sensitivities about international efforts on the IDP protection issue, though these were far from (and likely never will be) removed altogether.

However, beginning in 2000, after nearly ten years of international efforts that had progressively and measurably advanced the issue of IDP protection, a backlash of sorts began with a campaign, led by a small group of states,

---

[38] Guy S. Goodwin-Gill, 'Developments: United Nations Commission on Human Rights,' *International Journal of Refugee Law,* 4/2: 253-254 (1992), p. 254.

[39] Weiss and Korn, *Internal Displacement*, pp. 28-29, 34-35.

[40] E/CN.4/RES/1992/73 of 5 March 1992. This mandate, which initially was for a one-year period, subsequently has been renewed successively by the CHR and its successor the Human Rights Council. Serving in this position have been: Francis Deng from 1992 to 2004; and, with the slightly revised title of Representative of the Secretary-General on *the Human Rights of* Internally Displaced Persons, Walter Kälin from 2004 to the present [italics added]. See: http://www2.ohchr.org/english/issues/idp/mandate.htm, accessed 29 October 2009.

[41] Francis M. Deng, *Comprehensive Study on the Human Rights Issues related to Internally Displaced Persons,* Doc. E/CN.4/1993/35, 21 January 1993, (para. 286).

against the Guiding Principles.[42] This must be seen against the backdrop of the renewed and intensified debates concerning humanitarian intervention. These were given a forum following well-intentioned efforts by Secretary-General Kofi Annan to address the issue, and were fuelled in particular by the NATO air campaign in 1999 to halt ethnic cleansing and protect IDPs in Kosovo.[43] In certain circles, especially at the UN in New York, the term 'IDP' came to be conflated once again with humanitarian intervention, reminiscent of debates nearly a decade earlier and risking a rolling back of the progress made in recent years on the IDP protection issue. A particular low-point came in 2000 at the annual humanitarian segment of the UN Economic and Social Council (ECOSOC) in New York when Egypt worked to prevent the adoption of any resolution on humanitarian issues, including by filibustering into the early hours of the morning an otherwise innocuous reference to 'the continuing relevance of the Guiding Principles'; although in the end, this language did make it into the final document.[44] It is noteworthy that only months earlier, the CHR, in a resolution adopted by consensus, had 'welcome[d] the fact' that the RSG on IDPs 'has made use of the Guiding Principles in his dialogue with Governments and intergovernmental and non-governmental organizations, and requests him to continue his efforts in that regard,' while also encouraging 'the further dissemination and application of the Guiding Principles'.[45]

Following up on this task while at the same time using it as an opportunity to counter the efforts epitomized at ECOSOC, Deng launched a series of intensified consultations with groups of states, including with those that had begun to voice resistance to the Guiding Principles. By 2002-2003, these efforts had succeeded in quieting dissenting voices and shoring up support for the Principles.[46] As a result, international efforts on behalf of IDPs were able to pick up where, because of these concerns, to a certain degree they had left off.

At the same time, but surely more than coincidence, this period also saw the publication of the ICISS report introducing the doctrine of R2P which

---

[42] See Weiss and Korn, *Internal Displacement*, pp. 112-114; and Roberta Cohen and Francis Deng, 'The Genesis and the Challenges', *Forced Migration Review: Ten Years of the Guiding Principles on Internal Displacement,* Special Issue: 4-5 (2008), p. 4.

[43] See Evans, *The Responsibility to Protect*, pp. 31-34 and 37-38; and Alex J. Bellamy, *Responsibility to Protect: The Global Effort to End Mass Atrocities* (Cambridge: Polity Press, 2009), pp. 31-32.

[44] E/2006/L.13, 12 July 2006.

[45] E/CN.4/RES/2000/53, 25 April 2000, (paras. 6 and 7).

[46] Weiss and Korn, *Internal Displacement*, pp. 112-114; Cohen and Deng, 'The Genesis and the Challenges'.

reframed the debate on humanitarian intervention. Reflecting back on its impact, ICISS Co-Chair Gareth Evans notes that where other efforts had failed, R2P succeeded in securing 'a broad international consensus as to when and how the international community should respond to mass atrocity crimes'.[47] In so doing, it served to bring the debate to some form of conclusion. In this sense, as the UN Secretary-General's Special Adviser on the Responsibility to Protect, Edward Luck, has explained, 'the power of R2P is political, not legal.'[48] R2P has been instrumental in having opened up the necessary political space to spell out the procedures, and thereby also begin to open up new possibilities, for collective international action, which in exceptional circumstances, situations of internal displacement may demand.

Something Borrowed

According to the wedding rhyme, 'something borrowed' should be an item from a happily married couple, whose experience of good fortune is expected to carry over to and guide the way for the new couple. In a similar fashion, the central tenets of R2P were inspired by and expressly borrowed from an approach that had been tried and tested over the preceding decade in the context of efforts promoting effective protection for IDPs. More specifically, R2P built upon and benefitted from the consensus forged around the conceptual framework introduced and applied by Francis Deng to guide international efforts for the protection of IDPs.

Drawing upon his academic work with other scholars exploring issues of governance and conflict in Africa in the post-Cold War era, Deng applied to his work with IDPs the concept of 'sovereignty as responsibility'.[49] Providing part of the inspiration as well were the remarks by Jan Eliasson, then UN

---

[47] Evans, *The Responsibility to Protect*, p. 32.

[48] Interview by author, New York, 19 February 2009. See also Luck, 'The United Nations and the Responsibility to Protect', p. 8.

[49] Francis M. Deng, 'Reconciling Sovereignty with Responsibility: A Basis for International Humanitarian Action', in John W. Harbeson and Donald Rothschild (eds.), *Africa in World Politics: Post-Cold War Challenges*, (Boulder, Colo.: Westview, 1995); and Francis M. Deng, Sadikiel Kimaro, Terrence Lyons, Donald Rothchild and I. William Zartman, *Sovereignty as Responsibility: Conflict Management in Africa* (Washington, D.C.: Brookings Institution, 1996). See also the work of the Refugee Policy Group (RPG), in particular Roberta Cohen, Human Rights Protection for Internally Displaced Persons (RPG, June 1991), at: http://repository.forcedmigration.org/pdf/?pid=fmo:727; and RPG Conference on Human Rights Protection for Internally Displaced Persons, 24-25 1991, at: http://repository.forcedmigration.org/show_metadata.jsp?pid-fmo:3024.repository.forcedmigration.org/pdf/?pid=fmo:727.

Under-Secretary-General for Humanitarian Affairs and Emergency Relief Coordinator, who, in his response to a questionnaire that Deng had circulated, had pointed out that protecting and assisting IDPs and other populations at risk who were still within their own country was 'basically a question of striking a balance between sovereignty and solidarity with people in need'.[50] Deng then set about developing a formula for finding this balance. In presenting his first study on internal displacement to the CHR, he asserted:

> International concern with these fundamental human rights issues is in full accord with the cardinal principle of sovereignty. No Government can legitimately invoke sovereignty for the deliberate purpose of starving its population to death or otherwise denying them access to protection and resources vital to their survival and well-being. [...] if a Government is incapable of providing protection and assistance then the international community should act, either on the invitation of the host country or with international consensus, to fill the vacuum.[51]

The reaction of states to this recasting of sovereignty was far from embracing.[52] Nonetheless, Deng found that the reflex of suspicion harboured by states towards the international community's increasing engagement on the IDP protection issue could in large measure be effectively defused by agreeing with them that, indeed, protecting and assisting IDPs was an issue to be addressed, first and foremost, within the framework of state sovereignty. However, as Secretary-General Perez de Cuellar had posited in 1991, 'the principle of non-interference with the essential domestic jurisdiction of States cannot be regarded as a protective barrier behind which human rights could be massively or systematically violated with impunity.'[53] Deng accordingly argued that sovereignty had to be seen not in the negative sense of serving as a barricade against outside interference; rather, 'sovereignty carries with it [...] responsibilities for the population'; 'at a minimum it should guarantee food, shelter, physical security, basic health services and other essentials often denied the internally displaced'.[54] This means, he further explained:

> the guiding principle [...] is to assume that under normal circumstances, governments are concerned about the welfare of their people, will provide their people with adequate protection and assistance, and if unable, will invite or welcome

[50] Deng, *Comprehensive Study*, (para. 84); Francis M. Deng, *Protecting the Dispossessed: A Challenge for the International Community* (Brookings Institution, 1993), p. 18.

[51] Deng, *Comprehensive Study*, (para 151).

[52] For an indication, see Bellamy, *The Responsibility to Protect*, pp. 26-27.

[53] Javier Perez de Cuellar, *Report of the Secretary-General on the Work of the Organization*, Doc. A/46/1 (1991), pp. 10-11.

[54] Deng, *Protecting the Dispossessed*, pp. 18-19.

> foreign assistance and international cooperation to supplement their own efforts. Controversy arises only in the exceptional cases when the state has collapsed or the government is unwilling to invite or permit international involvement, while the level of human suffering dictates otherwise. [...] To fill the vacuum of moral responsibility created by such cleavages, international involvement becomes a moral imperative.[55]

Deng utilised this conceptual framework in carrying out all aspects of his mandate as RSG on IDPs, to the extent that it became his signature calling card. At the outset of virtually every meeting he held over the course of his mandate, and especially in discussions with governments, Deng routinely would sketch out his view of sovereignty as responsibility before then raising the specific IDP protection concerns that arose in each country situation.[56] This approach proved tremendously effective with governments the world over in attenuating the inevitable tensions surrounding what fundamentally is an internal issue and in opening channels fostering constructive dialogue on addressing internal displacement.

The concept of sovereignty as responsibility underpins and infuses the Guiding Principles. Principle 3 sets out as a general principle that '[n]ational authorities have the primary duty and responsibility to provide protection and humanitarian assistance to internally displaced persons within their jurisdiction.' The Principles then proceed to spell out what this responsibility entails in all phases of displacement: preventing arbitrary displacement; protection and assistance during displacement; and securing voluntary, safe, and durable solutions to internal displacement. The Principles also recognise that national responsibility to address internal displacement has an external dimension of seeking, or at least accepting, international assistance when national efforts fall short. Principle 25, after restating in paragraph (1) that '[t]he primary duty and responsibility for providing humanitarian assistance to internally displaced persons lies with national authorities,' then affirms:

> (2) International humanitarian organizations and other appropriate actors have the right to offer their services in support of the internally displaced. Such an offer shall not be regarded as an unfriendly act or an interference in a State's internal affairs and shall be considered in good faith. Consent thereto shall not be

---

[55] Deng et al., *Sovereignty as Responsibility*, pp. xxii-xxiii.

[56] By Deng's own account, the 'first five minutes are crucial' to allaying state concerns and facilitating constructive discussion of the concerns he would then raise. See Francis M. Deng, 'Displacement Studies and the Role of Universities', in Universität Kassel (ed.), *Universities and Rio +10: Paths to Sustainability in the Regions, an Interdisciplinary Challenge* (Kassel: Kassel University Press, 2003), p. 39.

> arbitrarily withheld, particularly when authorities concerned are unable or unwilling to provide the required humanitarian assistance.
>
> (3) All authorities concerned shall grant and facilitate the free passage of humanitarian assistance and grant persons engaged in the provision of such assistance rapid and unimpeded access to the internally displaced.

Principle 26 affirms that states and other authorities also have a responsibility to ensure that humanitarian personnel and supplies are 'respected and protected', and 'shall not be the object of attack or other acts of violence.' Further, Principle 27 makes clear that the scope of international humanitarian operations is not limited to assistance, but 'should give due regard to the protection needs and human rights of internally displaced persons and take appropriate measures in this regard.'[57]

The concept of sovereignty as responsibility that has guided international efforts for the protection of IDPs also provided a strong foundation for the architects of R2P. Although the ICISS report that articulated the R2P doctrine in 2001 did not formally acknowledge this parentage, ICISS members have since openly acknowledged the 'intellectual debt' owed to these efforts.[58] Former Canadian Foreign Minister Lloyd Axworthy, who established the ICISS group, recalls: 'The first time I heard the notion of 'responsibility to protect' was when Deng visited me in Ottawa and argued for a clear commitment by the international community to deal with the IDP issue.'[59]

Strong symmetry in approach is evident in the formulation of the R2P doctrine adopted by the 2005 World Summit. First, it unequivocally affirms 'that each individual State has the responsibility to protect its populations from genocide, war crimes, ethnic cleansing, and crimes against humanity' and specifies that this responsibility entails the 'prevention of such crimes, including their incitement.' Second, the international community should 'encourage and support States to exercise this responsibility', including by 'helping States build capacity to protect their populations' from mass atrocity crimes and 'assisting those which are under stress before crisis and conflicts break out.' Third, the international community 'also has the responsibility to use appropriate diplomatic, humanitarian and other peaceful means [...] to help protect populations'. Should peaceful means prove inadequate and national authorities

[57] *Guiding Principles on Internal Displacement.*

[58] Ramesh Thakur, *United Nations, Peace and Security* (Cambridge: Cambridge University Press: 2002), p. 255; Evans, *The Responsibility to Protect*, pp. 36-37.

[59] Lloyd Axworthy, *Navigating a New World: Canada's Global Future* (Toronto: Alfred A. Knopf, 2003), p. 414.

be 'manifestly failing to protect their populations' from the four stated crimes, it is 'prepared to take collective action, in a timely and decisive manner'.[60]

There is also symmetry between the two frameworks in terms of the temporal scope of protection responsibility. R2P, as articulated by ICISS and promoted by its chief architects still today, entails a responsibility: to *prevent* the occurrence of genocide, war crimes, ethnic cleansing and crimes against humanity; to *react* to protect populations when these situations nonetheless occur; and to *rebuild* in their aftermath.[61] This comprehensive approach dovetails nicely with the Guiding Principles spelling out responsibilities to prevent arbitrary displacement, to protect and assist IDPs once they become displaced, and to secure voluntary, safe and durable solutions to displacement. The strong emphasis placed by R2P on prevention and early warning is significant and stands to make an important contribution, if operationalised, to averting or at least attenuating many of the conditions that inevitably would cause internal displacement.

R2P goes one step further in spelling out a doctrine for invoking and implementing the international community's protection responsibility when national efforts to prevent and protect populations from these crimes clearly fall short. From the early days of his work on IDP issues, Deng had stressed that 'living up to the responsibilities of sovereignty implies a transcendent authority capable of holding the supposed sovereign accountable'.[62] Failure to fulfil these responsibilities should therefore carry international consequences, namely: 'calibrated actions ranging from diplomacy to political pressure, sanctions and as a last resort, military intervention'.[63] Towards the end of his tenure as RSG on IDPs, Deng began to express increasing frustration about the lack of effective mechanisms to hold states accountable to fulfilling their responsibilities. Without these accountability mechanisms, the credibility of 'sovereignty as responsibility', in particular its international dimensions, risked being called into question.[64] A key aspect of R2P's added value to IDP protection efforts is in elaborating a doctrine for invoking and exercising international responsibility to protect populations in grave peril in those cases where national responsibility is altogether absent and international offers of

---

[60] 'World Summit Outcome', (paras. 138-139).

[61] ICISS, *The Responsibility to Protect*; and Evans, *The Responsibility to Protect,* pp. 79-174.

[62] Deng, *Protecting the Dispossessed,* p. 19.

[63] Roberta Cohen and Francis M. Deng, 'Exodus Within Borders: The Uprooted Who Never Left Home', *Foreign Affairs*, 77/4: 12-16 (1998), p. 14. See also Cohen and Deng, *Masses in Flight*, pp. 276-284.

[64] Deng, 'Displacement Studies and the Role of Universities', pp. 39-41.

assistance are being refused. In other words, R2P not only borrows the concept of sovereignty as responsibility, but helpfully builds upon it by elaborating the process, through the United Nations and in particular the Security Council, and setting expectations for the international community to exercise its own protection responsibilities when national efforts patently fall short.

The idea that sovereignty is not absolute and inherently entails certain responsibilities of a state towards its population was not new; it has an extensive pedigree with 'long historical antecedents in both Western and non-Western political thought and doctrine'.[65] The concept nonetheless was given new focus with the introduction into international discourse of the concept of 'sovereignty as responsibility', in particular in the context of efforts on behalf of IDPs. Building upon these efforts, R2P must be situated within these evolving notions of sovereignty. Accordingly, as the Secretary-General's Adviser has suggested, R2P is better described as 'evolutionary rather than revolutionary'.[66]

...Something Blue?

According to the wedding custom, 'something blue' represents constancy, faithfulness and loyalty. As is well known, light blue also is the official colour of the United Nations; in fact, there exists a specific colour known as 'United Nations blue'.[67] How faithful and constant the UN will be in ensuring the realisation of the R2P doctrine and thus whether the R2P doctrine will add concretely, not only conceptually, to the protection of IDPs is still very much a question. Application of R2P in practice has been limited, inconsistent and, in the few instances when it has been applied, incomplete.[68]

Certainly, the World Summit Outcome document envisages a central role for the UN in the implementation of R2P. In cases of collective international

---

[65] Luck, 'The United Nations and the Responsibility to Protect', p. 2. See also Edward C. Luck, 'Introduction: The Responsible Sovereign and the Responsibility to Protect', in Joachim Müller and Karl P. Sauvant, *Annual Review of United Nations Affairs, 2006/7* (New York: Oceana, 2008), pp. xxxvi-xxxix; Bellamy, *Responsibility to Protect*, pp. 19-21.

[66] Luck, 'Introduction'.

[67] United Nations, *United Nations Flag Code and Regulations,* Doc. ST/SGB/132 (January 1967), available at: http://www.un.org/depts/dhl/maplib/docs/stsgb132.pdf, accessed on 7 November 2009.

[68] Erin Mooney, 'The Guiding Principles and the Responsibility to Protect', *Forced Migration Review: Ten Years of the Guiding Principles on Internal Displacement,* Special Issue: 11-13 (2008), pp. 12-13; Roberta Cohen, 'Reconciling R2P with IDP Protection', pp. 35-58, in this book.

action under Chapter VI and Chapter VII of the UN Charter, this role necessarily will be performed by the Security Council. Significantly, the Security Council has reaffirmed the R2P doctrine as set out in the World Summit Outcome and emphasised 'the responsibility of States to comply with their relevant obligations to end impunity and to prosecute those responsible for war crimes, genocide, crimes against humanity and serious violations of international humanitarian law'.[69] The Security Council recalled this resolution and referenced the World Summit Outcome paragraphs on R2P when it called in 2006 for the rapid deployment of additional UN peacekeepers to Sudan and in particular their deployment to Darfur with a mandate that included protection responsibilities relating to IDPs. Specifically, this force was expected 'to contribute towards international efforts to protect, promote and monitor human rights in Darfur, as well as to coordinate international efforts towards the protection of civilians with particular attention to vulnerable groups including internally displaced persons, returning refugees, and women and children'.[70]

Besides the Security Council, it is clear that implementation of R2P will require the combined efforts of diverse institutional actors within the UN system. After all, the Secretary-General's Adviser on R2P has extremely limited resources, lacking even an office in the UN. Similarly, the mandate of the RSG on IDPs never has received more than meagre support from the UN system; a voluntary position, it has been supported by one or two UN human rights officers and, as such, always had to rely on outside support, in particular the Brookings Project, to carry out many of its mandated tasks.[71]

More fundamentally, the three-dimensional responsibility – to prevent, to react, and to rebuild – in the context of actual or threatened genocide, war crimes, ethnic cleansing and crimes against humanity entails a geographic and substantive scope of such a magnitude as to depend upon an 'all hands on deck' approach. Key R2P actors within the UN would include: the human rights bodies and mechanisms (in particular the network of special procedures on particular countries or thematic issues), humanitarian and development agencies, international criminal tribunals, the Peace-building Commission, the Department for Peacekeeping Operations (DPKO) and of course the Secretary-General's Special Adviser for the Prevention of Genocide (a position

[69] UN Security Council Resolution 1674 of 28 April 2006, (paras. 5 and 8).

[70] S/RES/1706 (2006), (Preamble and para. 9). Cf. S/RES/1769 (2007), where the link to R2P is less explicit.

[71] For more on this arrangement, see Weiss and Korn, *Internal Displacement*, pp. 41-54 and 127-132.

currently filled, incidentally, by former RSG on IDPs Francis Deng). These different actors can bring to bear a range of expertise and decades of pre-existing and highly relevant experience to support the implementation of R2P. At the same time, and considering that each actor also brings its own perspective to R2P, there is an evident need to foster clearer understanding and consensus within the UN secretariat and agencies about R2P and expectations for how it should be realised.[72] Potentially relevant in this regard is the experience in the late 1990s to forge a common understanding among all the different relevant agencies of what is meant by 'protection' in the context of internal displacement and what can be expected of the different agencies in terms of their respective protection roles.[73]

One important issue requiring closer consideration and clarification within the UN is the scope of R2P's application, in terms of the situations that it covers. The wisdom of the official policy of the UN to confine the notion of R2P only to the four situations specified by the World Summit has been questioned, including from quarters within the UN: 'From the perspective of UNHCR, this is rather narrow. Why confine its use only to such situations flowing out of conflict? [...] the protection situation may be equally acute for an earthquake victim from Pakistan [...] or a victim of trafficking in Eastern Europe.'[74] While an expansion of the officially-sanctioned R2P doctrine in all of these directions seems excessive in terms of conceptual elasticity, at the very least the possibility that the lack of response to a natural disaster may risk crimes against humanity should be entertained. Especially after the experience of the 2008 Cyclone Nargis in Burma, it appears entirely conceivable for there to arise a case of an overwhelming natural or environmental catastrophe resulting in mass displacement, where the state is either unwilling or unable to respond effectively, or to request outside assistance, and where there risks, as a result, being significant loss of life.[75]

The activities of the RSG on IDPs, from the beginning of the mandate, in promoting effective international institutional arrangements and, since 2004, in 'mainstreaming the human rights' of IDPs 'into all relevant parts of the

[72] Interviews by author with UN agencies and offices, New York, 16-20 February 2009.

[73] IASC, *Protection of Internally Displaced Persons*, Policy Paper, December 1999, available at: http://www.humanitarianinfo.org/IASC/pageloader.aspx?page=content-products-products&productcatid=10, accessed 6 November 2009. On the genesis of this policy, see Weiss and Korn, *Internal Displacement*, pp. 86-87.

[74] Feller, 'Towards a Culture of Protection'.

[75] Lloyd Axworthy and Allan Rock, 'Responsibility to Protect? Yes,' *Globe and Mail* (9 May 2008); Roberta Cohen, 'The Burma Cyclone and the Responsibility to Protect', *Global Responsibility to Protect*, 1/2: 253-257 (2009); ICISS, *The Responsibility to Protect*, p. 33.

United Nations system'[76] may serve as useful building blocks for the implementation of R2P. Indeed, the UN Secretary-General, while acknowledging that UN agencies and programmes are already making important contributions to the elimination of mass atrocity crimes, has pointed out that they could do so 'much more effectively *if goals relating to the responsibility to protect, including the protection of refugees and the internally displaced*, were mainstreamed among their priorities, whether in the areas of human rights, humanitarian affairs, peacekeeping, peace-building, political affairs or development.'[77] Moreover, he notes that the lack of an effective international response to internal displacement, pointing specifically to Darfur, the Democratic Republic of the Congo (DRC) and Somalia, 'has undermined public confidence in the United Nations and our collective espousal of the principles relating to the responsibility to protect.'[78] There is therefore a clear recognition that the R2P and IDP protection frameworks are, in fact, highly interlinked and an expectation that these should be mutually reinforcing.

It is therefore all the more surprising that the issue of displacement has not been better integrated into the UN's implementation plan and UN-sponsored discussions of implementing R2P. The Secretary-General's report places strong emphasis throughout on the importance of existing protection standards, but makes no mention of the Guiding Principles on Internal Displacement. Moreover, the issue of protecting IDPs and refugees barely featured in recent discussions on R2P in the UN General Assembly. Considering the contentious nature of some of the discussions rehashing old debates on humanitarian intervention, it is perhaps fortunate that efforts to protect IDPs were not expressly enmeshed in these discussions. For, so long as states remain prickly about R2P for fear that it portends intervention, explicitly linking R2P to internal displacement and the Principles could risk conflating the latter anew with intervention in internal affairs, thereby undermining the wide acceptance of the Guiding Principles that has been so carefully cultivated over the past decade.[79] However, substantively, it does seem to be a missed opportunity that there was only scant attention to displacement. One analyst concludes from the July 2009 debate on R2P that in terms of priorities 'refugee and IDP protection is peripheral to the R2P doctrine' whereas 'forced displacement should be a central focus of R2P.'[80]

---

76 E/CN.4/RES/2004/55, 20 April 2004 (para. 23).

77 UN, *Implementing the Responsibility to Protect,* (para. 68) [italics added].

78 *Ibid.,* (para. 60).

79 Mooney, 'The Guiding Principles and the Responsibility to Protect', p. 13.

80 Harris-Rimmer, 'Refugees, IDPs and the R2P Doctrine', p. 20.

Beyond the UN, regional organisations also are recognised in the World Summit Outcome text as potential partners for the UN in the implementation of R2P. Here again, it may be valuable to build upon some of the work undertaken on behalf of IDPs. Beginning in 1998, the RSG on IDPs in collaboration with the Brookings Project convened regional seminars on internal displacement together with regional and sub-regional organisations across Africa, the Americas and Europe.[81] The inroads made at these meetings in building state consensus around the IDP protection issue could also be useful for advancing R2P. For instance, in the sub-region of the Inter-Governmental Authority on Development (IGAD) – of which six of its seven member states have IDP populations, collectively totalling more than 7.5 million IDPs currently – a Ministerial Declaration following the conference *inter alia* 'reaffirms that the primary responsibility of protecting and assisting the internally displaced and finding durable solution[s] lies with the national Governments and that the role of the international community is to complement the national effort'.[82] Moreover, the recent adoption of the African Union Convention on IDPs is significant not only for the expectation it brings for improved national and regional responses to internal displacement on the continent. As UNHCR points out, it also 'demonstrates that national sovereignty is fully compatible with the responsibility to protect' and 'serves as a reminder that the responsibility to protect its own citizens is first and foremost an individual state responsibility and that where the state fails to do so, there is a collective African responsibility to act.'[83]

Finally, but most importantly given that the central responsibility lies at the national level, UN member states have committed themselves to encourage and assist states to meet their R2P obligations. However, the Secretary-General's Adviser on R2P has observed that the paragraphs of the World Summit Outcome appear to 'offer no clue as to how to accomplish such feats.'[84] The experience of international efforts of working with states on issues of IDP protection can offer some insights and tools. In addition to the Guiding Principles, which spell out the specific responsibilities of states towards IDPs, a set of benchmarks for promoting, measuring and reinforcing national responsibility in addressing internal displacement has been developed and is

[81] The reports of many of these seminars are available at: www.brookings.edu/idp

[82] 'Khartoum Declaration', Ministerial Conference on Internally Displaced Persons in the IGAD Sub-Region, Khartoum, Sudan, 2 September 2003.

[83] Fleming and Hassan, 'African Union'.

[84] Luck, 'Introduction'.

being widely used, including by governments.[85] Further, a number of tools have been developed by the RSG on IDPs to assist governments in meeting these benchmarks, for instance in ensuring that the national legal framework protects the rights of IDPs and those at risk of displacement.[86] Technical assistance to governments, for instance, in the drafting and, critically, implementation of national legislation, policy and strategies on internal displacement has been an important focus of international efforts.The ultimate aim must be to restore the population's access to effective national protection.

Conclusion

The four situations with which R2P is concerned – genocide, war crimes, crimes against humanity and ethnic cleansing – invariably force people into displacement; with ethnic cleansing this is the very aim. The R2P doctrine, if operationalised, therefore should go a long way to averting or at least attenuating many of the situations forcing people to flee and to protecting IDPs against many of the risks and abuses to which they are exposed while displaced. On the flip side, mass displacement, whether internal or across borders, is often an indicator of situations of potential or actual genocide, war crimes, ethnic cleansing and crimes against humanity. The occurrence of internal displacement therefore can be a bellwether of situations which may warrant consideration under the R2P framework.

Yet, the convergence of R2P and protection efforts for IDPs goes deeper than causal links. Anchored in the same existing standards of international law and sharing the conceptual approach of sovereignty as responsibility, there is a natural compatibility between the R2P and IDP protection frameworks. Even

---

[85] *Addressing Internal Displacement: A Framework for National Responsibility* (Washington, D.C.: Brookings Institution – University of Bern Project on Internal Displacement, 2005). The *Framework*, developed by the author, also was presented to the United Nations Commission on Human Rights by the Representative of the Secretary-General on the Human Rights of Internally Displaced Persons, Walter Kälin, as UN Doc. E/CN.4/2006/71/Add.1 (23 December 2005). Translations of the *Framework* in more than a dozen languages, including Arabic, Azerbaijani, Russian, Serbian, Sinhala and Tamil, are available at: http://www.brookings.edu/projects/idp/20050401_nrframework.aspx (accessed 1 November 2009). See also Erin Mooney, 'National Responsibility and Internal Displacement: A Framework for Action', *Forced Migration Review - Protecting and Assisting the Internally Displaced: The Way Forward*, Special Issue: 11-14 (2004), available also in Arabic, French and Spanish at: http://www.fmreview.org.

[86] *Protecting Internally Displaced Persons: A Manual for Law and Policymakers* (Washington, D.C.: Brookings-Bern Project on Internal Displacement, 2008).

institutionally, there are similarities as to the Special Adviser's role (and paucity of resources). Many of his planned initiatives, such as mainstreaming the issue within the UN and working with regional organisations, also are very much akin to international efforts for the protection of IDPs initiated in the early 1990s and still ongoing. Most importantly, R2P goes further in setting out a framework for action by the international community to protect populations from mass atrocity crimes when national responses fail them. In so doing, R2P fills what always has been a critical gap in the international response to internal displacement: how to ensure accountability, in particular of the international community, to fulfil its own protection responsibilities. Given these areas of strategic overlap and complementarity, coordination of efforts and potential collaboration between the R2P and IDP protection frameworks can be beneficial and mutually reinforcing.

However, owing to fundamental differences between the two frameworks, R2P at best will offer only a partial response to addressing the global crisis of displacement. After all, the 'narrow but deep' scope of R2P currently being espoused, on the basis of the language endorsed by the World Summit, does not capture the range of scenarios in which internal displacement occurs. What is being suggested is not complete symmetry in the scope of application between the R2P and IDP protection frameworks; to include low-impact natural disasters and development projects, for instance, would broaden R2P to the risk of its becoming operationally unmanageable or, worse, irrelevant. Yet, it is entirely conceivable that there could be a case warranting consideration under R2P in the event of an overwhelming natural disaster, where the state is unable or unwilling to effectively respond and refuses offers of external assistance, and there is a risk, as a result of this denial of assistance, of significant loss of life. The UN and some leading R2P advocates have been too quick to dismiss this possibility – which the ICISS formulation of R2P recognised – and too dogmatic in asserting that R2P should never apply to natural disasters. Moreover, the concept of protection for IDPs that is spelled out in the Guiding Principles is much broader than the prescribed parameters for R2P. While there are important areas of convergence that could pay protection dividends, there also are certain significant differences between these two protection frameworks due to their distinct scope and purpose as well as their differing degrees of political traction and of practical implementation achieved to date.

The focus on R2P therefore must not overshadow the fact that more extensive of protection responsibilities exist, which also must be realised and often are equally demanding of attention and response.[87] Consequently, just as important as encouraging greater coordination in the areas of convergence, is to be aware of the 'spaces in between' wherein the R2P and IDP protection frameworks can complement one another and collectively produce a more comprehensive protection response. In this connection, it seems only fitting to conclude this inquiry into a marriage of concepts between R2P and IDP protection by citing another poem frequently heard at weddings, whereby Kahlil Gibran's 'The Prophet' offers the following advice on marriage:

> You were born together, and together you shall be forevermore.
>
> [...]
>
> But let there be spaces in your togetherness,
>
> [...]
>
> And stand together yet not too near together:
> For the pillars of the temple stand apart
> And the oak tree and the cypress grow not in each other's shadow.[88]

[87] Louise Arbour, 'Protection is Paramount', *Human Rights Tribune*, 29 June 2006.
[88] Kahlil Gibran, *The Collected Works* (New York: Alfred A. Knopf, 2007), p. 105.

Chapter Four

EU Migration Policy: Evolving Ideas of Responsibility and Protection

Emma Haddad[1]

Introduction

There is an open debate on humanitarian intervention to deal with political and economic instability, with the principle, enshrined within the idea of a responsibility to protect (R2P), remaining a moot point. Over the last two decades, intervention has been controversial both when it has happened and when it has failed to happen.[2] As Mayall has pointed out, while in the post-Cold War environment western states have taken the lead in promoting the discourse of human rights, 'their willingness to intervene in the domestic affairs of states whose governments transgressed these norms [has] remained highly selective, particularly where their own interests were not directly involved'.[3]

However, where there is a consensus it is around one of the corollaries of such instability, which makes its physical appearance in the form of refugee flows. Indeed it is laid down in international law that states party to the 1951 Convention have a responsibility to protect those fleeing persecution by way of non-refoulement. And this responsibility is even more advanced in the context of the Organisation of African Unity (OAU) Convention where the definition of the refugee is widened somewhat to include mass movements of people, thus bypassing the need for individual refugee determination. So while the jury is to some extent still out on whether the international community

---

[1] The views expressed in this article are personal and strictly those of the author and do not necessarily represent those of any institution to which she is affiliated.

[2] International Commission on Intervention and State Sovereignty, *The Responsibility to Protect* (Ottawa: International Development Research Centre, 2001), p. 1.

[3] James Mayall, *World Politics: Progress and its Limits* (Cambridge: Polity, 2000), p. 139.

has the right or duty to enter a state's sovereign territory when it is failing to protect its own citizens, that duty is quite clear and unequivocal when those people have crossed an international border.

The EU provides a good case study of how the concepts of both responsibility and protection are evolving in a world of increasing political and economic integration. It is an advanced case of such integration in which the single market shows that national borders are becoming arguably less important. At the same time, national borders remain fiercely guarded in the domain of EU migration and asylum policy, such that the debate often becomes one centring on *protectionism* rather than *protection*.

Taking a policy perspective, this chapter will first look at differing visions of responsibility that are currently being played out in the EU arena in terms of southern Member States pushing a physical burden-sharing conception of shared responsibility and northern Member States preferring an alternative vision focused on practical assistance. The second section will then discuss different types of protection that the EU promulgates, from the development of a Common European Asylum System within the EU to addressing the root causes of migration with countries outside the EU.

Differing visions of responsibility

It is around May each year that the high seas of the Mediterranean and the Atlantic become somewhat calmer than they have been during the winter months, and the media starts to show pictures of boats. These boats are usually overflowing with men from sub-Saharan Africa, although it is not uncommon to find women and children as well. The boats travel northwards aiming for the nearest bit of land: setting off from the coast of Libya, Malta is a mere 90 kilometres away, Lampedusa just a bit further. Those leaving the West African coastline head for the Canary Islands. Frequently the media reports of boats in distress and a debate over responsibility ensues between those countries considered to be the nearest and in whose search and rescue zone the boat finds itself. The tuna net episode in May 2007 was a highly visible example that caught the attention of the international community, when 27 migrants clung to nets in the middle of the Mediterranean as Malta, Spain and Libya argued it out.

Although events such as these have raised public consciousness of migratory flows into the EU, there are signs now that numbers of arrivals are undergoing a dramatic decline. In 2008 numbers arriving on Lampedusa and Sicily from

Libya hit a peak of 38,000 migrants, up 97% from 2007.[4] So far in 2009, however, arrivals have slowed to a trickle. In the period 6 May to 19 June 2009, less than 300 migrants arrived in Italy by boat compared to 2,500 in the same period in 2008. Meanwhile after 162 people arrived on Malta in January 2009 and 367 in February, there were no arrivals in March and April, 1 boat in May, a dry spell for the following 2 months, and then just a few people arriving again in late July. Slightly round the African coastline in the Atlantic, the Canary Islands saw a steep rise in 2006, but this year numbers have almost completely dried up.

What has caused these reductions in numbers arriving? Certainly the operations carried out by Frontex, the EU Border Agency, have had something to do with it. Frontex has put in place agreements with countries along the West African coastline which allows it to operate patrol boats within African waters, thus thwarting the attempts of migrants to set off in Cayucos. Operation Hera in the Atlantic is one such example. Similarly Frontex has recently reported that Operation Poseidon in the Central Mediterranean has been called off because boats are simply not trying to get from Turkey to Greece. Yet it is also evident that bilateral agreements put in place between individual southern Member States and their African neighbours have had an impact. Spain has now signed so-called second generation readmission agreements with a total of 10 countries of West Africa. They have held because they have actually offered partner countries something: legal migration channels for specific sectors of work, and assistance with development, in return for strict adherence to readmission of their illegal immigrants as well as third country nationals. Italy has now signed such agreements with both Algeria and Libya, and most believe that this is the clear reason for the dramatic fall in the number of boats arriving on Lampedusa in recent months. Libyan police are reported to be patrolling the coastline like never before, spread out at such short intervals so as to be able to see one another. Meanwhile, a recent boat intercepted by Italian patrols was sent straight back to Libya without being allowed to dock and the Libyan authorities accepted the boat back.

Such boat crossings are a clear example of today's mixed flows of economic migrants and refugees. Of the 38,000 who entered Italy by sea from Libya in 2008, 70% applied for asylum of which 50% were granted asylum or some kind of subsidiary protection. In Malta in July 2009 there were 1,523 beneficiaries of international protection, mainly Somali nationals but also a large

[4] All statistics from http://www.crimemalta.com/frontexwatch.htm unless otherwise stated.

number of Eritreans and Sudanese. 96% had been granted subsidiary protection and 4% refugee status. The vast majority were men aged between 18 and 34. Another 788 asylum-seekers were awaiting a decision on their claim. In other words, these high visibility border crossings have become a new location for the claiming of international protection.

Despite the fall in numbers, illegal immigration in the Mediterranean once again hit the highest levels of the European agenda this year such that it was up for discussion among EU Heads of State at the European Council in June 2009. Building on a commitment in the European Pact on Migration, agreed by all 27 Member States in October 2008, the southern Member States – Malta, Greece, Cyprus and Italy – called for a true system of physical burden-sharing within the EU to assist those under particular pressures. The Migration Pact had agreed to the coordination of voluntary intra-EU relocation of those granted international protection, and as if to show it meant what it said during its Presidency, between March and July 2009 France accepted 96 recognised refugees from Malta. At the same time the Commission initiated a pilot project to see how a coordination mechanism could work in Malta, and Member States have been asked to make pledges – a kind of beauty contest on international protection.[5] So the southern Member States see responsibility very much as joint, EU-wide responsibility focused on moving people around. They argue that the EU must provide protection for those in need, but this means all Member States taking their fair share and not just putting responsibility down to a question of geography.

Yet there are those in the non burden-sharing camp, including Austria and the Netherlands, who will not participate in the beauty contest. Internal relocation is not, they argue, the answer. If illegal immigrants know that if they now make it to Malta they will then be taken to live in any other part of the EU, such a system will simply act as a pull factor and so worsen the very problem it seeks to alleviate. Instead, these Member States put forward an alternative vision of responsibility based on practical assistance and working with countries outside the EU.

There are five elements to this vision. First, and importantly, this approach insists on a fair and fast asylum system. Resources are best dedicated to getting good quality decisions to ensure protection as quickly as possible for genuine refugees. This means simultaneously tackling abuse of the system by way of data sharing and carrying out checks on applicants – abuse simply hurts those

[5] 'Pilot burden-sharing project announced for Malta', The Times of Malta and The Financial Times, 4 June 2009.

with a real need of international protection. The second element is returns and is closely linked. To ensure confidence in European asylum systems, as well as to dissuade further waves of illegal immigration, those who are found not to be fearing persecution and who therefore have no basis on which to remain in the EU must be returned to their country of origin. Getting returns right – both forced and voluntary – is key, and Member States are looking to Frontex to coordinate more joint charter flights to help achieve this. But people cannot be returned to a country that will not accept them, so ensuring third countries accept back their nationals is of course also vital. This approach therefore insists on proper implementation of readmission clauses in international agreements.

The returns element of this vision of responsibility overlaps with practical assistance, the third strand. The southern Member States need help carrying out returns of those not in need of international protection, which means assistance with a range of issues including redocumentation of migrants, biometric checks, nationality identification and language and age analysis. Practical assistance also means giving these states the means to cope with the processing of applicants by way of actual caseworkers, interpretation and training. Help has also been offered by some Member States in debriefing migrants to try to identify trafficker and smuggler networks. In the more medium term, it seems clear that in some cases a real migration strategy to manage the phenomenon is lacking, and assistance could be provided in drawing up and implementing such a strategy, if states were amenable to such a proposal.

Financial assistance is the fourth element. The EU Solidarity Funds are being directed in large part towards the southern Member States to help them manage with arrivals of migrants. Since 2008, Italy has been allocated 77.2 million euro or 10.6% of the total money available, Greece 59.2 million euro or 8%, and Malta 21.1 million euro or 3%. These are significant sums but there are also other pots of EU money that could be tapped into. The external relations funding instruments are being used increasingly for migration purposes, but a greater allocation of such funds will be needed if the EU's external migration agenda is to be properly implemented. Indeed, the Rapid Reaction Mechanism was used in 2006 when Spain was experiencing unprecedented arrivals on the Canary Islands. This external relations funding instrument is now known as the Stability Instrument, but it has not since funded migration-related activities.

And this links with the fifth element of this responsibility agenda – the external dimension. This view sees work with countries outside the EU to address the reasons why people are migrating and the means they are using to do so as key parts of the EU's common migration and asylum policy, and a number of EU-funded and bilateral projects have been implemented over recent years with source and transit countries to this end. The Netherlands, for example, currently leads on a twinning project with Turkey, a key transit country into the EU, to assist in training, while the UK is a partner in a capacity building project in Ethiopia being carried out by the International Centre for Migration Policy Development (ICMPD) in conjunction with the Ethiopian Government and funded by the Thematic Programme for Cooperation on Migration with Third Countries which has a budget of around 380 million euro for the period 2007-13.

In short, the two competing visions of responsibility that currently prevail in the EU both view responsibility as something to be shared, no longer something that is solely national responsibility. However, such responsibility is viewed in two quite different ways, one in terms of moving people around and one that seeks to protect people in situ, either where they arrive or before they arrive. We will now look at the competing ideas of protection.

Different types of protection

The two ideas of responsibility outlined above hinge on two different conceptions of protection. When linked to the idea of burden-sharing of people, protection means ensuring a haven within the EU. When linked to the alternative vision of practical assistance and addressing the root causes of migration, protection takes on a broader meaning that is closer to the underlying idea behind the R2P principle, that of humanitarian intervention. Indeed, R2P is not only about forcible intervention in the domestic affairs of sovereign states – the third pillar of R2P – but also about the role of the international community in encouraging and assisting states to protect their populations – the second pillar of the principle.[6]

Protection within the EU is based on the idea of constructing 'a Europe of asylum', a commitment that was underlined in the European Pact on Migration. EU migration and asylum policy constitutes a strange mix between the inter-governmental and the federal. While national sovereignty remains as strong as ever in the domain of legal migration, joint cooperation on illegal

[6] Report of the UN Secretary-General, *Implementing the Responsibility to Protect* (UN Doc. A/63/677), January 2009.

immigration among the 27 Member States of the EU is accepted and fairly well developed. EU asylum policy sits somewhere in the middle.

The Hague Programme agreed in 2004 committed Member States to putting in place the first phase of the Common European Asylum System (CEAS), which was to be framed by the 1951 Convention. This has consisted of a number of elements including agreeing to common standards on reception, procedures for processing asylum claims and minimum standards for who qualifies as in need of international protection, as well as arrangements for the state responsible for processing an individual's claim (Dublin) and a system of fingerprinting asylum seekers which enables such Dublin removals (Eurodac). The second phase of the CEAS has been on the negotiating table since December 2008 and thus far comprises amendments to Dublin, Eurodac and the Reception Conditions Directive, as well as a proposal to establish a European Asylum Support Office. Amendments to the Procedures and Qualifications Directives were tabled in autumn 2009.

The negotiations over the second phase of the Common European Asylum System have brought into stark contrast the competing positions of Member States over EU asylum policy. Some are great supporters of further integration in this domain, and thus have an appetite for the second phase which they believe will lead to greater harmonisation of national laws on asylum so as to develop a truly level playing field and high standards of international protection across the EU. Others, notably Germany, feel efforts would first be better focused on ensuring proper implementation of existing measures and practical cooperation between countries, before thinking about further legislation. They point out the vastly different grant rates across Member States which can only be creating perverse push and pull factors and reasons for migrants to go 'asylum shopping'. Dealing with these kinds of issues only detracts resources from ensuring quick access to high quality protection for those with genuine claims for international protection. Whichever the case, the idea of protection promulgated by the Common European Asylum System remains focused on those seeking asylum within the EU.

The non burden-sharing approach links EU domestic asylum policy to cooperation with third countries and thus encompasses a somewhat more enlightened view of protection, one which to some extent hints at the limitations of a simple European migration policy and emphasises the need to integrate it into a wider framework linked to development, employment and foreign policy. The current political context for the development of the external dimension of EU migration and asylum policy is the 'Global Approach to

Migration', adopted by the European Council in 2005.[7] It is the most recent step in a series of Council Conclusions and Commission Communications adopted since the Tampere European Council in 1999, which made the first explicit commitment to integrating migration and asylum policy into the Union's external affairs. Tampere was a special Summit on Justice and Home Affairs, convened in the light of mass movements of refugees being created in Kosovo at the time. It committed the EU both to creating a common European asylum system as well as to working in partnership with countries of origin. The Conclusions demonstrated the first major reference to linking EU refugee policy with external relations. They stated:

> The European Union needs a comprehensive approach to migration addressing political, human rights and development issues in countries and regions of origin and transit. This requires combating poverty, improving living conditions and job opportunities, preventing conflicts and consolidating democratic states and ensuring respect for human rights... To that end, the Union as well as Member States are invited to contribute...to a greater coherence of internal and external policies of the Union.[8]

Thus European Heads of State and Government linked the domestic and the external in this field, explicitly, for the first time. The importance of addressing the root causes of migration in countries of origin was therefore underlined, while the Conclusions also called for full commitment to the obligations of the 1951 Convention and other relevant human rights instruments. Conclusions of the Laeken and Seville European Councils followed a similar theme. Laeken in December 2001 called for 'the integration of the policy on migratory flows into the European Union's foreign policy', and also referred to protection of refugees and the 1951 Convention.[9] Similarly, Seville in June 2002 reinforced the external dimension of asylum and migration by stating that 'an integrated, comprehensive and balanced approach to tackling the root causes of illegal immigration must remain the European Union's constant long-term objective'.[10]

In 2002 the Commission issued a Communication on *Integrating migration issues in the European Union's relations with third countries.*[11] This document

---

[7] Presidency Conclusions: 'The Global Approach to Migration: Priority actions focusing on Africa and the Mediterranean', European Council, Brussels, 15-16 December 2005.

[8] Presidency Conclusions, European Council, Tampere, 15-16 October 1999, paragraph 11.

[9] Presidency Conclusions, European Council, Laeken, 14-15 December 2001, para. 11.

[10] Presidency Conclusions, European Council, Seville, 21-22 June 2002, para. 10.

[11] European Commission, 'Communication on integrating migration issues in the European Union's relations with third countries', COM(2002) 703 final.

represented the Commission's first real attempt to push forward a strategy that used external relations tools to address the root causes of migration and forced migration, with prevention and protection measures clearly marked out as priorities and the Commission arguing for a complementary approach with existing development programmes. The Communication devoted attention to outlining the different Community actions in favour of refugees, including humanitarian assistance being provided to refugee populations. A further Communication issued by the Commission in June 2003, *Towards more accessible, equitable and managed asylum systems*, stressed that possible new approaches should be focused on action outside the EU, within a framework of genuine burden and responsibility sharing.[12] Preparatory actions were to be taken to test the ground for what could be done in regions of origin within this scope, and a budget line, B7-667, was set up for this purpose. Those projects selected were conducted through UNHCR and focused on issues such as gaps analyses of protection, how to strengthen international protection and institution-building of asylum systems in regions of origin.

Following a mandate from the Thessaloniki European Council in June 2003, the Commission then issued a Communication *On the managed entry in the EU of persons in need of international protection and the enhancement of the protection capacity of the regions of origin: "Improving access to durable solutions"*. It noted that:

> A reduction in the numbers of asylum seekers in the EU does not necessarily mean an overall reduction of the numbers of refugees and persons seeking international protection at a global level and it is clear that there remain many regions and countries in the world where human rights violations and consequent displacement cause protracted refugee situations, with still some 85% of these persons being hosted by the under-resourced neighbouring countries in regions of origin.[13]

Here the Commission clearly placed the focus on protection and attempted to show Member States that an emphasis solely on border control measures risked denying protection to refugees. The Communication noted that according to UNHCR 'there is a collective duty of the broader community of States…to equip States receiving or likely to receive asylum-seekers with the means to live up to international standards in their treatment of refugees'.[14]

---

[12] European Commission, 'Communication on towards more accessible, equitable and managed asylum systems', COM(2003) 315 final.

[13] European Commission, 'Communication on the managed entry in the EU of persons in need of international protection and enhancement of the protection capacity of the regions of origin: improving access to durable solutions', COM(2004) 410 final, para. 3.

[14] European Commission, 'Communication on the managed entry', para. 13.

This suggested that a system of international burden or responsibility sharing is implicit in international relations between states and, as such, showed that the international refugee regime creates obligations on sovereign states. The Communication committed the Commission to bringing forward a proposal for the creation of Regional Protection Programmes (RPPs) which would respond specifically to the world's protracted refugee situations – some thirty-three situations affecting 5.7 million refugees – in which the great majority of refugees continue to live in a state of limbo, unable to return home, unable to integrate in the country of asylum, and unable to find resettlement in a third country.[15] Moreover, programmes would be 'part and parcel of the overall strategy towards the country or region concerned and synergies with the various components of the strategy (in particular good governance, judiciary reform, institution building, democratisation and human rights etc) [would] be fully exploited'.[16]

RPPs were constructed around the idea of filling existing 'protection gaps'[17], offering protection to those in need as quickly and as close to home as possible and thus avoiding the need for dangerous border crossings in the bid to reach Europe. Their objective was to enhance the protection capacity of third countries and create the conditions for one of the three durable solutions to take place. Two Regional Protection Programmes were developed, one in the Great Lakes region round Tanzania and one in Moldova. They have proved to be a policy toolbox to address protracted refugee situations, comprising projects to improve protection capacity in host countries, establish an effective Refugee Status Determination procedure, improve reception conditions, benefit the wider local community, and provide training in protection issues for those dealing with refugees. They are flexible to each case but always protection-oriented, building on and complementing existing initiatives in the region by working closely with UNHCR and other international organisations.

Although Tampere is generally considered to mark the beginnings of attention on the external relations of asylum and migration, the Global Approach agenda has brought about a new impetus and focus on the external dimension, rebalancing the language of migration relations with third countries

[15] United Nations, Office of the United Nations High Commissioner for Refugees, *The State of the World's Refugees: Human Displacement in the New Millennium* (Oxford University Press, 2006), p.10. This figure does not include the 4.3 million displaced Palestinians who fall under the mandate of UNRWA – UNHCR, '2005 Global Refugee Trends', para. 3.

[16] European Commission, 'Communication on the managed entry', para. 17-18.

[17] European Commission, 'Communication on Regional Protection Programmes', COM(2005) 388 final, para. 3.

positively and comprehensively and shifting attention to working outside the EU in countries of migrant and refugee origin. As such it is similar in approach to the R2P principle of humanitarian intervention to deal with an issue inside a sovereign territory. It builds on the second pillar of R2P that underlines the duty of the international community to help states build their capacity to exercise their responsibility to protect their population.

Over the last three and a half years, the Global Approach has sought to reinforce the need to link external relations and migration policy. The purported aim of the Global Approach is to develop balanced policies on migration and asylum in partnership with third countries. It seeks to address the broad range of migration-related issues – from legal to illegal migration and combating trafficking and smuggling in human beings, and from strengthening protection for refugees to harnessing the positive links and synergies that exist between migration policy and development policy. As such, it brings together different policy areas – development, social affairs and employment, external relations and justice and home affairs – taking both short term actions as well as a longer term vision to address the root causes of migration and forced migration, including poverty and the lack of employment prospects.

The Global Approach to Migration has introduced a new way of working with third countries on migration issues. The emphasis has been on dialogue and concrete action focusing on the whole migration agenda in the interests of the EU, the partner countries and the migrants themselves. It has a strong theme of working in partnership with countries of origin and transit and underlines the need to formulate a comprehensive, balanced approach. The key concepts of 'partnership', 'solidarity' and 'shared responsibility' have become its mantra. Its commitment, as the Declaration of the Rabat Conference on Migration and Development nicely summed up, is 'to work together, in the framework of a global, balanced, pragmatic and operational approach, with respect to the fundamental rights and dignity of migrants and refugees, on the phenomenon of migratory routes'.[18] Thus it has given much attention to building cooperation with countries outside the EU, initially source and transit countries in Africa, but then widened to include a focus on the eastern and south-eastern regions neighbouring the EU.

The Global Approach has promoted dialogue on the whole range of migration issues with African countries and regional organisations in particular. At the continental level, Ministers from the whole of the EU and the whole of

[18] Declaration adopted at the EU-Africa Ministerial Conference on Migration and Development, Rabat, July 2006.

Africa met in Tripoli in November 2006 at a conference on migration and development. This was the first time ever that the EU and Africa met to take a joint commitment to working together on migration and development. Migration has also featured more and more prominently on the agendas of meetings between the EU and the African Union at both ministerial and official level events. Comprehensive dialogue and action has also been stepped up at the regional level. Ministers from EU Member States also met their counterparts of North and Sub-Saharan Africa in an EU-Africa conference on migration and development held in Rabat in July 2006, repeated in Paris in October 2008, which brought together some 60 source, transit and destination countries to talk about migration issues of common interest and concern for the first time. ECOWAS, the regional body representing West African states, drafted its own strategy on migration issues, and an EU-ECOWAS joint working group on migration was established and met for the first time in the margins of the EU-ECOWAS Troika held in April 2007. And at the bilateral level a series of EU 'migration missions' have taken place to specific third countries, including Ghana, Senegal, Mauritania, Mali, Cape Verde, Ethiopia and South Africa, to discuss issues of common concern. Such missions have resulted in joint conclusions being drawn up and signed by both sides.

Dialogue at the multilateral, regional and bilateral levels has tended to cover the broad range of migration issues of interest to both sides, looking specifically at where the EC can offer assistance in helping African countries to build capacity to better manage their own migration and asylum systems. Migration and development has been a key agenda item of this dialogue. The policy world now widely accepts that migration policy can be good for development policy and vice versa, and much time continues to be spent discussing ways to better harness the positive links and synergies that exist between the two policy areas. The High Level Dialogue on Migration and Development, held under the auspices of the United Nations in 2006, is an indication of this acceptance, a one-off event that has since evolved into an annual Global Forum on Migration and Development. States have discussed ways to facilitate remittance transfers and the developmental impact they may have, initiatives to better involve diaspora communities in the development of their countries of origin, opportunities for circular migration, and policy aimed at mitigating skill loss or brain drain and the negative impact it has on developing countries.[19]

[19] See European Commission, 'Communication on migration and development: some concrete orientations', COM(2005) 390 final.

'Cooperation platforms' on migration have been developed as a tool to further dialogue. The aim of such platforms is to promote coherence in policy implementation by bringing together migration and development actors in a country or region, including representatives of the country concerned, the main donors – EU Member States and the Commission – and international organisations such as the World Bank, the various UN agencies, the International Organization for Migration and the ILO, to coordinate the projects they are planning and to discuss progress, as well as to share best practice and experience and avoid any unnecessary duplication of efforts. A first such cooperation platform was set up in Ethiopia in 2008. Additionally, 'migration profiles' have been developed as a tool to help bring together all the information required to discuss and develop policy in the field of migration and development and to monitor the impact of policies implemented. Such profiles collate data and statistics on a range of issues including migratory flows in and out of a particular country, the labour market situation and any specific sectors suffering from a lack of skilled personnel, links with diaspora communities, and figures on remittance flows into the country. They have then been used to integrate migration into EC Country Strategy Papers by making suggestions for programming of development assistance in the field of migration.

Mobility partnerships have also been established as a tool to help cooperation between the EU and partner countries. The underlying thinking was that specific 'packages' could be established between the EU and interested third countries that contain something for both sides – incentives such as visa facilitation, quotas from certain Member States or circular migration schemes, in return for cooperation on fighting illegal migration and issues related to return and readmission. In this regard they mirror very much the bilateral agreements that Spain has put in place with a number of West African countries. The first two EU mobility partnerships were signed with Moldova and Cape Verde in 2008.

As part of the longer-term approach, the EU and Africa agreed a Joint EU-Africa Strategy at the EU-Africa Summit held in Lisbon at the end of 2007. It set out the steps that the EU will take with Africa between now and 2015 to support African efforts to build a peaceful, democratic and prosperous future for all its peoples, with the primary aim of achieving the Millennium Development Goals and the promotion of sustainable development, security and good governance in Africa. On migration specifically, the strategy set out to 'maximise the developmental benefits and minimize the negative aspects of migration and strengthen protection for refugees, through engaging in balanced dialogue and cooperation with the AU, other African organisations and states on a broad range of migration issues'. Migration was a key part of both the Strategy and the Summit, once again underlining the priority given to the domain by EU and African leaders alike.

In November 2006 the Commission reported on progress made so far with implementation of the Global Approach, and refugee protection featured as a section in its own right.[20] The Commission underlined in particular 'the need to ensure access to asylum processes for those in mixed migratory flows who might need international protection', noted the importance of keeping asylum and protection issues as a key element of dialogue with third countries, and suggested building on UNHCR's '10-Point Plan of Action' to foster operational cooperation in this domain.[21] It is interesting to note that refugee protection remained an integral part of EU external policy on migration, a fact that once again points back to the initial mandate of the Global Approach and its emphasis on addressing the whole migration agenda.

To sum up, the external dimension of migration and asylum policy demonstrates a wider understanding of protection, one which ignores the borders of the EU and thinks about why people migrate, the means they use to migrate, and the linkages with other policy areas to address the negative sides of migratory flows. It puts the locus of policy intervention in countries where migrants and refugees originate, in a manner not dissimilar to the idea of humanitarian intervention as assisting states in protecting their people. This contrasts with the Common European Asylum System which provides the more inward-facing perspective on protection.

Conclusions

Refugee flows are one of the starkest reminders of the failings of the modern state, and history has shown that the international community is more likely to step in to provide protection when these flows have crossed an international border – when the people moving have, according to international law, the right to international protection and refugee status. The European Union and its Member States are bound by the 1951 Convention, yet must grapple on a daily basis with today's phenomenon of 'mixed flows' that encompass refugees, economic migrants and lots of categories in between. The evolution of such mixed flows has led to differing views over what the responsibility to protect

[20] European Commission, 'Communication on the Global Approach to Migration one year one: Towards a comprehensive European migration policy', COM(2006) 735 final.

[21] European Commission, 'Communication on the Global Approach', para. 9.

actually means – physical burden-sharing or practical assistance – and the form in which the EU should provide protection to refugees – a common asylum policy within the EU, or an external relations approach that focuses on engagement with countries and regions of refugee origin that chimes more with the interventionist principle underlying the Responsibility to Protect.

It seems likely that both views of responsibility and protection will continue to persist. The EU migration and asylum policy arena is a complex one, illustrated with ever-changing political priorities, public opinion and real-world events, and these complexities impact on state responses to migratory and refugee flows. If these competing approaches can complement rather than contradict one another, there is no harm in their co-existence, indeed they could reinforce the R2P principle. It will remain fundamental, however, that the actual protection imperative stays at the top of the agenda in the continuing debate over what the EU's response to the duty of responsibility and the duty of protection should be.

Chapter Five

Regime-Induced Displacement and Decision-Making Within the United Nations Security Council: The Cases of Northern Iraq, Kosovo, and Darfur

Phil Orchard[1]

Introduction

Since the end of the Cold War, the nature of global forced displacement has changed. The 1951 Refugee Convention was created with a narrow purview to protect individuals fleeing state-based persecution. Yet today, the vast majority of refugees and internally displaced persons (IDPs) flee their homes for different reasons: either due to situations of generalised violence and civil war within their own country; or when governments deliberately displace their own populations. This latter category is particularly problematic because, as Cohen and Deng note, 'when governments become directly involved in uprooting minority populations they often see those they are uprooting not as their citizens but as "the other." This process of dehumanisation enables authorities to more easily explain away the high number of those killed or uprooted.'[2]

Cases of regime-induced displacement – situations in which the government or government-sponsored actors deliberately use coercive tactics to directly or indirectly cause large numbers of their own citizens to flee a given area – can easily blur into cases of ethnic cleansing, genocide, or policide as

---

[1] I would like to thank Alexander Betts, Alex Bellamy, Lesley Burns, Katrina Coleman, Sara Davies, Brian Job and especially Victoria Colvin for helpful comments, and Alexandra McCarter for research assistance. Support for this project has been provided through a Canadian Department of National Defence Security and Defence Forum Postdoctoral Fellowship and through the University of Queensland.

[2] Roberta Cohen and Francis M. Deng, 'Mass Displacement Caused by Conflicts and One-Sided Violence: National and International Responses,' in Stockholm International Peace Research Institute (ed.) *SIPRI Yearbook 2009* (Oxford: Oxford University Press, 2009), p. 20.

state-sponsored violence forces large numbers of civilians to flee. Recent work[3] has shown that in the 103 situations of mass displacement between 1991 and 2006 (affecting some 53 countries), regime-induced displacement was one of the primary causes of displacement in 62 (60 percent) of the cases.[4] Further, as Figure 1 shows below, while total incidents of mass displacement have declined since the early 1990s, the proportion of incidents of regime-induced displacement has increased. Thus, in 2007, civilians were targeted by their governments for real or perceived support to rebel forces in Colombia and the Central African Republic, while civilians were targeted in Iraq, Sudan (Darfur) and Kenya as a means of clearing areas of people with certain ethnic, religious, or political ties.[5]

The international response to these problems, however, remains limited. The existing international refugee regime – based around the Refugee Convention and the United Nations High Commissioner for Refugees (UNHCR) – and the emerging humanitarian regime designed to protect IDPs[6] – based around the guiding principles on internal displacement and a number of international organisations including UNHCR – remain poorly equipped to respond to states that deliberately displace their own populations.

[3] Phil Orchard, 'The Perils of Humanitarianism: Refugee and IDP Protection in Situations of Regime-Induced Displacement,' *Refugee Survey Quarterly*, Forthcoming.

[4] Mass displacement refers to cases where either 100,000 refugees or IDPs were created within a year. A case may include multiple years if this threshold is crossed each year. In many cases, one or more causes of displacement may be present. In three quarters of the cases (77) civil wars or internationalised civil wars were one of the causes and in four cases interstate war was one of the causes. Thus, there is a high correlation between civil wars and regime-induced displacement – 50 of the cases (49 percent) had both causes present in the same year, lending support to the argument that 'intentional killing of civilians during war is often a calculated military strategy designed to combat powerful guerrilla insurgencies.' Benjamin Valentino, Paul Huth, and Dylan Balch-Lindsay, '"Draining the Sea": Mass Killing and Guerrilla Warfare,' *International Organization*, 58/2 (2004), p. 376. However, it is not invariably linked: Zimbabwe in 2006 is a case of regime-induced displacement without a civil war present, while in Rwanda in 1994 the civil war reignited following the genocide which displaced hundreds of thousands of Tutsis. The complete list of countries and cases is provided in Orchard 'Perils of Humanitarianism', as is this discussion in more substantial detail.

[5] Internal Displacement Monitoring Centre, *Internal Displacement: Global Overview of Trends and Developments in 2007* (Geneva: Norwegian Refugee Council, 2008), p. 15.

[6] Alexander Betts, 'Institutional Proliferation and the Global Refugee Regime,' *Perspectives on Politics* 7/1 (2009).

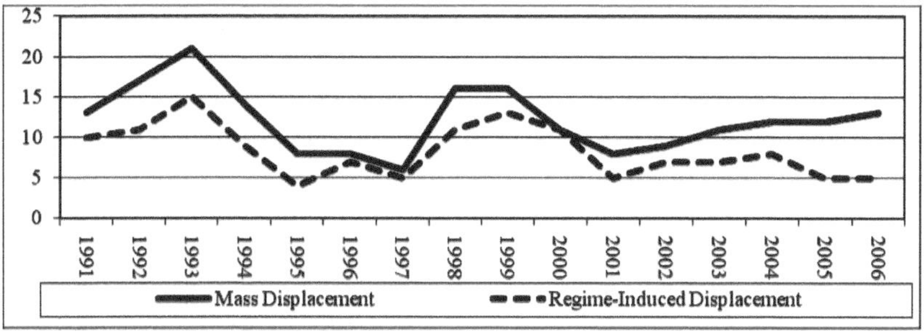

Figure 1: Incidents of Mass Displacement by Year (1991-2006)

Instead, what is needed is for situations of regime-induced displacement to be dealt with at a higher level of institutional authority, notably through the UN Security Council. The Council is pivotal in this regard as it is one of the few international institutions with a clear enforcement capability. Moreover, the Responsibility to Protect doctrine (R2P), which argues that military interventions for human protection purposes are justified to halt or avert either large scale loss of life or large scale ethnic cleansing, whether carried out 'by killing, forced expulsion, acts of terror or rape,'[7] provides a clear mechanism for Council involvement in the most extreme cases of regime-induced displacement. The ICISS report noted that the primary arbiter for such decisions should be the UN Security Council[8], a view reinforced by the 2005 World Summit Declaration which positioned it as the only authoritative body.

Unfortunately, while the Council has incorporated protecting refugees and IDPs into its purview, leading Gil Loescher to suggest that armed interventions against states where refugee flows are generated 'is becoming a norm,'[9] Council action remains limited in two ways. The first is that 'international action has on most occasions attempted to limit [refugee] crises and to provide relief after the damage has been done.'[10] The second is that the record of

---

[7] International Commission on Intervention and State Sovereignty (ICISS), *The Responsibility to Protect: Report of the International Commission on Intervention and State Sovereignty* (Ottawa: International Development Research Centre, 2001), p. 32.

[8] Ibid., pp. 48-49.

[9] Gil Loescher, 'Refugees as Grounds for International Action,' in Edward Newman and Joanne van Selm (eds.) *Refugees and Forced Displacement: International Security, Human Vulnerability, and the State* (Tokyo: United Nations University Press, 2003), p. 23.

[10] Ibid., p. 23.

the Security Council authorising explicit humanitarian interventions without the consent of the state when regime-induced displacement is occurring is non-existent. Even the record of states acting outside the Council since 1991 includes only two interventions: in Northern Iraq in 1991 and in Kosovo in 1999.

By examining these two cases and one where a humanitarian intervention did not occur – Darfur – I argue that the Security Council faces two dilemmas when responding to situations of regime-induced displacement: the problems of political will and of consent. Critically, the Council has not authorised an intervention without the consent of the concerned state. This is a particular problem since in cases of regime-induced displacement it is the state itself that is responsible for mass displacement and atrocities. The two cases of intervention are aberrant because in both cases, groups of states had the political will to intervene without Council authorisation, driven by humanitarian concerns as well as by the international implications of large-scale refugee flows. Darfur represents a more vexing problem, when neither political will exists to intervene, nor state consent is forthcoming. Yet as Darfur shows, the lack of consent and the omnipresent threat of the veto within the Security Council can be used by its members as a shield and cover for not having the will to take action. This suggests that without change, even as regime-induced displacement becomes a greater problem for the international community, the international body best suited to deal with it will frequently fail to take action. Therefore, I end by briefly discussing two routes to ameliorate the veto problem: the need for agreement among the five permanent members (P-5) to restrict use of the veto in situations of regime-induced displacement which are serious enough to cross the R2P threshold, or revitalising the 'Uniting for Peace' protocol within the General Assembly. Otherwise, in a future case of regime-induced displacement where political will does exist to intervene, it will likely occur outside of the Council.

The Security Council and the Protection of Internally Displaced Persons

Throughout the 1990s, as refugee and IDP flows increased dramatically (see Figure 2 below), the Security Council increasingly saw mass displacement of civilians as threats to international peace and security. The UN Charter establishes under Chapter VII that the Council has the primary responsibility for the maintenance of international peace and security. Since the end of the Cold War, this responsibility has been successfully redefined by the Council to include such actions as 'the use of extreme violence by governments against large populations [that] could generate massive refugee flows, illegal arms trafficking, and the rise of paramilitary guerrilla armies, all of which could disrupt neighbouring states and regional stability.'[11] Through resolutions, the Council has expanded its purview to protect refugees and internally displaced persons (IDPs), whether by declaring ethnic cleansing to be an illegal practice[12] or by emphasising vulnerable groups including IDPs, such as in 'resolution 1261 that condemns the targeting of children, resolution 1265 on the protection of civilians in armed conflict, resolution 1325 that specifically addresses the impact of war and women, and resolution 1400 that extends the UN mission in Sierra Leone mainly on the basis of IDPs,' as well as referencing the R2P.[13]

This signals an important rhetorical shift in Council views on the protection of refugees and IDPs. However, what is the likelihood of the Council taking action under the R2P doctrine to protect those displaced by their own governments? In this, the record of action remains decidedly limited. As the recent Preventing Genocide Task Force report notes, 'the Security Council rarely authorizes peace operations or peace enforcement missions when a state is targeting its own civilians.'[14] Its practice towards protecting civilian populations exposed to state violence has been 'highly inconsistent… [with the Council] often choosing to avoid becoming involved in situations where these practices occur…'[15]

---

[11] Bruce Cronin, 'International Consensus and the Changing Legal Authority of the UN Security Council,' in Bruce Cronin and Ian Hurd (eds.) *The UN Security Council and the Politics of International Authority* (London: Routledge, 2008), p. 72; see also Simon Chesterman, 'Legality Versus Legitimacy: Humanitarian Intervention, the Security Council, and the Rule of Law,' *Security Dialogue* 33/3 (2002).

[12] Cronin, 'International Consensus and the Changing Legal Authority of the UN Security Council,' p. 75.

[13] Thomas G. Weiss and David A. Korn, *Internal Displacement: Conceptualization and Its Consequences* (Oxford: Routledge, 2006), p. 102; S/RES/1674, 28 April 2006.

[14] Madeleine K. Albright and William S. Cohen, *Preventing Genocide: A Blueprint for US Policymakers* (Washington: United States Institute of Peace, 2008), p. 72.

[15] Cronin, 'International Consensus and the Changing Legal Authority of the UN Security Council,' p. 73.

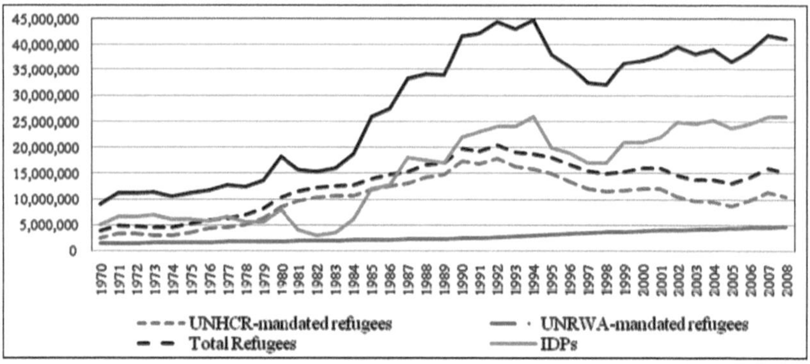

Figure 2: Total Displaced Persons, 1970-2008[16]

Humanitarian interventions without the consent of the state concerned remain extremely rare. In only the cases of Northern Iraq and Kosovo is it clear that the operations were undertaken without that consent. When forces were deployed to Somalia in 1992, Secretary-General Boutrous-Ghali argued that 'no government exists in Somalia that could request and allow use of such a force.'[17] A similar finding that 'the collapse of effective government constituted a threat to peace and security in the region' led to the deployment of a multinational force in Albania in 1997.[18] In Haiti in 1994[19] and again in East

[16] UNHCR data: http://www.unhcr.org/statistics/ (figures since 2007 include people in refugee-like situations and are not directly comparable); UNRWA data: Report of the Commissioner-General of the United Nations Relief and Works Agency for Palestine Refugees in the Near East, A/35/13, 30 June 1980, and Annually 1982-2007. Reports available at the UN Information System on the Question of Palestine, http://www.unispal.un.org, accessed 10 April 2009. Data for 1981 is missing, and has been extrapolated from 1980 data based on annual growth rate of 2.2%. See BADIL *Annual Growth Rate of Registered Palestinian Refugees (1953-2000),* http://www.badil.org/Statistics/population/Statistics.htm., accessed 10 April 2009; IDP Data: United States Committee for Refugees, *World Refugee Survey [Yearly 1997-2004]* (Washington: US Committee for Refugees); Internal Displacement Monitoring Centre, *Internal Displacement: Global Overview of Trends and Developments,* [Yearly 2004-2008] (Geneva: Norwegian Refugee Council, 2005-2009); Norwegian Refugee Survey, *Internally Displaced Persons: A Global Survey* (London: Earthscan Publications, 1999), p. 28.

[17] 'Letter from the Secretary General Addressed to the President of the Security Council' S/24868, 30 Nov 1992, p. 3.

[18] Christine Gray *International Law and the Use of Force* (Oxford: Oxford University Press, 2000), p. 188.

[19] In the case of Haiti, last minute diplomacy resulted in the coup leaders consenting and avoiding an intervention authorised by the Council in Resolution S/RES/940, 31 July 1994. John Ballard, *Upholding Democracy: The United States Military Campaign in Haiti, 1994-1997* (Westport: Praeger, 1998), p. 96.

Timor in 2000, the government consented to the intervention. While the French-led *Operation Turquoise* deployed with a Security Council mandate in 1994, there were significant questions around whether the government of Rwanda, which had lost significant territory to the Rwandese Patriotic Front, had the capacity to consent.[20]

Yet, while in neither Northern Iraq nor Kosovo did the Security Council provide explicit authorisation for the intervention prior to the fact, in both cases the intervening forces claimed legitimacy based on prior Security Council resolutions. Two other factors are important in explaining this difference. The first is that in both cases a group of states were willing to operate outside of the Council to intervene: the United States, Great Britain, and France in the first case; the North Atlantic Treaty Organization (NATO) in the second. Further, in both cases their justifications focused on the regional or international threats posed by *refugee flows*; protecting the internally displaced (and the civilian population more generally) if discussed at all was a second priority. As will be discussed below, this suggests that humanitarian interventions to protect internally displaced persons from regime-induced displacement will remain unlikely for two reasons: first, a high likelihood that any resolution favouring such an operation without the consent of the state concerned will face a veto in the Council; and because of the relative infrequency of a group of actors having the political will to stage an operation outside of the Council. The lack of interventions over this period – only two since 1991 – does mean that these conclusions are suggestive only. However, the case of Darfur provides a clear example that even with the rhetorical expansion that has occurred within the Council the issue of consent remains a critical impediment to successful action.

Safe Havens and Mass Displacement in Northern Iraq

Following the Gulf War in 1991, uprisings among the Kurdish and Shiite populations of Iraq were crushed by Saddam Hussein, causing massive displacement. Beginning in April, 1991, at least 1.5 million refugees fled Iraq and sought asylum in Iran and Turkey. An additional one million more were

---

[20] Thomas G. Weiss and Don Hubert, *The Responsibility to Protect: Research, Bibliography, Background* (Ottawa: International Development Research Centre, 2001), pp. 97-117; Nicolas J. Wheeler, *Saving Strangers: Humanitarian Intervention in International Society* (Oxford: Oxford University Press, 2000).

internally displaced in the north after Turkey closed its borders with Iraq.[21] The result was a humanitarian crisis of epic proportions, with a death rate of between 400 and 1,000 per day among the IDPs due to 'hypothermia, exposure, exhaustion, and bacteria-ridden drinking water, which led to pneumonia, diarrhea, and cholera.'[22]

Initially, there was no international response. While sustained refugee flows began in early March,[23] it was not until 3 April that the issue was raised at the Security Council level. Yet within two weeks the American and British governments had committed to deploying troops inside Iraqi territory. Two important shifts led to this change. The first was internationally, with the Turkish, French, and Iranian governments raising the issue at the Security Council. Equally important was a shift in public opinion at the domestic level in the United States, Great Britain, and other western countries, fuelled by the media who remained in the region following the end of the Gulf War.[24]

The French government first raised it at the Council, arguing that 'the Security Council has a duty to say something about this situation.'[25] The next day, the Iranian and Turkish governments argued that refugee flows from Iraq across their respective borders 'posed a threat to the security and stability of the region…'[26] The French government also argued that there was a need to protect the Kurdish population as a whole. Roland Dumas, the French Foreign

[21] U.S. Committee for Refugees, 'April is the Cruellest Month: The Flight of the Iraqi Refugees,' *Refugee Reports*, March/April (1991), p. 1; UNHCR, *The State of the World's Refugees 2000: Fifty Years of Humanitarian Action* (Oxford: Oxford University Press, 2000), pp. 211-12. Little condemnation of Turkey occurred, Sadako Ogata notes, because of the need for coalition member states to use Turkish air bases. Sadako Ogata, *The Turbulent Decade: Confronting the Refugee Crises of the 1990s* (New York: W.W. Norton & Company, 2005), pp. 28-29.

[22] Thomas G. Weiss, *Military-Civilian Interactions: Intervening in Humanitarian Crises* (Lanham, MD: Rowman & Littlefield, 1999), p. 50.

[23] Hikaru Yamashita, *Humanitarian Space and International Politics: The Creation of Safe Areas* (Aldershot: Ashgate, 2004), p. 35.

[24] Weiss, *Military-Civilian Interactions,* p. 52; Daniel Schorr, 'Ten Days That Shook the White House,' *Columbia Journalism Review* 30/2 (1991).

[25] Rochereau de La Sabliere, France, S/PV.2981, 3 April 1991, p. 94. However, the Iraqi government claimed that the Kurdish refugees were being coerced and intimidated by the rebels to flee and that the claims were being used as pretexts to 'interfere in Iraq's internal affairs.' Al-Anbari, Iraq, Ibid., pp. 136-37.

[26] Jane E. Stromseth, 'Iraq's Repression of Its Civilian Population: Collective Responses and Continuing Challenges,' in Lori F. Damrosch (ed.) *Enforcing Restraint: Collective Intervention in Internal Conflicts* (New York: Council on Foreign Affairs, 1993), p. 85. See also 'Letter from the Turkish Ambassador to the President of the Security Council,' S/22435, 2 April 1991; and 'Letter from the Iranian Ambassador to the President of the Security Council,' S/22447, 4 April 1991.

Minister, suggested there needed to be an 'international "duty to intervene," to prevent gross violations of human rights and the rights of minorities' in such situations, while French President Francois Mitterrand suggested that the political and moral authority of the Council would be seriously affected if it failed to take action.[27] While both views were framed in the ensuing debate in the Council, it was the refugee flows – which thereby constituted an *international* problem – which was used as the primary justification for Council action.

Thus, while Resolution 688 condemned the repression 'of the Iraqi civilian population in many parts of Iraq...' it went on to note 'the consequences of which threaten international peace and security in the region.' The Council demanded a rather tepid response: that Iraq end the repression and allow immediate access for humanitarian organisations.[28] Of the countries that spoke in favour of the resolution, only Britain and France raised explicit humanitarian claims, with Britain arguing that Article 2(7) of the Charter, which bans interference in the domestic jurisdiction of states, 'did not apply to human rights because they were "not essentially domestic." '[29]

The other states who spoke in favour of 688 saw the crisis as a threat to international peace and security due to the large refugee flows into neighbouring countries. The Turkish representative, for example, noted that 'there is no way in which what is going on in northern Iraq can be justified as an internal affair of that country... Turkey will not allow its border provinces to be overwhelmed by such a flood of displaced persons.'[30] Thus, as David Malone notes, the resolution 'did not condemn the repression itself as a threat to international peace and security—only its transboundary effects— nor take steps under Chapter VII to put a stop to it.' This shift allowed the USSR to support it and China to abstain.[31] Only Cuba, Yemen, and Zimbabwe voted against the resolution, arguing that the problem did not threaten international peace and security,[32] that it was a 'domestic political conflict,'[33] and that while there

[27] Robert Cottrell, 'French Government Steps up the Pressure on UN for Stand against Iraqi Reposession [Sic] of Kurds,' *The Independent*, 4 April 1991, p. 10.

[28] S/RES/688, 5 April 1991, p. 6.

[29] Wheeler, *Saving Strangers*, p. 145.

[30] Askin, Turkey. S.PV/2982, 5 April 1991, p. 6. This claim was echoed by the Soviet and Ecuadorian ambassadors. Vorontsov, USSR, Ibid., p. 61; Ayala Lasso. Ecuador, Ibid., p. 36.

[31] David M. Malone, *The International Struggle over Iraq: Politics in the UN Security Council 1980-2005* (Oxford University Press, 2006), p. 86-87. The Chinese delegate noted that the refugee flows were concerning, but that a state's internal affairs were involved. Li Daoyu, China, S.PV/2982, 5 April 1991, pp. 54-55.

[32] Al-Ashtal, Yemen, Ibid., p. 27.

[33] Zenenga, Zimbabwe, Ibid., p. 31.

were legitimate humanitarian concerns, the Council had 'no right to violate the principle of non-intervention.'[34] Thus, Jane Stromseth notes that 688 was precedential in indicating the Council was willing 'to condemn internal repression as a threat to international peace and security, at least when it results in substantial cross-border refugee flows.'[35]

The resolution did not presage the deployment of military troops – it was only after the resolution was passed, on 7 April, that Turkey's president first proposed the idea of creating protected areas within Iraq. British Prime Minister John Major then proposed the creation of 'safe enclaves' (later changing to 'safe havens' to avoid suggesting an autonomous Kurdish area would be created) within Northern Iraq to a European Community Summit in Luxembourg. Major said the plan would be taken to the Council as it would not constitute interference because it was based on 'protection of a population from persecution.'[36]

Initially, the American government was cool to the idea. Both President Bush and Secretary of Defence Richard Cheney pointed to the need for the UN to be involved. The President noted 'when you have a refugee problem of this enormous consequence, then that comes under the heading of United Nations business,' while Cheney suggested 'the US might want to go back to the UN for "some kind of mechanism or process that would provide an area where they (the Kurds) would be safe." '[37]

There were also concerns within the UN about taking action without Iraqi consent. Eric Suy, the Secretary-General's Special Envoy to Northern Iraq, argued that such havens would require the consent of the Iraqi government, while Secretary-General Pérez de Cuéllar, when asked:

> whether a Western military presence could be established under UN authority without Iraqi consent, he replied 'No. No. No. We have to be in touch first of all with the Iraqis.' At the same time, though, he seemed prepared to look the other way if Western forces chose to act alone, so long as the UN was not asked to use force: '... if the countries involved do not require the United Nations flag, then that is quite different.'[38]

---

[34] Alarcon de Quesada, Cuba, Ibid., p. 46.

[35] Stromseth, 'Iraq's Repression of Its Civilian Population' p. 79; see also Malone, *International Struggle Over Iraq*, p. 86.

[36] Alan Riding, 'After the War; Europeans Urging Enclave for Kurds in Northern Iraq,' *New York Times*, 9 April 1991, p.1; David Usborne, Sarah Lambert, and Leonard Doyle, 'Major Urges Enclave for Kurds in Iraq,' *The Independent*, 9 April 1991, p. 1.

[37] Peter Riddell, 'US May Seek UN Protection for Kurds: Creation of "Safe Zone" in Northern Iraq for Refugees Suggested,' *Financial Times*, 8 April 1991, p. 1.

[38] Malone *International Struggle Over Iraq*, p. 90-1; see also Yamashita, *Humanitarian Space and International Politics*, p. 53.

As the Americans began to favour the plan, led in part by Secretary of State James Baker who had visited the border and argued that 'the international community has to respond quickly and effectively,' but also by a widespread shift in domestic public opinion,[39] the Iraqi government rejected the proposal. The governments of the Soviet Union and China began expressing reservations to the plan, with Chinese Ambassador Li Daoyu stating the move 'went beyond the council's mandate in the Gulf Crisis…'[40]

In spite of this opposition, the British and American governments persisted, with the British Minister of State at the Foreign Office, Douglas Hogg, arguing they had the authority to do so in Resolution 688 'in order to ensure the safety of the Kurds and this is a method of devising that, delivering that.'[41] President Bush noted that forces were being deployed to work closely with relief organisations and provide security. He went on to note that while 'some might argue that this is an intervention into the internal affairs of Iraq…I think the humanitarian concern, the refugee concern, is so overwhelming that there will be a lot of understanding about this.'[42]

Initially, 12,000 troops were deployed from the US, Britain, France, the Netherlands, Italy and Turkey (at its height the operation had 22,000 troops). Both the American and British governments made clear that their goals were limited – forces would be mobilised 'only insofar as they would contribute to humanitarian efforts… [the haven] would only have to be large enough to provide a temporary shelter until the displaced felt secure enough to go home.'[43]

While the allied forces were deployed in Northern Iraq for less than two months, turning over responsibility for relief operations to UNHCR on

---

[39] Thomas L. Friedman, 'After the War; Baker Sees and Hears Kurds' Pain in a Brief Visit at Turkish Border,' *New York Times*, 9 April 1991, p. 1. The President's vacillation on the issue "had helped to bring down his approval rating from 92 to 80 percent in a *Newsweek* poll (78 percent in a Gallup poll)." Schorr, 'Ten Days That Shook the White House,' p. 23. The Turkish government was also pushing the Bush administration to accept the safe haven idea. Samantha Power, *A Problem from Hell: America and the Age of Genocide* (New York: HarperCollins, 2002), pp. 240-241.

[40] Lionel Barber, Robert Mauthner, Michael Littlejohns, and Tony Walker, "US Orders Kurd Safety Zone: Saddam Told to Keep Air and Ground Forces out of Northern Iraq," *Financial Times*, 11 April 1991, p. 1.

[41] Cited in Wheeler, *Saving Strangers*, p. 152.

[42] George H. W. Bush, 'Remarks on Assistance for Iraqi Refugees and a News Conference,' 16 April 1991, in John T. Woolley and Gerhard Peters (eds.) *The American Presidency Project*, http://www.presidency.ucsb.edu/ index.php, accessed 1 May 2009.

[43] Yamashita, *Humanitarian Space and International Politics*, p. 51; see also UNHCR, *State of the World's Refugees 2000*, p. 216.

7 June, the operation has generally been perceived as a success. On one level, while the troops left, the American government did establish a residual force in Turkey. This, coupled with negotiations between the Kurds and the Iraqi government, and the no fly zones which remained in place, allowed the Kurds a measure of autonomy in the north. At the same time, assistance was set up rapidly by the military and provided to the Kurdish IDPs on a massive scale, while Kurdish refugees took the allied security presence as a positive indicator and returned quickly, with nearly 200,000 returning in the first two weeks of the mission and by early June the number had reached 600,000.[44]

The intervention also encouraged the Iraqi government to work with the UN to deploy monitors from the UN's own security personnel and to create confidence as well as provide access and humanitarian assistance.[45]As Freedman and Boren note, 'if it had to have a foreign presence on its soil it much preferred this to be civilian UN workers rather than Western soldiers.'[46]

The coalition did successfully stop a humanitarian crisis already in progress by providing secure areas within Northern Iraq to protect the Kurds who could not flee and to facilitate the return of those who had. As an example of a successful intervention, however, it must be tempered by four caveats. The first is that the intervention did not occur for over a month from the start of massive population displacement. Nor, of course, did it receive Security Council approval. Thirdly, it was successful in part because it facilitated more autonomy for the Kurds domestically, but also ensured that they were protected by an allied air umbrella which was used frequently over the ensuring twelve years. Finally, the Western states were unwilling to pressure Turkey to open its own borders. Thus, the easiest solution – asylum – was unavailable to many Kurds. As then UN High Commission for Refugees Sadako Ogata noted in a 1996 speech:

> it was the converging interests of the Coalition Forces... to protect the strategic oil producing region of the Gulf that forced them to military action. They recognized Turkey's security concerns not to allow the inflow of Kurdish refugees. Consequently, refugees were stopped at the mountainous borders and a safe area established in northern Iraq to allow people to return.[47]

---

[44] Ibid., 216-17.

[45] Yamashita, *Humanitarian Space and International Politics*, pp. 52-54.

[46] Lawrence Freedman and David Boren, '"Safe Havens" for Kurds,' in Nigel S. Rodley (ed.) *To Loose the Bands of Wickedness* (London: Brassey's, 1992), p. 61.

[47] Sadako Ogata, 'World Order, Internal Conflict and Refugees,' 28 October 1996, http://www.unhcr.org, accessed 1 Oct 2009. Ogata has noted that the decision to help the Kurdish IDPs was opposed within UNHCR as a substitute for asylum, but she had no choice once the

What does the intervention in Northern Iraq suggest about Council behaviour? As both Stomseth and Wheeler note, the most interesting response was the *lack* of an outcry by Council members about the operation. Stomseth argues that while Operation Provide Comfort revealed a Council with a clear reluctance to 'explicitly authorize the use of force to stop a state from repressing its own citizens,' it showed the Council would implicitly tolerate military measures taken by some member states.[48] Wheeler similarly notes that while the Soviet Union, China, and other non-western States were anxious about this precedent, 'none of these states wanted to be exposed publicly as opposing a rescue mission that was saving lives and they were shamed into silence.'[49]

The intervention in Northern Iraq, consequently, represents a potent mixture of humanitarian and state interests at play, including the needs of a close ally – Turkey – and fears over the destabilising effects of the refugee flows. These factors led the coalition to challenge Council practice and create a novel solution for the Iraqi IDPs and refugees, based in an existing resolution as precedent. It succeeded only because widespread displacement was dealt with quickly and the political will existed to provide long-term protection.

Rifts Emerge: The Council and the NATO Intervention in Kosovo

Similar dynamics drove the Council's response to the Kosovo crisis eight years later. Beginning in 1996, the Kosovo Liberation Army (KLA) attacked Serb targets. Early in 1998, the Serbian government responded by deploying large numbers of troops and increasingly killing civilians.[50] By October, the UN Secretary-General argued that 'civilians increasingly have become the main target in the conflict… there are concerns that the disproportionate use of force and actions of the security forces are designed to terrorise and subjugate

safe areas were announced. Gil Loescher, *The UNHCR and World Politics: A Perilous Path* (Oxford: Oxford University Press), p. 288; Ogata, *The Turbulent Decade*, p. 38. A 2003 report notes 'the coalition's decision to back Turkey and therefore to mitigate the effects of that country's refusal to open its borders to persons who should have become refugees… in fact created massive internal displacement and thus necessitated the international attention that followed.' OCHA Internal Displacement Unit, *No Refuge: The Challenge of Internal Displacement* (Geneva: United Nations Publications, 2003), pp. 16-17.

48 Stromseth, 'Iraq's Repression of Its Civilian Population,' p. 79.

49 Wheeler, *Saving Strangers*, p. 154.

50 Thomas M. Franck, *Recourse to Force: State Action Against Threats and Armed Attacks* (Cambridge: Cambridge University Press, 2002), pp. 163-64; Wheeler, *Saving Strangers*, pp. 257-59.

the population…'[51] At that point, a half-million Kosovars were internally displaced and an additional 200,000 had sought asylum.[52]

The Security Council began by condemning violence on both sides in Resolution 1160, which was passed under Chapter VII.[53] By the fall, however, the Council demanded not only that both sides take steps to avert an 'impending humanitarian catastrophe' but singled out the Yugoslavian government, demanding that it 'cease all action by the security forces affecting the civilian population and order the withdrawal of security units used for civilian repression.'[54] Both Resolutions 1199 (passed on 23 September 1998) and 1203 (passed on 24 October 1998) were passed under Chapter VII.

Following 1199, US officials began to consider using NATO to stage an intervention arguing that there was no further authorisation required from the Council. While the Russians acquiesced to the resolution, in part due to irritation that Serbian President Slobodan Milosevic had violated commitments made with Russian President Boris Yeltsin in a joint statement that June, their ambassador noted that 'no use of force and no sanctions are being imposed…'[55]

This proved to be little impediment to NATO once the Serbian government rejected an agreement proposed by the Contact Group at Rambouillet in March 1999. They justified the intervention for humanitarian reasons and used the earlier resolutions as justifications. NATO Secretary-General Javier Solana argued that their objective was 'to prevent more human suffering and more repression and violence against the civilian population of Kosovo. We

[51] Kofi Annan, Report of the Secretary-General prepared pursuant to resolution 1160 and 1199 of the Security Council, S/1998/912, 3 October 1998, p. 3.

[52] Jim Whitman, 'The Kosovo Refugee Crisis: NATO's Humanitarianism Versus Human Rights,' *The International Journal of Human Rights* 4/3 (2000), pp. 168-69.

[53] S/RES/1160, 31 March 1998. This resolution also imposed an arms embargo. Serbia continued to be under some 'outer wall' sanctions from the Bosnian war, linked to the human rights situation in Kosovo. Alex J. Bellamy, *Kosovo and International Society* (New York: Palgrave Macmillan 2002), p. 55. The six country contact group also imposed sanctions in March and April 1998. Alessandra Stanley, 'U.S. and Allies Put Pressure on Yugoslavia to Negotiate,' *The New York Times*, 30 April 1998, p. A10.

[54] S/RES/1199, 23 September 1998, p. 3.

[55] John M. Goshko, 'US, Allies Inch Closer to Kosovo Intervention; UN Council to Vote on Key Resolution,' *The Washington Post*, 23 Sep 1998, p. A21; Lavrov, Russian Federation, S/PV.3930, 23 September 1998, p. 3. The Russian government abstained on the other two resolutions, arguing it was an internal affair. Fedotov, Russian Federation, S/PV.3868, 31 March 1998, p. 10. The Chinese government abstained on all three resolutions. Shen Guofang, China, S/PV.3868, 31 March 1998, p. 11-12.

[56] Press Statement by Javier Solana, Secretary General of NATO, 23 March 1999. http://www.nato.int/docu/pr/1999/p99-040e.htm, accessed 2 July 2009.

must also act to prevent instability from spreading in the region...'[56] President Clinton argued in an address to the nation: 'Do our interests in Kosovo justify the dangers to our armed forces?... I am convinced that the dangers of acting are far outweighed by the dangers of not acting – dangers to defenseless people and to our national interests.'[57] The Security Council, French Prime Minister Lionel Jospin suggested, 'wasn't in a position to [act], because it had become a matter of urgency, it was up to us to shoulder all our responsibilities, particularly in the Atlantic Alliance.'[58] Similarly, the British Foreign Office argued that 'force can be justified on the grounds of overwhelming humanitarian necessity without a UNSC [Resolution]' based in part on 'extreme humanitarian distress on a large scale, requiring immediate and urgent relief.'[59]

And yet, as Katrina Coleman notes, none of the resolutions actually provided a firm basis:

> ...although Security Council Resolutions 1199 and 1203 invoke Chapter VII of the UN Charter they do not explicitly authorize the use of force against the [Federal Republic of Yugoslavia]. By convention, UN resolutions mandating the international use of force authorizes states to use 'all necessary means' to address a particular crisis. The Security Council resolution on Kosovo did not contain this phrase.[60]

Further, both Russia and China had made it clear with each resolution that they would 'veto any proposal for military action against Yugoslavia regarding its conduct in its own territory.'[61]

The Russian ambassador quickly took the matter to the Council. Here, NATO sought to justify the intervention as necessary to avert a humanitarian catastrophe coupled with massive refugee flows.[62] Thus the American ambassador justified NATO's actions by arguing not only that 'Belgrade's brutal persecution of Kosovar Albanians... foreshadow a humanitarian catastrophe

---

[57] William J. Clinton 'Address to the Nation on Airstrikes Against Serbian Targets in the Federal Republic of Yugoslavia,' 24 March 1999, Woolley and Gerhard Peters (eds.) *The American Presidency Project*, accessed 1 Oct 2009.

[58] Cited in Katharina P. Coleman, *International Organisations and Peace Enforcement: The Politics of International Legitimacy* (Cambridge: Cambridge University Press, 2007), pp. 198-99.

[59] Cited in Adam Roberts, 'NATO's "Humanitarian War" over Kosovo,' *Survival* 41/3 (1999), p. 106.

[60] Coleman, *International Organisations and Peace Enforcement*, p. 200; see also Michael Byers and Simon Chesterman, 'Changing the Rules About Rules? Unilateral Humanitarian Intervention and the Future of International Law,' in J.L. Holzgrefe and Robert O. Keohane (eds.) *Humanitarian Intervention: Ethical, Legal, and Political Dilemmas* (Cambridge: Cambridge University Press, 2003), pp. 181-83.

[61] Roberts, 'NATO's "Humanitarian War" over Kosovo,' p. 104.

[62] Bellamy, *Kosovo and International Society*, p. 69.

of immense proportions' but also that it 'is generating refugees and creating pressures on neighbouring countries, threatening the stability of the region.'[63] These views were echoed by other NATO members and by states as diverse as Slovenia, Bahrain, Gambia, and Malaysia. Of the states that spoke against the intervention, both Namibia and Gabon argued they were against the use of military force to create a solution, while China, India, and Russia framed the intervention as illegal since it was a domestic matter and had not been approved by the Council.[64] As Adam Roberts notes, 'a crumb of legal comfort,' but little else, was given to the intervention when a draft resolution sponsored by Russia and which called for 'an immediate cessation of the use of force against the Federal Republic of Yugoslavia' 'had only three states (Russia, China and Namibia) [vote] in favour, and 12 against.'[65]

The intervention itself failed in its goal of averting a humanitarian catastrophe. Serb forces responded to the bombings by dramatically escalating attacks on the Albanian population of Kosovo. Executions occurred as a means to 'eliminate resistance and to demonstrate the costs of remaining in Kosovo... All told, Milosevic's forces drove more than 1.3 million Kosovars from their homes, some 740,000 of whom flooded into neighbouring Macedonia and Albania.' An estimated 10,000 were killed.[66] While UNHCR had made contingency plans, the mass flight 'overwhelmed the response capacity of the host government and humanitarian organizations.'[67]

The matter of Kosovo returned to the Security Council on 10 June with the end of the conflict. Resolution 1244 placed Kosovo under UN administration and authorised an 'international security presence' without mentioning NATO explicitly.[68] This followed negotiations between the American and Russian governments and Russian pressure on the Serbian government to agree to NATO's terms. The Russian government played a key role in the Council in 'persuading the Chinese not to use their veto. Ambassador Lavrov argued that it was better to create a UN administration than to force NATO to create a protectorate outside UN auspices.'[69] In so doing, it has been suggested the resolution 'retroactively endorsed the NATO campaign, if only by necessary

[63] Burleigh, United States of America, S.PV/3988, 24 March 1999, p. 4.

[64] S.PV/3988, 24 March 1999.

[65] Roberts, 'NATO's "Humanitarian War" over Kosovo,' p. 105.

[66] Samantha Power, *A Problem from Hell*, pp. 549-50; Bellamy, *Kosovo and International Society*, p. 199; see also the Independent Commission on Kosovo, *The Kosovo Report: Conflict, International Response, Lessons Learned* (Oxford: Oxford University Press, 2000).

[67] UNHCR, *State of the World's Refugees 2000*, p. 234.

[68] S/RES/1244, 10 June 1999, p. 2.

[69] Bellamy, *Kosovo and International Society*, p. 200.

implication.'[70] The following year, the Independent International Commission on Kosovo argued that the intervention was:

> illegal but legitimate. It was illegal because it did not receive prior approval from the United Nations Security Council. However, the Commission considers that the intervention was justified because all diplomatic avenues had been exhausted and because the intervention had the effect of liberating the majority population of Kosovo from a long period of oppression under Serbian rule.[71]

In Kosovo, like in Northern Iraq, individual states possessed the political will to act outside of the Council when faced with the veto, though in this case the intervention triggered further mass displacement. In both cases, interventions were undertaken because of the potential consequences of regime-induced displacement: in particular, fears of the destabilising effects of refugee flows.

Council (in)action in Darfur

In December 2003, Jan Egeland, then the UN Emergency Relief Coordinator, declared that 'the humanitarian situation in Darfur had quickly become one of the worst in the world.'[72] While fighting there had begun in February, the Council would not even address the crisis until the following May. As a contrast to Northern Iraq and Kosovo, Darfur provides a more typical view of Security Council practice in situations of regime-induced displacement where political will is lacking: the issue of consent and of state sovereignty is used 'by Western states as a convenient excuse for not doing more.'[73]

Origins of the Current Conflict

Fighting began in February 2003 when two rebel groups – the Sudan Liberation Army (SLA) and the Justice Equality Movement (JEM)[74] – began a series of

---

[70] Nigel S. Rodley and Basak Cali, 'Kosovo Revisited: Humanitarian Intervention on the Fault Lines of International Law,' *Human Rights Law Review* 7/2 (2007), p. 282.

[71] The Independent Commission on Kosovo, *The Kosovo Report*, p. 4.

[72] Cited in Gerard Prunier, *Darfur: The Ambiguous Genocide*, (Ithaca: Cornell University Press, 2007), p. 90.

[73] Cristina G. Badescu and Linnea Bergholm, 'The Responsibility to Protect and the Conflict in Darfur: The Big Let-Down" *Security Dialogue* 40/3 (2009), p. 296.

[74] Adding to the complexity of the Darfur situation, both groups have since split. Estimates of the number of rebel groups range as high as fifty. Johan Brosché 'Darfur: Dimensions and Dilemmas of a Complex Situation' *Uppsala University Department of Peace and Conflict Research UCDP Paper No. 2*, http://www.pcr.uu.se, accessed 9 Sept 2008, p. 30.

attacks against government buildings and military installations. When the rebels were initially successful, the Sudanese government rapidly moved from negotiations to a military solution. Unwilling to trust the Sudanese armed forces – many of whom had been recruited from Darfur – the government decided to use the existing Arab *janjaweed* militias, made up of bandits, highwayman, demobilised soldiers, criminals, and the young unemployed.[75]

High levels of violence have been used against the civilian population by the *janjaweed* throughout the conflict – including 'killings, abductions, forced expulsions, systematic sexual violence, and deliberate destruction of crops, livestock, and important cultural and religious sites.'[76] However, four distinct phases mark the conflict. The initial violent campaign during the second half of 2003 concentrated the civilian population in the larger urban centres, methods that Alex De Waal has referred to as 'counter-insurgency on the cheap.'[77] Therefore, while brutal, the primary goal was to displace the population to centres where they could more easily be controlled. An initial cease-fire agreement broke down in December 2003, after which the government substantially escalated the level of violence, including more systematically targeting the civilian population and their livelihoods as well as blocking international observers and food aid.[78]

By mid-2004, the conflict moved into its third phase, as international pressure, a new cease-fire agreement, and a growing international humanitarian presence caused the government to reduce direct violence against the civilian population. However, this was a shift in tactics rather than an end to the violence. As Gerard Prunier notes:

> open violence slowly receded, but without really ending. The [Government of Sudan], now submitted to hard diplomatic pressure but feeling safe from military intervention, began to rely more on the parlous food and medical situation to finish off the job that the militias had started....[79]

---

[75] Prunier, *Darfur,* p. 97.

[76] Paul D. Williams and Alex J. Bellamy, 'The Responsibility to Protect and the Crisis in Darfur,' *Security Dialogue* 36/1 (2005), p. 30; see also 'Report of the International Commission of Inquiry on Darfur to the United Nations Secretary-General: Pursuant to Security Council Resolution 1564 of 18 September 2004,' 25 January 2005, pp. 73-77.

[77] Alex De Waal, 'Counter-Insurgency on the Cheap,' *London Review of Books* 26/15 (2004).

[78] Prunier, Darfur, p. 108; Cheryl O. Igiri and N. Lyman Princeton, *Giving Meaning To 'Never Again': Seeking an Effective Response to the Crisis in Darfur and Beyond* (New York: Council on Foreign Relations, 2004), p. 5; International Criminal Court, 'Situation in Darfur, The Sudan, Prosecutor's Application under Art. 58(7),' *ICC-02-05*, 27 Feb 2007, pp. 36-37.

[79] Prunier, *Darfur*, p. 116.

In early 2008, the conflict entered a fourth stage, with the government using regular military personnel to engage the rebels in large-scale offences, and to engage in aerial bombardments in violation of a UN ban on military overflights, while *janjaweed* forces attacked IDP camps and peacekeepers, a process that has continued in 2009.[80] At the same time, the *janjaweed* themselves have splintered and suggestions are that the government of Sudan no longer exercises substantial control over them.[81]

The Council's Response

International reporting on the conflict began soon after it started in 2003, with Amnesty International on 28 April 2003 highlighting 'horrifying attacks against civilians in villages by war planes, soldiers, and pro-government militias.'[82] For the next year, however, little action occurred in spite of claims, such as that by the UN Resident Humanitarian Coordinator for Sudan, Mukesh Kapila, in March 2004 that 'the violence in Darfur appears to be particularly directed at a specific group based on their ethnic identity and appears to be systemized. This is akin to ethnic cleansing.'[83]

There are a number of possible steps prior to a humanitarian intervention, including effectively targeted sanctions[84] or the deployment of a protection of civilians-oriented peacekeeping force with the consent of the host state.[85] Where Council practice varied in the case of Darfur from those of Northern Iraq and Kosovo was in adopting a fourth form of practice: not recognising the crisis until May 2004, a year since mass displacement had begun and the period during which the most widespread mass killings[86] and the bulk of

---

[80] Eric Reeves, '"Chaos by Design": Khartoum's Patterns of Violence in Darfur, 2008,' http://www.sudanreeves.org/Article224.html, accessed 09 November 2008; 'Sudan: Restrictions on Force Dropped,' *Africa Research Bulletin* (2008), 17435. Ban Ki-moon, 'Report of the Secretary-General on the Deployment of the African Union-United Nations Hybrid Operation in Darfur,' S/2008/781, 12 December 2008.

[81] Julie Flint, *Beyond 'Janjaweed': Understanding the Militias of Darfur*, (Small Arms Survey, Geneva, 2009). By August 2009, most fatalities were as a result of armed clashes and lawlessness. Alex de Waal, 'Violent Deaths in Darfur: August', *Making Sense of Darfur*, http://blogs.ssrc.org/Darfur/2009/09/16/violent-deaths-in-darfur-august, accessed 1 October 2009.

[82] Cited in Igiri and Princeton, *Giving Meaning To 'Never Again'* p. 5.

[83] Cited in Ibid., p. 6. In 2003-2004 UNHCR did undertake operations to move 150,000 Sudanese refugees in Chad away from the border. UNHCR *State of the World's Refugees, 2006*, (UNHCR: Geneva, 2006), p. 95.

[84] ICISS, *The Responsibility to Protect*, pp. 29-30.

[85] Bellamy, *Responsibility to Protect*, pp. 147-49.

[86] The authoritative CRED report estimated 120,000 excess deaths in Darfur and East Chad directly attributable to the conflict between September 2003 and January 2005. Debarati

displacement occurred.[87] Jan Pronk, the former Special Representative of the Secretary-General for Sudan, has argued that 'the Security Council did not want to act… requests to put this on the agenda were directed at the US and UK in particular and they refused to do it. They had their reasons – diplomatic and political reasons.'[88]

The Council's response after this time, as de Waal argues, has consisted "chiefly of ad hoc steps rather than a systematic or strategic approach to the crisis."[89] In July 2004 it issued a resolution under Chapter VII of the Charter demanding the government disarm the *janjaweed* militias and condemning acts of violence with an ethnic dimension, as well as endorsing the African Union plan to deploy international monitors.[90] And yet while the Council's members argued that it 'cannot be passive and indifferent… to the ongoing humanitarian crisis' they focused on the need to find a political solution to the crisis.[91] Even the US government noted simply that the resolution 'anticipates sanctions…'[92] Sanctions were not formally imposed until March 2005,[93] but Human Rights Watch noted that they risked 'amounting to little more than a symbolic gesture given the divisions on the Security Council.'[94] Subsequent action included referring the situation to the International Criminal Court

Guha-Sapir, Olivier Degomme, and Mark Phelan 'Darfur: Counting the Deaths,' *Centre for Research on the Epidemiology of Disasters,* http://www.cred.be/docs/cedat/DarfurCountingTheDeaths-withClarifications.pdf, accessed 28 Sept 2009, p. 6.

[87] Of the 250,000 Darfuri refugees in Chad, UNHCR estimates that 180,000 sought asylum between May 2003 and June 2004. Of the estimated 2.7 million IDPs still in Darfur, almost 1.5 million had been displaced prior to September 2004. Dominik Bartsch and Nagette Belgacem, 'Real-Time Evaluation of UNHCR's Response to the Emergency in Chad' *Evaluation and Policy Analysis Unit* (UNHCR: Geneva, 2004), p. 3; OCHA, 'Darfur Humanitarian Profile No. 34', 1 January 2009 http://www.reliefweb.int/rw/RWFiles2009.nsf/FilesByRWDoc UnidFilename/EGUA-7QPR45-full_report.pdf/$File/full_report.pdf, accessed 1 October 2009.

[88] Interview with Jan Pronk by Rebecca Hamilton, 27 May 2009, http://bechamilton.com/?feed=podcast, accessed 4 October 2009; see also Igiri and Princeton, *Giving Meaning To 'Never Again'*, pp. 11-12.

[89] Alex De Waal, "Darfur and the Failure of the Responsibility to Protect," *International Affairs* 83/6 (2007), p. 1041; see also Badescu and Bergholm, 'The Responsibility to Protect and the Conflict in Darfur', p. 295; Alex J. Bellamy, 'Responsibility to Protect or Trojan Horse? The Crisis in Darfur and Humanitarian Intervention after Iraq,' *Ethics and International Affairs* 19/2 (2005), p. 32

[90] S/RES/1556, 30 July 2004.

[91] Baali, Algeria, S/PV.5015, 30 July 2004, pp. 5-6.

[92] Danforth, United States, Ibid., p. 4.

[93] S/RES/1591, 29 March, 2005.

[94] Human Rights Watch, *Entrenching Impunity: Government Responsibility for International Crimes in Darfur* (New York: Human Rights Watch, 2005), p. 85.

(ICC),[95] and authorising the creation of a joint African Union-UN assistance mission to Darfur, UNAMID.[96]

Individual states were far more ready to condemn the Sudanese government. Great Britain argued that Darfur was 'the most serious humanitarian emergency in the world today.'[97] The US Congress passed a resolution labelling Darfur a genocide, followed by statements from Secretary of State Colin Powell and President George W. Bush using the term.[98] Secretary-General Annan also argued that international action was necessary: 'the international community cannot stand idly by… [but] must be prepared to take swift and appropriate action. By "action" in such situations I mean a continuum of steps, which may include military action.'[99] But such actions, as Scott Straus notes, 'did not – contrary to expectations – electrify international efforts to intervene in Sudan.'[100]

The Council did not take further actions, Alex Bellamy argues, because anti-interventionists used the R2P language 'to legitimize arguments against action by claiming that primary responsibility in certain contested cases still lies with the state, and not (yet) with an international body.'[101] Thus, 'Pakistan, China, and Russia believed that the scale of human suffering in Darfur was insufficient to provoke serious reflection on whether Sudan was fulfilling its responsibilities to its citizens, and the United States, the U.K., and France were reluctant to force them to do so.'[102] The US was constrained by its

---

[95] S/RES/1593, 31 March 2005. This decision led to the Court issuing an arrest warrant for Sudanese President Omar al-Bashir in March 2009 on charges of war crimes and crimes against humanity; the Prosecutor had also charged him with genocide though the Court ruled that reasonable grounds for the charge did not exist. International Criminal Court, 'ICC Issues a Warrant of Arrest for Omar Al Bashir, President of Sudan' (2009), http://www.icc-cpi.int/NR/exeres/0EF62173-05ED-403A-80C8-F15EE1D25BB3.htm, accessed 24 March 2009. In response, the Sudanese government expelled over a dozen aid organisations from Darfur. Lynsey Addario and Lydia Polgreen, 'Aid Groups' Expulsion, Fears of More Misery,' *New York Times*, 23 March 2009, p. A6.

[96] S/RES/1769, 31 July 2007.

[97] DFID Press Release 'UK presses Sudan government for urgent action on Darfur,' 08 June 2004, http://www.dfid.gov.uk/News/files/pr-sudanurgentaction8june04.asp, accessed 2 Oct 2008.

[98] Colin L. Powell, 'The Crisis in Darfur: Testimony before the Senate Foreign Relations Committee,' (Washington: U.S. Department of State, 2004); Scott Straus, 'Darfur and the Genocide Debate,' *Foreign Affairs* 84/1 (2005); IRIN, 'More Violence Reported in Darfur,' http://www.irinnews.org/report.aspx?reportid=52302, accessed 2 Oct 2008.

[99] Williams and Bellamy, 'The Responsibility to Protect and the Crisis in Darfur,' p. 31.

[100] Straus, "Darfur and the Genocide Debate."

[101] Bellamy, 'Responsibility to Protect or Trojan Horse?' p. 33.

[102] Ibid., pp. 41-42.

support for the peace process in the South and for a government friendly to the war on terror, while the European Union had neither the forces nor the political will[103] – as one EU official noted 'however much hand-wringing there is, we're simply not up to something like this yet.'[104] Former Secretary of State Condoleezza Rice noted that no Council members wanted to take action along the lines of the R2P:

> I think we thought the Responsibility to Protect meant something...Almost not a day passes in this office that we're not trying to find some way to get more forces into Darfur. To make the Sudanese government live up to the multiple agreements that it has made and then walked away from. We go to the Security Council, and nobody wants there to be consequences, well, not nobody, sorry, some don't wish there to be consequences. And so we end up sanctioning again, unilaterally. The Europeans do some things but other interests seem to then trump the responsibility to protect.[105]

Even the deployment of the less controversial peacekeeping force was fraught with difficult negotiations. The initial African Union Protection Force, authorised by Resolution 1556, until October 2004 had no mandate to protect civilians.[106] The alternative UN force, meanwhile, was delayed for over three years. This was due to the unwillingness of the Sudanese government to consent, fearful that a UN peacekeeping force might exercise International Criminal Court arrest warrants or slowly lead to Darfur's independence in an echo of Kosovo.[107] It finally consented only due to diplomatic pressure from China.[108]

This intransigence by the Sudanese government gave it considerable negotiating power, allowing it to force concessions which, as Reeves notes, 'would prove disastrous for the "hybrid" mission: an unprecedented and hopelessly confused command and control structure; language that permitted Khartoum to insist that it had veto power over which non-African nations could deploy as part of the mission; and a reliance on African resources that simply did not exist.'[109] This has meant that a number of states, including Sweden and

---

[103] Ibid., pp. 34-35; see also Badescu and Bergholm, 'The Responsibility to Protect and the Conflict in Darfur', p. 294.

[104] The Economist, "Sudan: The World Notices Darfur," 31 July 2004.

[105] Helene Cooper and Scott L. Malcomson, 'Welcome to My World, Barack- an Exit Interview with Condoleezza Rice,' *New York Times Magazine*, 13 Nov 2008.

[106] Williams and Bellamy, "The Responsibility to Protect and the Crisis in Darfur," p. 29.

[107] De Waal, 'Darfur and the Failure of the Responsibility to Protect,' pp. 1045-46.

[108] Brosché, "Darfur," p. 60.

[109] Reeves, 'Chaos by Design'; see also De Waal, "Darfur and the Failure of the Responsibility to Protect."

Norway, decided against sending troops for the missions due to opposition from the Sudanese government, and that the mission was still 5,000 personnel short of its authorised strength in October 2009.[110]

It is unclear if an intervention could have succeeded.[111] However, between 2003 and 2004, when *janjaweed* attacks, mass killings, and mass displacement were at their height, the Council failed to take any action at all, even though this is the type of crisis envisioned by the R2P doctrine. Instead, some fourteen months passed before the matter was even raised at the Council. Even once the Council was engaged with the crisis, the threat of the veto and debates within the Council delayed effective action such as sanctions for some further eight months and five years passed before the first UN peacekeepers were deployed.

Conclusions: Paths to Legitimate Humanitarian Intervention

Wheeler and Egerton have argued 'the real test of the [2005] Summit Declaration is whether it increases the likelihood of the Council mustering the political will to act to prevent and halt future humanitarian crises.'[112] While there is no question that Darfur – whether as a case of regime-induced displacement, of ethnic cleansing, or of genocide – falls within the criteria envisioned by the drafters of the ICISS report and the World Summit declaration, the Council neglected the issue for a year and has been slow and hesitant even since. Kosovo and Northern Iraq reflected a different problem: political will existed, but the Council's permanent members, in particular Russia and China, were unwilling to approve interventions without the consent of the affected state.

---

[110] Cited in 'Sudan: UNAMID Seeks Support,' *Africa Research Bulletin* (2008), p. 17398. S/RES/1769, 31 July 2007; http://www.un.org/depts/dpko/missions/unamid/facts.html, accessed 9 December 2009.

[111] De Waal, for example, argues that '[p]racticality dictates that a peacekeeping force in Darfur cannot enforce its will on any resisting armed groups without entering into a protracted and unwinnable counter-insurgency.' Alex de Waal, 'The Book was Closed too Soon on Peace in Darfur', *The Guardian,* 29 September 2006. Francis Deng, then Representative of the Secretary-General for Internally Displaced Persons, similarly argued in 2004 that 'the chances are that far from alleviating the suffering of the people of Darfur, it would complicate and aggravate the situation.' Francis Deng, 'Mission to the Sudan- The Darfur Crisis' E/CN.4/2005/8, 27 September 2004, p. 14.

[112] Nicholas J. Wheeler and Frazer Egerton, 'The Responsibility to Protect: "Precious Commitment" or a Promise Unfulfilled?,' *Global Responsibility to Protect* 1/1 (2009), p. 128.

Requiring the consent of the Council, as the 2005 Declaration does, established not auger well for future interventions to protect the internally displaced and refugees who are forced to flee their own government. But this is in no one's interests – either such crimes will continue without international action, or interventions will be launched without Council authorisation. In effect, the R2P doctrine will gradually be marginalised and actions will reflect the patterns of the 1990s.

Reform of the Council would alleviate the second problem and temper the first by removing the veto as a procedural way to hide the unwillingness of Council members to take action. The ICISS report itself argued the P-5 should restrict the use of the veto, a plan which was discarded in the 2005 negotiations.[113] Recently, such calls have been renewed as the General Assembly considers broad-based Security Council reform,[114] with the Secretary-General urging the P-5 'to refrain from employing or threatening to employ the veto in situations of manifest failure to meet obligations relating to the responsibility to protect... and to reach a mutual understanding to that effect.'[115] This has been echoed by the American Genocide Prevention Task Force, which has recommended that the United States government negotiate an agreement among the P-5 for non-use of the veto in cases of genocide or mass atrocities unless three permanent members are prepared to use it.[116]

An alternative is the 'Uniting for Peace' procedures within the UN General Assembly, which can pass a matter from the Council to the Assembly as a non-vetoable procedural matter.[117] As participants in the ICISS consultations noted, the Assembly 'while flawed, is still the most democratic of the existing international bodies, and it is, at the very least, a better reflection of world public opinion.'[118] There are two distinct limitations to this procedure,

[113] Alex J. Bellamy, 'Whither the Responsibility to Protect? Humanitarian Intervention and the 2005 World Summit,' *Ethics & International Affairs* 20/2 (2006), p. 167.

[114] General Assembly Decision 62/557, http://www.un.org/ga/63/plenary/I_sc_representation_members.shtml, accessed 30 March 2009; UN Department of Public Information 'Press Conference on Security Council Reform Negotiations' 13 February 2009, http://www.un.org/News/briefings/docs/2009/090213_SC_Reform.doc.htm, accessed 30 March 2009.

[115] Ban Ki-moon, *Implementing the Responsibility to Protect: Report of the Secretary-General*, A63/677, 12 January 2009, p. 27.

[116] Albright and Cohen, *Preventing Genocide*, p. 106. The Task Force also points to the problem with the status quo, noting 'it is unacceptable to ignore a threat of mass atrocities or genocide. If the Security Council is unable to act, there may be other appropriate options.' Ibid., p. 97. See also Lloyd Axworthy and Allan Rock, 'R2P: A New and Unfinished Agenda,' *Global Responsibility to Protect* 1/1 (2009), p. 61.

[117] ICISS, *The Responsibility to Protect*, p. 53.; General Assembly Resolution 377 (V) "Uniting for Peace" was passed in November 1950.

[118] Weiss and Hubert, *The Responsibility to Protect,* p. 378, see also David Chandler, 'The Responsibility to Protect? Imposing the "Liberal Peace",' *International Peacekeeping* 11/1 (2004).

however. The first is that the Council is unlikely to support the move. In the lead-up to the Kosovo intervention, Adam Roberts raised this possibility, but the UK Foreign Office argued that it was uncertain that the two-thirds majority could be met, and 'that the General Assembly is a somewhat cumbersome instrument.'[119] Paul Heinbecker, the Canadian ambassador to the UN at the time, put it more nakedly: 'the P-5 didn't want it... because none of them wants to deprecate the value of the veto.'[120] The second is that while the International Court of Justice, in the *Certain Expenses* advisory opinion of 1962, ruled that the Assembly could play such a role, it noted that enforcement actions must be referred to the Security Council.[121]

The R2P doctrine positions the Security Council as the body able to take action in the most extreme cases of regime-induced displacement. This is a role the Council has rhetorically established for itself by framing situations of mass displacement as an issue of international peace and security in successive resolutions. While interventions have occurred in two such cases – Northern Iraq and Kosovo – in both individual member states chose to not seek Council authorisation. These were unusual cases both because interventions occurred in spite of the Council and because these member states had the political will to intervene. By contrast, the case of Darfur represents more typical behaviour, with the lack of consent and the threat of the veto being used to shield a lack of political will to take more decisive action. This pattern of practice, therefore, suggests that it is unlikely the Council will take decisive action in situations of regime-induced displacement and when states have the political will to do so, they will go around the Council. Returning to the pattern of the 1990s, as this suggests, is in no one's interests: either the Council's authority will be weakened by its failure to act, or it will be weakened by interventions undertaken outside its purview. Yet the R2P doctrine, endorsed by the Council, was deliberately formulated as a mechanism to get around these issues. While the Uniting for Peace protocol in the General Assembly provides an alternative to the Council, it is a weak one. Rather, it is in the interest of the P-5 to agree to limit the power of the veto in cases of regime-induced displacement which cross the R2P threshold in order to ensure the continued validity of the Council.

---

119 Cited in Chesterman, 'Legality Versus Legitimacy,' p. 296.

120 Cited in Jean Krasno and Mitushi Das, 'The Uniting for Peace Resolution and Other Ways of Circumventing the Authority of the Security Council,' in Bruce Cronin and Ian Hurd (eds.) *The UN Security Council and the Politics of International Authority* (London: Routledge, 2008), p. 187.

121 Gray, *International Law and the Use of Force*, p. 149; Franck, *Recourse to Force*, pp. 38-39.

Chapter Six

Protecting Civilians in Uncivil Wars

Alex J. Bellamy and Paul D. Williams

Introduction

It is mainly civilians that die as a result of contemporary armed conflicts.[1] Although most of them succumb to disease and the effects of malnutrition a significant number are slaughtered or suffer other forms of violent death.[2] This fact is not unique to the contemporary era but the period since the end of the Cold War has witnessed an unprecedented level of international activity ostensibly aimed at reducing levels of civilian suffering during armed conflicts. Such activity resulted from the confluence of moral, political, legal and prudential considerations. First, the world's governments have intensified their political commitment to protect civilians in light of a strengthening moral norm that genocide and mass atrocities are unacceptable wherever and whenever they occur.[3] Second, there has been growing international support for the idea that states have a legal responsibility to respond to atrocities that are considered crimes under international human rights and humanitarian law.[4] Third,

---

[1] Although precise figures are impossible to ascertain, one study of nine conflicts in sub-Saharan Africa put the average proportion of civilian casualties as between 87 and 92 percent of the total number of casualties. Bethany Lacina and Nils Petter Gleditsch, 'Monitoring Trends in Global Combat: A New Dataset of Battle Deaths', *European Journal of Population*, 21/2-3: 145-166 (2005).

[2] For every direct civilian death caused by war an estimated 4-10 additional people suffer indirect deaths. See Human Security Centre, *Human Security Report 2005* (Oxford: Oxford University Press, 2005), pp. 127-134.

[3] See the moral and political commitments to protect human rights set out in, among other places, the UN Charter (1945), the Universal Declaration of Human Rights (1948), the UN General Assembly's World Summit Outcome Document (2005) and a variety of recent UN Security Council resolutions.

[4] The key documents here are the Convention on the Prevention and Punishment of the Crime of Genocide (1948) and the Rome Statute (1998) as well as a variety of UN Security Council resolutions.

a variety of prudential calculations have persuaded states to take civilian protection issues more seriously. Specifically, it is widely recognised that it is harder to build peace and maintain order in environments where atrocities go unaddressed;[5] it is also well known that civilian deaths damage the legitimacy of counter-insurgency operations and make them harder to win; and it has become clear that relief workers face greater risks in circumstances where the combatant/non-combatant distinction is blurred.

Yet despite these commitments peacekeepers and other actors are not well prepared to deal with the daunting challenges posed by civilian protection agendas. As one analysis of the twentieth century concluded, '[n]o century had better norms and worse realities' when it came to the protection of civilians in war.[6] Sometimes, the world reacted to crimes against civilians by despatching peacekeepers 'without sufficient capacity, clear guidance and doctrine, adequate training, or a solid concept of operations to uphold mandates to 'protect civilians'.'[7] More often, no troops were dispatched at all to protect civilians. Not only have these sins of omission and commission badly damaged the reputation of liberal states and international institutions, they have facilitated the massacre of thousands of civilians in the world's war zones.

Efforts to strengthen the protection of civilians are inhibited by a lack of consensus on what protection ought to entail, where the sources of protection lay and how those sources relate to one another, which actors should be engaged in protection, and how their activities should be coordinated. As a result, whilst considerable activity has occurred, the contemporary agenda remains limited and incoherent in some important respects. This chapter aims to advance the debate in three ways. First, we propose a framework for thinking about the different dimensions of a comprehensive and coherent civilian protection agenda: the nature of the problem i.e. threats facing civilians during armed conflict; the sources of the contemporary protection agenda; the pillars upon which the protection agenda should rest; and the principal agents of protection. Second, we identify several problems with the current agenda: the gap between capabilities and expectations; the lack of operational guidance;

---

[5] In 2000, the UN Panel on Peace Operations – the so-called Brahimi Report – insisted that 'peacekeepers – troops or police – who witness violence against civilians should be presumed to be authorized to stop it, within their means, in support of basic United Nations principles.' *Report of the Panel on UN Peace Operations* (New York: UN doc. A/55/305-S/2000/809, 2000), p. x.

[6] David Reiff, *A Bed for the Night* (New York: Simon & Schuster, 1993), p. 70.

[7] Victoria K. Holt and Joshua G. Smith, *Halting Widespread or Systematic Attacks on Civilians* (Washington DC: Henry L. Stimson Center, 2008), p. 40.

coordination and coherence problems; the tensions between internal and external modes of protection; and the role of the state. We finish by suggesting four important areas for further research and action: enhancing state capacity in relevant areas; bolstering the resilience of local communities at risk of harm; strengthening the ability of peacekeepers to protect civilians; and developing capacities to conduct effective humanitarian interventions.

The Problem: Threats to Civilians during Armed Conflict

Many factors contribute to civilian suffering during periods of armed conflict. Viewed in the abstract, this makes for a broad and daunting agenda which can encourage a tendency to prioritise everything and thereby nothing. However, establishing priorities is easier to do with reference to specific empirical settings. The starting point for analysis and action must therefore be identifying the ways in which civilians are threatened in both a general sense and with reference to specific armed conflicts. Or as the ICRC has put it, analysis must start with an assessment of who does what to whom?[8]

In general terms it is useful to distinguish between direct and indirect forms of harm.[9] In some instances civilians will be the direct target of atrocities committed by a potentially wide range of actors. Any list of atrocities is potentially very long but a useful starting point is the seventeen types of violations identified by the Truth and Reconciliation Commission of Sierra Leone in its study of that country's civil war. These were: abduction, amputation, arbitrary detention, assault/beating, destruction of property, drugging, extortion, forced cannibalism, forced displacement, forced labour, forced recruitment, killing, looting, physical torture, rape, sexual abuse, and sexual slavery. Civilians can also be harmed indirectly. Among the most common forms of indirect harm are those which occur through loss of livelihood and displacement (which are central factors exacerbating the likelihood of civilians succumbing to disease or malnutrition) and instances of mistaken or unintentional killing through inaccurate bombardment and/or targeting or the use of indiscriminate weapons (e.g. antipersonnel mines and cluster bombs).

---

[8] ICRC, *Enhancing Protection for Civilians in Armed Conflict and Other Situations of Violence* (Geneva: ICRC, September 2008), p. 15.

[9] For an alternative characterisation of 'seven spheres' of civilian suffering see Hugo Slim, *Killing Civilians: Method, Madness and Morality in War* (New York: Columbia University Press, 2008), p. 39.

With this broad distinction in mind it is important to understand which actors threaten civilians in armed conflicts and why. Here four categories of actors are particularly important:

- Local armed forces: these are likely to cause harm to civilians either when they are ordered to do so, or when they are undisciplined and/or unprofessional.[10]
- Unofficial, non-state armed actors: including insurgencies, paramilitaries, militias and organised groups of thugs.[11]
- Self-defence groups: which might emerge from noble motives (such as defending livestock or community property) but degenerate into more predatory organisations.[12]
- Foreign peacekeepers, soldiers and/or contractors: Whether it is the scandals at Abu Ghraib, the behaviour of Blackwater employees in Iraq, or UN peacekeepers engaging in organised criminal activities and/or sexual exploitation and abuse of locals, local civilians often suffer harm at the hands of foreigners.[13]

The subsidiary question is why, despite the very clear prohibition of such acts, civilians are targeted. Although the relevant literature remains divided, it seems clear that both the direct and indirect targeting of civilians requires some form of justificatory ideology.[14] These ideologies have tended to take two forms: those that reject the application of civilian immunity to certain racial, national, ethnic, religious, linguistic, sexual or physical groups (e.g. Nazism, extreme nationalism, doctrine of collective responsibility, Stalinism) and those that privilege perceived necessity over the moral and legal restraints on war.[15]

---

[10] This underlines the importance of attempts to professionalise Africa's military forces called for by Herbert Howe in *Ambiguous Order: Military Forces in African States* (Boulder, CO: Lynne Rienner, 2001).

[11] On the ways in which some of these non-state actors can be harnessed to state agendas see John Mueller, 'The Banality of Ethnic War', *International Security*, 25/1: 42-70 (2000).

[12] Examples might include the White Army in southern Sudan or the *kamajors* in Sierra Leone.

[13] See, for example, Karen J. Greenberg and Joshua L. Dratel (eds.), *The Torture Papers* (Cambridge: Cambridge University Press, 2005); Sandra Whitworth, *Men, Militarism and UN Peacekeeping* (Boulder, CO: Lynne Rienner, 2004); Peter Andreas, *Blue Helmets and Black Markets* (Ithaca, NY: Cornell University Press, 2008).

[14] See Slim, *Killing Civilians*; Alexander B. Downes, *Targeting Civilians in War* (Ithaca, NY: Cornell University Press, 2008); Stathis N. Kalyvas, *The Logic of Violence in Civil War* (Cambridge: Cambridge University Press, 2006).

[15] Slim, *Killing Civilians*, pp. 1, 179; Downes, *Targeting Civilians*, p. 121.

Both types are more likely to facilitate the targeting of civilians in contexts of impunity, where there are no immediate negative consequences for violating the norm of civilian immunity.[16] In such contexts, belligerents may target civilians in order to achieve tactical goals at lower costs to themselves (e.g. as a strategy of counter-insurgency or a tactic for recruiting child soldiers), to accomplish strategic objectives by claiming and 'cleansing' particular territories and eliminating whole groups; to punish communities for supporting the enemy; and to violently assert control over the civilian populations.[17] In addition, leaders might create a culture of impunity towards the abuse of the civilian population as payment for military services – civilians can be killed, raped, kidnapped into (often sexual) servitude and have their assets taken or destroyed as a form of payment.[18]

From this necessarily brief overview of how and why civilians are targeted in war, it is clear that the protection agenda needs to include measures designed to challenge the enabling conditions and sometimes stand between the civilian population and their tormentors.

Sources of Protection

Contemporary interest in protection stems from six interconnected streams of thought and policy which developed in reaction to different aspects of civilian suffering during war:

- the development of international humanitarian law (IHL);
- the adoption of protection agendas by humanitarian agencies;
- the UN Security Council's focus on civilian protection;
- the incorporation of protection mandates for peace operations;
- the embracing of protection by some regional organisations;
- the political commitment to the Responsibility to Protect.

---

[16] Gregory Stanton, 'Could the Rwandan Genocide have been Prevented?', *Journal of Genocide Research*, 6/2 (2004), p. 216.

[17] As identified by Downes, *Targeting Civilians in War;* Kalyvas, *The Logic of Violence in Civil War* and Benjamin Valentino, *Final Solutions: Mass Killing and Genocides in the Twentieth Century* (Ithaca: Cornell University Press, 2005).

[18] One documented case of this is the war in Darfur, when the Government of Sudan created a culture of impunity as payment for *janjawiid* assistance. See Julie Flint, testimony before the US Senate Foreign Relations Committee, 15 June 2004, available at http://www.globalsecurity.org/military/library/congress/2004_hr/040615-flint.pdf.

Although interrelated, the streams reflect the particular concerns and interests of the respective norm carriers and thus emphasise different components of protection. This has left important gaps and tensions in the contemporary protection agenda which are addressed in part 5 of this chapter.

The Development of International Humanitarian Law

The global effort to strengthen IHL – as well as the concomitant development of international criminal law – has become the legal bedrock for civilian protection. As is well known, IHL had its origins in the mid-late nineteenth century with the development of the US Government's 'General Orders No. 100' (better known as the Lieber code) and the emergence of the Red Cross movement inspired by Henry Dunant.[19] After the Second World War, IHL was developed and codified in the four Geneva Conventions (1949), two additional protocols (1977), and in a range of protocols covering the use of Certain Conventional Weapons (1980, 1995, 1996, 2008). Of particular importance were Common Article 3 of the 1949 Geneva Conventions, which committed parties in non-international conflicts to respect the human rights of all those placed *hors de combat*, and the Convention on the Protection of Civilian Persons (Convention IV), which—among other things—offered legal protection to non-combatants in occupied territories.[20] The first Geneva Protocol (1977) extended the protection afforded to non-combatants by insisting that armed attacks be strictly limited to military objectives (Article 52, Protocol I). Combatants were forbidden from attacking non-combatants or their property, though so-called 'dual use' facilities remained lawful targets. Article 51(5) outlawed attacks on military objects which 'may be expected to cause' excessive civilian casualties, and forbade the indirect targeting of non-combatants. Protocol I also insisted that in cases of doubt, people should be assumed to be non-combatants. The principle of discrimination set out in the Protocol also provided the legal and moral foundation for subsequent campaigns for conventions banning weapons considered inherently

---

[19] The General Orders No. 100 are reproduced in full and discussed in Richard Shelly Hartigan, *Lieber's Code and the Law of War* (Chicago: Precedent, 1983). On Dunant and the Red Cross see David Forsythe, *The Humanitarians* (Cambridge: Cambridge University Press, 2005) and Caroline Moorhead, *Dunant's Dream: War, Switzerland and the History of the Red Cross* (New York: Carroll and Graf Publishers, 1998).

[20] See Alwyn V. Freeman, 'War Crimes by Enemy Nationals Administering Justice in Occupied Territory', *American Journal of International Law*, 41/3 (1947), p. 581 and Olivier Durr, 'Humanitarian Law of Armed Conflict: Problems of Applicability', *Journal of Peace Research*, 24/3 (1987), p. 268.

indiscriminate and is now a core part of international criminal law.[21] IHL has thus created a normative standard of civilian protection that not only restricts the use of certain weapons and behaviour but also seeks to punish perpetrators of individual or mass crimes.

Humanitarian Agencies

Traditionally, humanitarian agencies viewed 'protection' as the responsibility of 'mandated actors' such as the International Committee for the Red Cross (ICRC), the UN Children's Fund (UNICEF) and the UN High Commissioner for Refugees (UNHCR) to promote the legal protection of individual human rights. As such, ICRC officials tended to equate 'protection' mainly with the verification of government compliance with IHL in cases of detention.[22] For its part, UNICEF was mandated to develop country-level reporting mechanisms in relation to the protection of children in armed conflict while UNHCR was mandated by the 1951 Refugee Convention and subsequent protocol (1967) to provide legal protection to refugees.[23] To the extent that other emergency relief organisations referred to protection, they typically saw it as a natural counterpart to the impartial delivery of humanitarian assistance. This began to change in the 1990s when some organisations recognised that effective humanitarian assistance was dependent on security and stability.[24] In extreme cases, this view noted that assistance without protection could produce the so-called 'well fed dead' – civilians given food, housing and medical support by humanitarian agencies only to be killed by armed groups. The result was a broader approach to protection by a variety of actors; from Oxfam to the international financial institutions.[25] This, in turn, produced a raft of different theories and strategies for the development, management and

[21] Louise Doswald-Beck, 'The Civilian in the Crossfire', *Journal of Peace Research*, 24/3 (1987), p. 253.

[22] Forsythe, *The Humanitarians*, p.168 and Jean-Francois Quéguiner, 'Precautions Under the Law Governing the Conduct of Hostilities', *International Review of the Red Cross*, 88/864: 793-821 (2006).

[23] Sorcha O'Callaghan and Sara Pantuliano, *Protective Action: Incorporating Civilian Protection in Humanitarian Response* (Overseas Development Institute, Humanitarian Policy Group, Report, 26 December 2007), p. 10.

[24] Mark Duffield, 'NGO Relief in War Zones: Towards an Analysis of the New Aid Paradigm', *Third World Quarterly*, 18/3: 527-542 (1997).

[25] See O'Callaghan and Pantuliano, *Protective Action*, p.13; Oxfam International, *Beyond the Headlines: An Agenda for Action to Protect Civilians in Neglected Conflicts* (Oxford: Oxfam GB for Oxfam International, 2003); Hastie et al, *Protection: Mainstreamed, Integrated or 'Stand Alone'*

assessment of protection programs.[26] While the expansion of the protection agenda was important, it highlighted significant areas of ambiguity to humanitarian work and in some cases, perhaps most notably Médecins Sans Frontières (MSF), encouraged a reaction against the idea that humanitarian agencies alone can deliver protection.[27]

The UN Security Council

Since 1998, the UN Security Council has explicitly debated a relatively broad and unfocused civilian protection agenda that has encompassed compliance with IHL, operational issues connected to peace operations and humanitarian access, as well as the Council's role in responding to emergencies and tackling disarmament issues.[28] On 17 September 1999, the Council unanimously adopted Resolution 1265. This expressed the Council's 'willingness' to consider 'appropriate measures' in response 'to situations of armed conflict where civilians are being targeted or where humanitarian assistance to civilians is being deliberately obstructed;' called on states to ratify key human rights treaties and work towards ending the 'culture of impunity' by prosecuting those responsible for genocide, crimes against humanity and 'serious violations of international humanitarian law;' and expressed the Council's willingness to explore how peacekeeping mandates might be reframed to afford better protection to endangered civilians.[29]

Programmes? (Oxford: Oxfam Discussion Paper, 2007); Paul Collier, *The Bottom Billion* (Oxford: Oxford University Press, 2008).

[26] Recent examples are Deborah Mancini-Griffoli and Andre Picot, *Humanitarian Negotiation; A Handbook for Securing Access, Assistance and Protection for Civilians in Armed Conflict* (Geneva: Centre for Humanitarian Dialogue, 2004); Hugo Slim and Andrew Bonwick, *Protection: An ALNAP Guide for Humanitarian Agencies* (London: ALNAP/Overseas Development Institute, 2005), Liam Mahoney, *Proactive Presence: Field Strategies for Civilian Protection* (Geneva: Centre for Humanitarian Dialogue, 2006). Others are in development.

[27] These, and other, criticisms are aired in Fiona Fox, 'New Humanitarianism: Does it Provide a Moral Banner for the 21st Century?', *Disasters*, 25/4: 275-89 (2001); Rieff, *A Bed for the Night*, Fiona Terry, *Condemned to Repeat? The Paradoxes of Humanitarian Aid* (Ithaca, NY: Cornell University Press, 2002). On MSF's position see O'Callaghan and Pantuliano, *Protective Action*, p. 8 and OCHA, *Special Report: Civilian Protection in Armed Conflict* (New York, OCHA Integrated Regional Information Network, 2003).

[28] At Canada's request, the Council adopted a presidential statement calling for the Secretary-General to submit periodic reports on how the UN might improve the protection of civilians. See UN doc. S/1998/318, 13 April 1998. For an overview see Security Council Report, *Protection of Civilians* (Cross-Cutting Report No. 2, 14 October 2008).

[29] The resolution enjoyed broad support within the Council and the wider membership, which was invited to participate in the dialogue. UN doc. S/PV.4046, 16 September 1999.

In 2004, the Council issued an *Aide Memoire* on civilian protection, which was subsequently adopted and developed by the UN's Office for the Coordination of Humanitarian Affairs (OCHA) to guide its work.[30] The Security Council issued a further landmark resolution (number 1674) on the protection of civilians in April 2006. This reiterated its demand for access to be granted to humanitarian agencies, stated the Council's willingness to take action in cases where civilians are deliberately targeted and reaffirmed the Responsibility to Protect principle (see below). In 2007, new Secretary-General Ban Ki-moon called for measures to strengthen the right to humanitarian access and the creation of a working group to explore avenues for translating the Council's commitment to protection into tangible outcomes for endangered populations.[31] Neither elicited much support.

Peacekeeping Mandates

The Council has also supported the civilian protection agenda through the mandates it has crafted for peace operations. Although peacekeeping operations have sometimes contained human rights components, it was very rare for civilian protection to be considered a core part of the mission.[32] It was not until the publication of the UN's Panel on Peace Operations – the so-called 'Brahimi Report' – in 2000 that peacekeepers who witnessed violence against civilians should officially 'be presumed to be authorized to stop it, within their means'.[33] Starting in 1999 with the UN mission in Sierra Leone (UNAMSIL), the Security Council has regularly invoked Chapter VII of the UN Charter to

---

However, there were some notable exceptions. India and Egypt, for example, expressed scepticism about the Secretary-General's approach. See S/PV.4046 (resumption 1), 17 September 1999.

[30] OCHA, *Aide-Memoire for the Consideration of Issues Pertaining to the Protection of Civilians* (New York, OCHA Policy Development and Studies Branch, 2004); and Mark Bowden, 'The Protection of Civilians' in Bertrand G. Ramcharan (ed.), *Human Rights Protection in the Field*, special issue of *International Studies in Human Rights*, 87 (2006), p. 61. OCHA proposed a revised version in early 2009, which was welcomed by the Security Council, S/PV.6066, 14 January 2009.

[31] Ban Ki-moon, *Report of the Secretary-General on the Protection of Civilians in Armed Conflict*, UN doc. S/2007/643, 28 October 2007. For the Council's reaction see UN doc. S/PV.5781, 20 November 2007.

[32] See Katarina Månsson, 'Use of Force and Civilian Protection: Peace Operations in the Congo', *International Peacekeeping*, 12/4: 503-519 (2005) and Katarina Månsson, 'Integration of Human Rights in Peace Operations: Is There an Ideal Model?', *International Peacekeeping*, 13/4: 547-563 (2006).

[33] Brahimi Report, p. x.

create protection mandates, albeit while inserting some important geographical, temporal and capabilities-based caveats.[34]

Regional Arrangements

The protection agenda has also been fostered at the regional level, especially in Europe and Africa. The foundations for Europe's engagement with civilian protection were laid in the 1970s with the Helsinki Accords. Over time, these provided the basis for a Conference on Security and Cooperation in Europe (CSCE) mechanism which by the 1990s incorporated specific references to protection issues, including the protection of children and protection against torture.[35] When the CSCE was transformed into an organisation – the OSCE – in 1995, it was given additional institutional capacities in relation to human rights. Among those capacities was the establishment of the High Commissioner for National Minorities (HCNM). This was intended to employ quiet diplomacy to help states protect the rights of national minorities and prevent the escalation of ethnic divisions into violent conflict.[36] Beginning with its engagement in the Bosnian conflict, NATO has also incorporated the protection of civilians into its crisis management work more broadly.[37] As part of its common foreign and security policy the EU also started to develop a civilian protection role, exemplified by the French-led multinational force in eastern DRC (*Operation Artemis*, 2003). Although less well established, the African Union (AU) has also provided a vehicle for the development of civilian protection. Article 4(h) of the AU's Constitutive Act enshrines the Union's right to intervene in the affairs of its member states in issues relating to genocide, war crimes and crimes against humanity, and the AU peace operation in Darfur (AMIS) included a civilian protection mandate.[38]

---

[34] For details see Victoria K. Holt and Tobias C. Berkman, *The Impossible Mandate? Military Preparedness, The Responsibility to Protect and Modern Peace Operations* (Washington, DC: The Henry L. Stimson Center, 2006).

[35] S. Neil McFarlane and Yuen Foong Khong, *Human Security and the UN* (Bloomington: Indiana University Press, 2006), p. 183.

[36] See Walter A. Kemp, *The OSCE in a New Context* (London: Royal Institute of International Affairs, 1996).

[37] Macfarlane and Khong, *Human Security*, p. 174.

[38] Richard Gowan and Ian Johnstone, *New Challenges for Peacekeeping* (New York: International Peace Academy Working Paper series, March 2007) and Paul D. Williams, 'From Non-Intervention to Non-Indifference: The Origins and Development of the African Union's Security Culture', *African Affairs*, 106/423: 253-79 (2007).

The Responsibility to Protect

In late 2005, world leaders unanimously adopted the Responsibility to Protect (RtoP) principle in paragraphs 138-140 of the UN World Summit Outcome Document. In April 2006 the Security Council reaffirmed the principle in Resolution 1674.[39] As agreed by Member States, the RtoP rests on three pillars.[40] The first is the responsibility of each state to use appropriate and necessary means to protect its own populations from genocide, war crimes, ethnic cleansing and crimes against humanity, and from their incitement. The second pillar refers to the commitment of the 'international community' to encourage and help states to exercise this responsibility. The third pillar refers to the international responsibility to respond through the UN in a timely and decisive manner when national authorities are manifestly failing to protect their populations from the four crimes identified above. The Secretary-General, Ban Ki-moon identified translating the RtoP 'from words to deeds' as one of his main priorities and appointed a Special Adviser on the matter.[41] The principle has also become part of the working language of international engagement with political crises such as the UNAMID operation in Sudan and the diplomatic efforts to resolve the post-election conflict in Kenya. However, its exact scope and meaning remain the subject of debate, not least when in May 2008 Bernard Kouchner invoked RtoP to legitimise the forcible delivery of humanitarian assistance to Myanmar and in August of the same year, the Russian Foreign Minister claimed that his country was exercising its RtoP by invading Georgia in support of South Ossetian separatists.

Pillars of Protection

Ironically, one of the principal strengths of the civilian protection norm—the breadth and depth of the normative consensus underpinning it—is also a source of weakness because there is little agreement across the six streams about what protection means, what it entails and which agents are best placed

[39] For more details see Alex J. Bellamy, *Responsibility to Protect* (Cambridge: Polity, 2009); Gareth Evans, *The Responsibility to Protect* (Washington DC: Brookings Institution, 2008).

[40] Ban Ki-moon, 'On Responsible Sovereignty: International Cooperation for a Changed World', speech, Berlin, SG/SM/11701, 15 July 2008.

[41] Ban Ki-moon, 'Annual Address to the General Assembly', 25 September, SG/SM/11182, 25 September 2007.

to provide it. In our view, a unified and comprehensive conception of protection should rest on three pillars:

1. the physical protection from immediate harm;
2. the satisfaction of needs essential for the sustenance of life;
3. the freedom to exercise fundamental human rights.

Although each element is usually emphasised by particular agents of protection (i.e. the first by military peacekeepers, the second by humanitarian agencies, the third by mandated actors), any holistic conception of protection must incorporate all three.

Physical protection from immediate harm

This entails numerous tasks but it is useful to distinguish two broad types. *Direct* protection implies measures designed to protect civilians under immediate threat of physical harm. Measures such as guarding and demilitarising refugee and IDP camps, patrolling villages and establishing checkpoints, protecting safe corridors, using force to maintain humanitarian access or coerce perpetrators of abuses, as well as providing personal protection to vulnerable individuals can be considered direct forms of protection because they involve the use of military and/or police personnel to deter threats and protect civilians who are likely to come under attack. Although non-military actors can play a part in risk reduction and reporting it is important to recognise that unarmed civilian organisations are rarely able to directly protect civilians in imminent danger.[42] *Indirect* measures contribute to the establishment of an environment conducive to civilian protection but do not provide immediate protection. Military and police measures such as enforcement operations against armed groups, securing humanitarian access, and apprehending those suspected of crimes against the civilian population and civilian measures such as disarmament and demobilisation, capacity-building and training, integrating protection considerations into activities such as camp design, improving the quality of information provided to local communities, and measures to strengthen the rule of law, may create the necessary environment for protection and reduce the likelihood of attacks but they do not protect civilians in immediate danger.[43]

---

[42] Andrew Bonwick, 'Who Really Protects Civilians?', *Development in Practice*, 16/3-4 (2006), p. 274.

[43] Holt and Berkman, *The Impossible Mandate?*, pp. 37-42.

The satisfaction of needs essential for the sustenance of life

As noted above, most civilian casualties of war result from indirect effects, such as disease and deprivation, and these indirect risks are intensified and multiplied by displacement.[44] As such, protection should be concerned with preventing and mitigating the most damaging indirect effects that armed conflicts have on civilians. Oxfam, for example, envisage protection as involving the provision of the necessities of life (food, shelter, medicine, means of earning a living) and freedom from impediments on those necessities.[45] Among other things, the satisfaction of needs requires support for local coping strategies, access to stricken populations, the prevention of displacement where possible, and provision of safe havens when needed.[46]

The freedom to exercise fundamental human rights

This involves maintaining an environment conducive to the satisfaction of rights granted to individuals by international human rights and humanitarian law. One of the first attempts to develop a protection agenda for humanitarian agencies, spearheaded by the ICRC (1996-2000), produced a consensus that protection encompassed 'all activities aimed at ensuring full respect for the rights of the individual in accordance with the letter and the spirit of the relevant bodies of law, i.e. human rights law, international humanitarian law, and refugee law.'[47] Focusing on already existing rights helps to clarify the extent and focus of the protection agenda, set minimum standards, and provide common benchmarks for evaluating behaviour. However, there are inherent limits to what a rights based approach can achieve. The scope of rights is limited because not all states have ratified the relevant treaties and there is a fundamental disconnect between formal obligations and levels of compliance. Moreover, educating people about their rights is only part of the

---

[44] See Lacina and Gleditsch, 'Monitoring Trends in Global Combat'. On the heightened risks caused by displacement see Roberta Cohen and Francis M. Deng, *Masses in Flight: The Global Crisis of Internal Displacement* (Washington DC: Brookings Institution, 1998).

[45] Oxfam, *Beyond the Headlines*, p. 6.

[46] Ibid., pp. 16-17.

[47] S. Giossi Caverzasio, (ed.), *Strengthening Protection in War: A Search for Professional Standards* (Geneva: ICRC, 2001), p. 19. This definition was also adopted by the UN's Inter-Agency Standing Committee (IASC) which comprises all the UN's major agencies and offices Inter-Agency Standing Committee, *Protection of Internally Displaced Persons: Inter-Agency Standing Committee Policy Paper Series*, No. 2 (New York: United Nations, 2000), p. 4.

equation: they also need to be able to exercise those rights. In the eye of the storm, such opportunities are rarely available.[48]

Agents of Protection

To be effective over time, protection clearly requires action in all three areas identified above. However, we also need to be clear about the strengths and limitations of the different agents of protection. We suggest that there are five main agents of protection: states, local communities, humanitarian agencies, peacekeepers and international judicial institutions. Each agent acts according to its own conception of protection and while there is sometimes coherence and coordination, this is ad hoc and patchy at best. This section evaluates the role of each of these agents in order to identify critical limitations in the contemporary protection agenda.

States

States not only have the primary responsibility to protect civilians, they are also usually the principal agent of protection. Indeed, a variety of social contract theories insist that the first duty of states is to protect their populations from insecurity.[49] As such, it is only when a government fails to protect its population that the question of alternative agents of protection arises. This might occur for a number of reasons. In one scenario, well-meaning governments might lack the capacity to effectively protect their citizens from rebel groups. In other cases, governments may be divided, with some factions committed to protecting their populations but lacking the capacity to effectively control the state's military forces. In situations of state collapse there ceases to be any meaningful distinction between the government's armed forces and various militia groups. On other occasions governments pursue a deliberate policy of targeting segments of their population.[50]

These different dynamics are important because the precise nature of the state's failure to protect will shape the opportunities for and constraints upon the adoption of external measures. Clearly, states lacking the capacity to

---

[48] Bonwick, 'Who Really Protects Civilians?', p. 271.

[49] See Thomas Hobbes, *Leviathan* (Oxford: Oxford University Press, 1998), p. 111; Michael W. Doyle, *Ways of War and Peace* (New York: Norton, 1997), pp. 214-8.

[50] See Slim and Bonswick, *Protection*, pp. 27-8.

protect populations from rebels or external forces are more likely to request international assistance than those that have deliberately targeted civilians. In these latter cases external agents will be confronted by major additional obstacles associated with the norm of sovereignty and non-intervention. Most notably, humanitarian agencies will not be granted unfettered access and will be forced to negotiate and cooperate with the perpetrators of crimes against civilians to gain limited access. In addition, the UN Security Council's deep reluctance to authorise peace operations without host state consent means that a mixture of diplomatic skill and coercion will be required to permit the deployment of peacekeepers. These political problems are eased somewhat in cases of state collapse but they present a different range of logistical and security problems.[51] In most cases, however, external agents of protection will be required to cooperate with a government that has failed to protect its civilian population either because of volition, neglect or incapacity.

The range of measures that states can take to protect their populations is too vast to list here in any but the most perfunctory fashion, but it is useful to think of the state's role in relation to the three pillars of protection identified above. First and foremost, physical protection requires that states abide by IHL and ensure that their security forces understand and respect the law. In addition, states should uphold the rule of law and ensure that key crimes against civilians – genocide, war crimes, ethnic cleansing and crimes against humanity – are written into the domestic penal code and that individual criminal responsibility for these crimes is established.[52]

States also play a significant role in the satisfaction of life-sustaining needs. Many famines and disease outbreaks that accompany armed conflict and disproportionately affect the civilian population were products of either deliberate policy or wilful neglect by states.[53] The Ethiopian famine in 1984 provides the best example of the former and the 2008 cholera outbreak in Zimbabwe is

[51] China acquiesced in the US-led intervention in Somalia in late 1992 on the grounds that because no central government existed, Somalia was no longer sovereign and therefore intervention could not be a violation of a sovereign's right to non-interference. See Nicholas J. Wheeler, *Saving Strangers: Humanitarian Intervention in International Society* (Oxford: Oxford University Press, 2000), p. 186.

[52] Kofi Annan, *The Rule of Law and Transitional Justice in Conflict and Post-Conflict Societies*, UN doc. S/2004/616, 23 August 2004 and Chandra Lekha Sriram, 'Prevention and the Rule of Law: Rhetoric and Reality' in Angnes Hurwitz with Reyko Huang (eds.), *Civil War and the Rule of Law* (Boulder: Lynne Rienner, 2008), pp. 80-82.

[53] See Kurt Jonassohn with Kain Solveig Björnson, *Genocide and Gross Human Rights Violations in Comparative Perspective* (New Brunswick, NJ: Transaction Publishers, 1998), p. 44; David Keen, *The Benefits of Famine* (Princeton, N.J.: Princeton University Press, 1994).

a good example of the latter. States that are incapable of meeting the basic needs of their population as a result of incapacity or because of unexpected shocks such as rebellions or natural disasters can request external assistance to meet those needs.

In relation to the protection of fundamental rights, the most obvious way in which states can protect civilians is by signing, ratifying and – most importantly – implementing relevant legal treaties, including the nine 'core' treaties identified by the UN High Commissioner for Human Rights and the guiding principles relating to the treatment of IDPs.[54] When states lack the resources or technical expertise to properly implement these core human rights treaties, external assistance is also available through institutions such as the Office of UN Human Rights Commissioner. One hopeful development is the establishment of National Human Rights Institutions.[55] Although there are various models, these institutions share certain similarities in their role and function.[56] They are a particularly important component of a state's protection regime because they can ensure that rights are interpreted and implemented in a context-specific fashion, monitor patterns of rights violation, oversee the integration of rights into national policy, and provide an institutional setting for individuals to lodge complaints.

---

[54] The former include the 1948 UN Convention on the Prevention and Punishment of the Crime of Genocide, the 1949 Geneva Conventions (I-IV), the 1977 Geneva Protocols (I-II), 1980 Convention on the Prohibitions or Restrictions on the Use of Certain Conventional Weapons and additional protocols (I-IV), 1997 Ottawa Convention on the Prohibition, Use, Stockpiling, Production and Transfer of Anti-Personnel Landmines, and the 2008 Convention on certain Cluster Munitions. The nine core human rights treaties are: International Convention on the Elimination of All Racial Discrimination; International Covenant on Civil and Political Rights; International Covenant on Economic, Social and Cultural Rights; Convention on the Elimination of All Forms of Discrimination Against Women; Convention Against Torture and other Cruel, Inhuman or Degrading Treatment or Punishment; International Convention on the Protection of the Rights of All Migrant Workers and Members of their Families; International Convention for the Protection of All Persons from Enforced Disappearance, Convention on the Rights of Persons with Disabilities. On the guiding principles see Roberta Cohen, 'Developing an International System for Internally Displaced Persons', *International Studies Perspectives*, Vol. 7, No. 2 (2006) pp. 81-101.

[55] The National Human Rights Institutions Forum estimated that 117 of the world's States had some form of institution on 6 January 2009.

[56] National Human Rights Institutions should be compatible with the 1993 Paris Principles, which reflect a global consensus on the appropriate role and characteristics of national human rights institutions. The Paris Principles were set out at the first International Workshop on National Institutions for the Promotion and Protection of Human Rights in 1991 and relate to the functioning of national institutions. They were subsequently adopted by the UN Human Rights Commission (Resolution 1992/54, 1992) and by the General Assembly (Resolution 48/134, 1993).

In situations where a state is failing to protect its population, the foremost aim of international engagement must be to encourage the state to change course and fulfil its obligations, either by ceasing attacks, stepping up efforts to uphold the rule of law, or requesting external assistance. The principal means to achieve this is diplomacy.[57] Thus, Kenyan civilians were eventually protected from further bloodshed in the wake of the post-election violence there in 2007 by an internationally brokered power-sharing agreement that followed calls for both parties to fulfil their responsibilities to protect civilians by prominent global figures such as Kofi Annan and Ban Ki-moon.[58] Likewise, diplomatic efforts by the UN Secretary-General and ASEAN persuaded the government of Myanmar to protect its population from deprivation by granting access to humanitarian agencies in wake of Cyclone Nargis.[59] Sometimes, persuasion will not suffice and coercive techniques may be required. Part of the problem is that coercion (whether military or economic) has a poor record of success.[60]

Local Communities

External actors often overlook the fact that populations in danger usually take (often quite effective) measures to protect themselves.[61] External actors are seldom present in large numbers in the eye of an emergency when most of the killing and displacement is actually underway.[62] Typically, international assistance arrives after the peak of the violence.[63] In the inevitable gap between a

---

[57] The Genocide Prevention Task Force (GPTF) provides a useful summary of the cooperative and coercive tools states can use to secure compliance. See GPTF, *Preventing Genocide: A Blueprint for US Policymakers* (Washington, DC: US Institute for Peace, 2008), p. 61.

[58] Roberta Cohen, 'How Kofi Annan Rescued Kenya', *The New York Review of Books*, 55/13, 14 August 2008.

[59] Jurgen Haacke, 'Myanmar, the Responsibility to Protect, and the Need for Practical Assistance', *Global Responsibility to Protect*, 1/2 (2009); Asia-Pacific Centre for the Responsibility to Protect, *Cyclone Nargis and the Responsibility to Protect* (2008), at http://www.r2pasiapacific.org/documents/Burma_Brief2.pdf

[60] See Robert J. Art and Patrick M. Cronin (eds.), *The United States and Coercive Diplomacy* (Washington DC: USIP Press, 2003) and David Cortright and George A. Lopez, *Sanctions and the Search fro Security* (Boulder, CO: Lynne Rienner, 2002).

[61] Bonwick, 'Who Really Protects Civilians?', p. 274; Slim and Eguren, *Humanitarian Protection.*

[62] Bonwick, 'Who Really Protects Civilians?', p. 274.

[63] For example, at the beginning of the Darfur emergency in 2003 there were very few agencies present in either Darfur or in Chad and no peacekeepers or military observers. It was not until May 2004 – approximately eighteen months after the killing and displacement began – that international agencies began arriving in the region in significant numbers. See David Keen, *Complex Emergencies* (Cambridge: Polity, 2008), p. 146.

crisis erupting and outside help arriving (if it does at all), civilians have to make provision for their own protection by escaping violence, protecting their property and reducing threats.[64]

Modes of self-protection fall into three broad types: *in situ* self-protection; flight from danger; and armed resistance. *In situ* self-protection involves measures to protect the community from direct attack and from the deprivation caused by violent conflict. Tactics include travelling only by particular routes or only at night, gathering in large groups for added protection or dispersing into smaller groups for concealment, spending time in different locales by tending farms during the day and hiding in the surrounding countryside at night, concealing vulnerable groups or belongings at night, establishing 'neighbourhood watch'-type systems to provide early warning of impending risk, and paying bribes (in cash, food or assets) to government agents, rebels or vigilante groups in return for protection.[65] Protection against deprivation is fostered through the development of 'coping economies.'[66] Groups use their ever-decreasing asset base in whatever way they can to either survive or prop-up their declining standard of living. Where possible, they might engage in illegal production and smuggling to augment their income or pillage money, supplies and assets from neighbours, ethnic minorities, groups associated with the 'enemy,' or international humanitarian agencies. Indeed, humanitarian workers tend to be targeted more by small armed groups looking for cash, supplies and assets than by larger armed groups, even in cases where these larger groups are responsible for most of the attacks on civilians.[67]

A second self-protection strategy is flight: leaving the area under threat. Decisions about flight are rarely arbitrary.[68] People typically flee to where they believe it will be safer, either because of familial or identity based relationships or the promise of assistance from national authorities or humanitarian agencies. Often, people flee several times in search of safety. Although flight in the face of imminent danger is a good means of physical protection in the short-term, as noted above, those who flee are often left relatively unprotected in the longer-term and much more vulnerable to threats associated with deprivation.

---

[64] O'Callaghan and Pantuliano, *Protective Action,* p. 4.

[65] Bonwick, 'Who Really Protects Civilians?', p. 274; O'Callaghan and Pantuliano, *Protective Action*, p. 4; C. Dolan and L. Hovil, *Humanitarian Protection in Uganda: A Trojan Horse?* (London: HPG Background Paper for the Overseas Development Institute, 2006), p. 5.

[66] Michael Pugh and Neil Cooper, *War Economies in a Regional Context* (Boulder, CO: Lynne Rienner, 2004), p. 9.

[67] O'Callaghan and Pantuliano, *Protective Action,* p. 4.

[68] ibid., p. 4.

Most of the world's displaced are deprived the 'essentials of life,' namely 'shelter, food, medicine, education, community and a resource base for self-reliant livelihood.'[69] Indeed, mortality rates among IDPs are higher than among any other group, with the possible exception of those who stay behind.[70] Compounding the obvious humanitarian problems associated with displacement is the political problem that IDPs remain under the nominal authority of the government that has either directly threatened them or manifestly failed to protect them.[71] As we noted earlier, those authorities often deny humanitarian agencies the access they need to support displaced people, intensifying the challenge of operating in an insecure environment.

A third way in which local communities might respond to imminent threats is through violent resistance. One tactic is to send money, assets and recruits to major rebel groups. In 1998-99, for example, many Kosovar Albanians joined the Kosovo Liberation Army (KLA) simply as a way of protecting their properties and families. People might also band together to establish community militia to protect themselves. An example of this was the various self-defense groups (*kamajors*) that emerged during the civil war in Sierra Leone.[72] But the phenomenon is more common than generally acknowledged. In Darfur, for example, one of the reasons for the apparent fragmenting of the rebel movements was the emergence of dozens of small armed organisations, many of which were groups of armed men formed to protect their community.

All these activities create additional risks. The decision to remain *in situ* in order to protect property and belongings leaves local communities exposed to potential attack, and the risks usually increase with time. While the various *in situ* coping strategies tend to produce better outcomes than flight, the longer a conflict persists the less feasible those strategies usually become as a community's asset base dwindles over time. Likewise, paying government agents, militia groups or vigilantes for protection might enhance physical protection in the short-term, but is likely to create further risks in the future. Payments encourage predatory behaviour on the part of established armed groups and

---

[69] Francis M. Deng, 'Divided Nations: The Paradox of National Protection', *The Annals of the American Academy of Political and Social Science*, Vol.603 (2006), p. 218.

[70] Cohen and Deng, *Masses in Flight*, p. 227.

[71] Deng, 'Divided Nations', p. 218. Nor are refugees always in a much better position, see K. Morjane, 'The Protection of Refugee and Displaced Persons' in B. G. Ramcharan (ed.), *Human Rights Protection in the Field*, special issue of *International Studies in Human Rights*, Vol. 87 (2006), p. 79.

[72] See Paul Richards, *Fighting for the Rain Forest: War, Youth and Resources in Sierra Leone* (Oxford: James Currey, 1996), pp. 152-4.

create an incentive structure for the establishment of new groups. Moreover, insurance payments tie a local community to a particular armed faction and expose the civilian population to retribution and punishment from other armed groups. Similarly, other coping strategies such as engaging in illegal trade or using force to seize assets from other groups might buy a degree of short-term protection but inadvertently contribute to the further deterioration of security, exposing the community to potentially heightened risks further down the line. As noted above, flight is a particularly high-risk strategy. Although it may sometimes represent the only feasible form of physical protection, displaced people suffer heightened deprivation and the community risks losing most, if not all, of its assets, including its land. Finally, although armed resistance might provide a short-term palliative, it makes matters worse just as often as it helps. Sometimes, armed resistance provokes reprisals against civilians as in the case of Kosovo where the KLA's use of violence prompted the Serbian authorities to escalate from a strategy of political and civil rights violations to a campaign of ethnic cleansing.[73] In other circumstances, as in Darfur, self-defense groups become part of the problem. Less well equipped and funded than larger militia groups, self-defense groups use violence against civilians, aid agencies and sometimes peacekeepers to secure assets, money and weapons.[74] In short, therefore, flight, resistance and succumbing to extortion may all buy a degree of short-term protection, but this protection is uncertain, incomplete, risky and might increase risks in the longer-term.

Humanitarian Agencies

The traditional view of humanitarian agencies was that they could contribute to protection in three main ways: 1) they could deliver life-sustaining assistance; 2) they could use their influence to support individuals and groups within government that can promote respect for civilians; and 3) they could 'bear witness' to crimes against civilians (the hope being that the prospect of NGOs reporting on the actions of perpetrators might affect the latter's

---

[73] See Alan J. Kuperman, 'Humanitarian Hazard: Revising the Doctrine of Intervention', *Harvard International Review*, 26/1: 64-68 (2004) and Alan J. Kuperman, 'The Moral Hazard of Humanitarian Intervention: Lessons from the Balkans', *International Studies Quarterly*, 52/1: 49-80 (2008).

[74] It seems that the 2007 attack on AMIS forces in Haskanita was primarily motivated by a desire for equipment, following government attacks that left the rebels depleted. See Julie Flint and Alex de Waal, *Darfur: A New History of a Long War* (London: Zed Books, 2008), pp. 262-67.

calculations).[75] Unfortunately, the evidence suggested that humanitarian presence tended to have only marginal impact on the protection of civilians, especially in frontline regions. In Darfur, for example, humanitarian presence did decrease the reported harassment of civilians and improved freedom of movement but these effects were most noticeable in areas not considered strategically important by the belligerents and only in the immediate vicinity of the respective agency's offices. Elsewhere, presence had little bearing on the protection of civilians.[76]

More recently, it has been recognised that humanitarian agencies can add to their potential protection activities not least by discouraging local communities from adopting risky behaviour and improving local lines of communication and hence decision-making.[77] One recent report identified six strategies in particular that have been used by humanitarian agencies:

1. Use humanitarian assistance to reduce vulnerability by targeting aid at vulnerable groups or at groups that might cause harm to others as part of their coping strategies.
2. Help prevent displacement by providing secure access to land, helping communities to sustain themselves and reducing dependency on displacement camps.[78]
3. Reduce civilians' exposure to threat, for example by supplying stoves that require less firewood thus reducing the need to leave the camps and villages to acquire fuel, providing paid work to reduce the need to adopt risky coping strategies, competition for resources and perceived incentives associated with joining armed groups, and designing camps to maximise safety by including fences and reducing exposure to vulnerable areas.
4. Place conditions on the delivery of assistance, for example by requiring that national authorities guarantee access and provide a safe and secure environment.
5. Help local communities to make better informed decisions about their

[75] See Lisa Mahoney, *Proactive Presence: Field Strategies for Civilian Protection* (Geneva: Centre for Humanitarian Dialogue, 2006), pp. 14-27; ICRC, *Enhancing Protection*, p. 27. As discussed below, the potential role of judicial organisations depends in large part upon such witness testimony to provide the evidentiary basis for future prosecutions. See Mahoney, *Proactive Presence*, p. 13.

[76] Bonwick, 'Who Really Protects Civilians?', p. 276.

[77] The following six points are set out in O'Callaghan and Pantuliano, *Protective Agenda*, pp. 34-8.

[78] ICRC, *Annual Report: Sudan* (Geneva: ICRC, 2005), pp. 116-7.

own protection by providing accurate information about the presence of threats and location of assistance.[79]

6. Report abuses to stimulate responses from more appropriate actors such as states and international organisations.

Each of these activities carries the potential for backlash, especially when attempted in isolation, because humanitarian agencies rely on the consent and cooperation of local communities, armed groups and governments in environments where goodwill is in very short supply. Targeting resources at vulnerable populations without the armed protection of peacekeepers might make those groups more attractive targets to predatory armed groups; providing aid to those who might become threats to the civilian population risks encouraging and rewarding the abuse of civilians; although it is clearly preferential for individuals to remain in their homes, it is important to recognise that this is sometimes simply not possible and the strategy of preventing displacement is only viable in regions not directly affected by armed conflict; and finally, attaching conditions to aid only works if the government wants to reduce (or wants to be seen to be reducing) civilian suffering.[80]

Peacekeepers

As noted above, most peace operations created after 1999 have included civilian protection mandates and since 2002 the UN's Standing Rules of Engagement for peace operations have authorised the use of force 'to defend any civilian person who is in need of protection'.[81] Typically, the protection of civilians by military peacekeepers involves one or both of two types of activity. The first involves the positioning of military forces between the civilian population and those that threaten them in order to deter and respond to attacks.[82] The second, less frequent type of activity involves measures designed to eliminate or restrict the activities of armed groups that threaten civilians.

---

[79] Slim and Bonwick, *Protection,* pp. 95-6 and O'Callaghan and Pantuliano, *Protective Agenda,* p. 35.

[80] N. Leader, *The Politics of Principle: The Principles of Humanitarian Action in Practice* (London: HPG Report 2 for the Overseas Development Institute, 2000), p. 47.

[81] These are not a matter of public record but are cited in Daniel S. Blocq, 'The Fog of UN Peacekeeping: Ethical Issues Regarding the Use of Force to Protect Civilians in UN Operations', *Journal of Military Ethics*, 5/3 (2006), p. 205.

[82] Thomas G. Weiss, 'The Humanitarian Impulse' in David M. Malone (ed.), *The UN Security Council* (Boulder, CO: Lynne Rienner, 2004), p. 48.

In the first type, protection usually involves measures short of offensive force such as erecting military barriers around civilian populations, patrolling at-risk areas, and gradually reducing threats through negotiated disarmament.[83] Sometimes, even if forces are not explicitly mandated or configured for civilian protection tasks, the areas in and around peacekeeping bases and offices get treated as de facto 'safe havens' as civilians relocate there in search of protection.[84] Specific tasks given to peacekeepers include, discouraging the abuse of civilians and improving stability by patrolling, defending civilians under imminent threat, protecting civilians in transit and upon return to their homes, taking special measures to protect women and girls from sexual and gender-based violence, supporting institution-building in areas such as human rights and law enforcement, protecting and assisting humanitarian workers by defending their camps and convoys and securing access to needy populations, delivering humanitarian assistance, defending displacement and refugee camps from external attack and providing security inside camps, separating combatants from non-combatants in refugee camps, and defending 'safe zones' for civilians.[85] Peacekeepers may use force more coercively to protect civilians by conducting rescue operations to free civilians kidnapped by criminal groups or repel attacks on the civilian population.[86]

The second type of military activity involves the use of force against the perpetrators of attacks on civilians in order to eliminate them, degrade their military capabilities or restrict their activities. These activities are much rarer than the first type. At the more limited end of the scale they may involve the apprehension of indicted war criminals by peacekeepers, as in the Balkans. At the other end of the scale, military peacekeepers may conduct campaigns to

[83] Holt and Berkman, *The Impossible Mandate?*, p. 52.

[84] For example, when a Uruguayan MONUC battalion entered Bunia in eastern DRC in 2003, thousands of civilians sought shelter near its bases despite the fact that the battalion was neither configured nor mandated for civilian protection duties. DPKO (2004), *Operation Artemis: The Lessons of the Interim Emergency Multinational Force* (Peacekeeping Best Practices Unit, Military Division, October 2004), p. 7.

[85] This list draws on three Reports of the UN Secretary-General on the Protection of Civilians in Armed Conflict: UN docs S/1999/957, 8 September 1999; S/2004/431, 28 May, 2004; S/2005/740, 28 November 2005. A more detailed list was articulated by Holt and Berkman on the basis of consultations with military leaders. See Holt and Berkman, *The Impossible Mandate?*, p. 46.

[86] For example, in October 2008 MONUC used helicopter gunships to halt the advance of Laurent Nkunda's CNDP forces towards the major centre of civilian population at Goma, some thirty miles north at Kimbumba. See UN Radio, 'MONUC Battles Rebel Fighters in Eastern DRC', 28 October 2008 and Michelle Faul, 'UN Attacks Rebels to Protect Civilians in Congo', *Associated Press*, 27 October 2008.

degrade the ability of certain groups to attack the civilian population.[87] For example, NATO responded to the August 1995 attack on the Sarajevo marketplace with *Operation Deliberate Force*, an air and artillery bombardment of Bosnian Serb forces aimed at eliminating their capacity to target Sarajevo's civilians.[88] In 2000, British troops used force to eliminate a rebel group in Sierra Leone known as the 'West Side Boys' that had attacked civilians, kidnapped and raped women and girls and seized British peacekeepers.[89] More recently, in 2005 MONUC forcibly disarmed groups in Ituri district and adopted a robust civilian protection posture in South Kivu, targeting Hutu *Forces Démocratiques de Libération du Rwanda* (FDLR) militia associated with the 1994 Rwandan genocide and subsequent abuse of civilians in the DRC. When the FDLR refused to cooperate, MONUC used helicopter gunships to destroy up to sixteen of its camps.[90]

Although some positive developments have occurred in the design and conduct of peace operations, many remain incapable of protecting civilians from attack. For example, in 2008/9 MONUC was unable to prevent a wave of violence against civilians sparked by a conflict between Laurent Nkunda's *Congrès national pour la défense du peuple* (CNDP) and the FDLR which displaced approximately 200,000 civilians. Shortly afterwards, because it was not deployed in the far north-east of the DRC and lacked the necessary resources, MONUC could not protect civilians from the Lord's Resistance Army (LRA) which conducted a series of massacres in north eastern DRC in response to a concerted military offensive against it by Uganda, the SPLA and the FARDC.[91] Peace operations in Afghanistan, Burundi, Côte d'Ivoire, Darfur, Sierra Leone, Somalia, and Sudan, amongst others, have confronted similar challenges and proven unable to protect civilians from attack. There are at least three reasons for this.

The first is the enduring gap between expectations and capabilities caused by a combination of demand-side and supply-side factors. On the demand side, states are typically reluctant to consent to the intervention of a large and well-equipped peacekeeping force unless they calculate that it is in their interests to do so, which is rare. On the supply-side, international society – and its

---

[87] See GPTF, *Preventing Genocide*, p. 83, table 3.

[88] The objective of *Operation Deliberate Force* was 'to reduce the threat to the Sarajevo safe area and to deter further attacks there or on any other safe area'. See Henning-A. Frantzen, *NATO and Peace Support Operations 1991-1999* (London: Frank Cass, 2005), p. 66.

[89] See Richard Connaughton, 'Operation Barass,' *Small Wars and Insurgencies*, Vol.12, No. 2 (Summer 2001), pp. 110-119.

[90] Holt and Berkman, *The Impossible Mandate?*, p. 165.

[91] Thanks to William Durch for this point.

wealthiest members especially – have grown increasingly reluctant to commit troops to civilian protection missions outside their areas of strategic interest.[92] As a result, most operations do not have the capabilities needed to provide comprehensive protection to civilian populations.[93] This is evident if we recall two rules of thumb commonly used to calculate the necessary force size for civilian protection operations.[94] The first is based on the assumption that 2-10 troops are required for every 1,000 inhabitants within the crisis zone. The second method is based on the protection force being at least the size of the largest indigenous armed force. On these indicators several peace operations remained significantly under-staffed (see table 1).

The result is that even relatively large peacekeeping missions are seldom able to provide protection throughout their area of operations. Consequently, military protection efforts usually focus on specific geographic areas, be they 'safe havens/areas/zones,' 'safe corridors' for transit, or undesignated areas close to the peacekeepers' bases. The rationale for designating safe areas is that through

Table 1: Ideal and Actual Size of Peace Operations with Civilian Protection Mandates[95]

Region	Local Population	Mission	Required Size: Method 1	Required Size: Method 2	Actual Size (Dec. 2008)
Darfur, Sudan	c.6 million	UNAMID	12,000-60,000	40,000-45,000	15,130
South Sudan	c.8 million	UNMIS	16,000-80,000	40,000	10,025
North Kivu, DRC	c.5 million	MONUC	10,000-50,000	20,000	6,000

[92] Alex J. Bellamy and Paul D. Williams, 'The West and Contemporary Peace Operations', *Journal of Peace Research*, 46/1: 39-57 (2009).

[93] Thus, between 2000 and 2004, the UN Secretary-General advised against the adoption of protection as a core role for MONUC, even after it had been mandated by the Security Council, on the grounds that the mission lacked the necessary resources. See Månsson, 'Use of Force and Civilian Protection', pp. 507, 512.

[94] Michael O'Hanlon and Peter W. Singer, 'The Humanitarian Transformation: Expanding Global Intervention Capacity', *Survival*, 46/1 (2004), p. 97, n. 7.

[95] Sources: 'Report of the International Commission of Inquiry on Darfur to the UN Secretary-General: Pursuant to Security Council resolution 1564, 18 September 2004', Geneva, 25 January 2005, p. 27, para.78; Amnesty International, *Democratic Republic of Congo: Crisis in North Kivu* (21 Nov. 2008), at http://www.amnesty.org/en/library/info/AFR62/014/2008/en.

the concentration of force, peacekeepers can carve out secure areas.[96] The problem with this approach is that it only protects those civilians that are able to make it into the safe zone, encourages displacement as civilians flee their homes for the safety of the safe zone, and facilitates the concentration of civilian populations making them more vulnerable to atrocities if the peacekeepers fail to defend the zone (as happened in Srebrenica in 1995). In addition, protecting civilians in one area leaves them vulnerable to violence elsewhere: by default, creating 'safe zones' renders other areas 'danger zones'.[97]

The second problem is that there is no clear doctrine to guide military forces in their civilian protection activities. The UN's recent 'principles and guidelines' document for peacekeeping operations identifies civilian protection as requiring 'concerted and coordinated action among the military, police and civilian components' of a peace operation and that it 'must be mainstreamed into the planning and conduct of [the UN's] core activities.' Yet it did not spell out what protection entails or how it could be achieved.[98] Similarly, key states such as Canada, the United States, the UK, the Netherlands, France and India as well as organisations like NATO, the EU, ECOWAS and the AU have also been slow to include specific guidelines on civilian protection in their military doctrines.[99] While their doctrine points to civilian protection as a possible role, none singles it out or elaborates on how military force should be used for protection purposes.[100] As such, civilian protection activities remain *ad hoc* and dependent on the initiative and ingenuity of individual commanders.[101] This poses a particular problem in multinational operations where national rotations and priorities make it difficult to establish or implement long-term strategies.

Third, it has proven difficult to eliminate threats to civilians entirely and using force against militia groups may make it harder to secure their cooperation in the future. Cases where peacekeepers succeed in eliminating threats are rare – the British assault on the West Side Boys in Sierra Leone and NATO's

---

[96] Mary Kaldor, *New and Old Wars* (Cambridge: Polity, 1999), p. 125.

[97] Ian Johnstone, 'Dilemmas of Robust Peace Operations', in *Annual Review of Global Peace Operations 2006* (Boulder, CO: Lynne Rienner, 2006), p. 7.

[98] UN DPKO, *UN Peacekeeping Operations: Principles and Guidelines* (New York: UN, 2008), p. 24.

[99] Arguably the most advanced attempt to develop military planning tools to respond effectively to mass atrocities is the Mass Atrocity Response Operations (MARO) Project run out of Harvard University with the collaboration of the US Army's Peacekeeping and Stability Operations Institute. See http://www.hks.harvard.edu/cchrp/maro/index.php

[100] Holt and Berkman, *The Impossible Mandate?*, pp. 114-28.

[101] Holt and Smith, *Halting Widespread or Systematic Attacks on Civilians.*

strikes against the Bosnian Serbs provide the best examples but the former involved a small and politically insignificant militia group and the latter came in the context of wider military reverses on the ground. More often, armed groups are weakened but may regroup and return to attack civilians. Although it succeeded in weakening the FDLR and restricting its freedom of movement, MONUC neither destroyed the militia nor forced it to disarm.[102] The FDLR responded by negotiating an alliance with the DRC government, prompting the 2008 conflict with the CNDP which had devastating effects on the civilian population. The point here is that in most cases, military efforts by themselves are unlikely to eliminate threats to the civilian population.

International Judicial Institutions

International judicial institutions such as the International Criminal Court (ICC), special tribunals such as those created for the former Yugoslavia and Rwanda, and hybrid national tribunals (e.g. in Sierra Leone and Cambodia) contribute to protection by holding some of the perpetrators of atrocities to account. Proponents argue that by ending impunity such institutions will help deter would-be perpetrators of atrocities and afford legal protection to the victims.[103]

The idea that some crimes are so heinous as to fall under universal jurisdiction is not new but efforts to internationalise and institutionalise individual criminal responsibility in the wake of the Nuremberg and Tokyo trials were stymied by political disputes. The first tentative steps were taken in the mid-1990s when the Security Council established *ad hoc* tribunals to prosecute the perpetrators of grave crimes in Bosnia and Rwanda.[104] The Rome Statute establishing the ICC in 1998 held that the court's jurisdiction could be invoked when a state party proved unwilling or unable to investigate evidence pointing to the commission of widespread and systematic war crimes, crimes against humanity and genocide. The ICC prosecutor could initiate proceedings in cases where s/he was able to persuade a panel of judges that a case fell under the court's jurisdiction, where a complaint was made by a signatory state, or when a case was referred to the prosecutor by the Security Council.

---

[102] Holt and Berkman, *The Impossible Mandate?*, pp. 166-7.

[103] William Schabas, *An Introduction to the International Criminal Court* (Cambridge: Cambridge University Press, 2008), p. 57.

[104] Gary J. Bass, *Stay the Hand of Vengeance* (Princeton, NJ: Princeton University Press, 2000), p. 221 and Richard J. Goldstone, *For Humanity: Reflections of a War Crimes Investigator* (New Haven: Yale University Press, 2000).

The Security Council also reserved the right to postpone investigations by one year. To date, the Security Council has referred the situation in Darfur to the ICC and the governments of the DRC, Uganda and the Central African Republic have requested that the ICC investigate and prosecute crimes committed in their countries. The court opened its first case in January 2009, against the Congolese militia leader Thomas Lubanga.

It is thus far too early to pronounce on the court's effectiveness or its potential to deter the commission of atrocities. Early anecdotal evidence from Darfur and Uganda, however, suggests that while the threat of prosecution is sometimes factored into perpetrators' calculations, it has failed to prevent the commission of crimes.[105] This brings us to an additional problem, which is that criminal proceedings might undermine political efforts to end crimes against civilians because the threat of future prosecution provides a disincentive for leaders to negotiate an end to violence, accept the deployment of peacekeepers or step down from power.[106] This issue has been widely debated in relation to the ICC's attempts to indict Sudan's President Bashir and the leader of Uganda's Lords Resistance Army, Joseph Kony.

Gaps and Tensions in the Protection Agenda

Although recent decades have witnessed considerable activity directed towards the protection of civilians in war and significant progress has been made, especially in the humanitarian sector, important gaps and tensions remain.

The first, and arguably most significant, is the gap between *expectations and capabilities*. In short, across each actor type identified in the previous section there are profound gaps between what agents are expected to deliver (either by insiders or outsiders) and what they are capable of, or committed to, delivering. Thus: some states simply lack the capacity to protect their citizens, and many others lack the political will to do so; humanitarian agencies cannot sustain life in the face of immediate physical threats and find it difficult to deliver aid effectively in insecure environments; although military peacekeepers

---

[105] See Flint and de Waal, *Darfur*, pp. 241, 257, 262 and Jan Egeland, *A Billion Lives: An Eyewitness Report from the Frontlines of Humanity* (New York: Simon and Schuster, 2008), pp. 197-214.

[106] See Jack Snyder and Leslie Vinjanmuri, 'Trials and Errors: Principle and Pragmatism in Strategies of International Justice', *International Security*, 28/3: 5-44 (2003-04); Daniel Sutter, 'The Deterrent Effects of the International Criminal Court', *New Political Economy*, 23/1: 9-24 (2006).

have the theoretical capacity to provide physical security more often than not they are deployed without the numbers, equipment or expertise necessary to complete a civilian protection mandate; and while IHL promises an end to impunity it lacks the judicial authority or policing capacity to deliver protection on the ground. In these four instances, expectations about what ought to happen do not match reality. In some cases, this may be because those expectations are unrealistic. As MSF has repeatedly argued, it is a mistake to think that humanitarian agencies are able to protect civilians from direct harm. But in other cases, the gap is a product of choice prompted by countervailing interests. The clearest example here is the peacekeeping gap. The principal reason for the gap between the number of peacekeepers needed to protect civilians and the number deployed is international society's inability to muster sufficient political will.

Even if sufficient resources were found to close the expectations-capabilities gap, lack of *operational guidance* for the UN and regional organisations would remain a problem. Put simply, while there has been an outpouring of guidance for humanitarian NGOs, the proliferation of civilian protection mandates has not been met with a similar proliferation of guidance about how to 'do' civilian protection in the field. This problem is most acute in relation to the role of host states and peacekeepers but it is also apparent in relation to the way that humanitarian agencies provide protection and in the absence of guidance on how local communities might better protect themselves. In relation to peacekeepers, although the Security Council has increased the frequency of its civilian protection mandates it has not issued clear guidance as to what this entails. This includes a failure to clarify the meaning of caveats referring to the mission's 'areas of deployment,' 'capabilities' and the need to protect civilians 'without prejudice to the responsibility' of the host country.[107] In the absence of clear guidance, actors are left to make decisions on an *ad hoc* basis, without the benefits of past lessons learned and best practices.

A third problem is the lack of coherence and effective coordination.[108] Although civil-military coordination in complex emergencies has been significantly strengthened in the past two decades, the preceding analysis identified a number of areas in which protection activity in one area might negatively impact upon activities in another. For example, there is the potential that

---

[107] Holt and Smith, *Halting Attacks on Civilians*, p. 11.

[108] For a relevant discussion see Roland Paris, 'Understanding the "coordination problem" in postwar statebuilding' in Roland Paris and Timothy Sisk (eds.), *The Dilemmas of Statebuilding* (London: Routledge, 2008), pp. 53-78.

political efforts to persuade the government to fulfill its obligations might impair humanitarian work by casting doubt on its impartiality. This fate befell the UN's Humanitarian Coordinator in Darfur, Jan Pronk, when he publicised his concerns about the government of Sudan's failure to comply with its obligations towards its civilian population and used public diplomacy to persuade the government to change course. In response, the government of Sudan accused Pronk of politicising aid and deported him.[109] Likewise, the controversies surrounding the indictment of Joseph Kony and Omar al-Bashir by the ICC, points to the potential for the judicial arm of the civilian protection agenda to undermine political efforts to bring the targeting of civilians to an end. Similarly, where NGOs and peacekeepers coordinate their activities and – for instance – peacekeepers protect aid workers, perceptions of humanitarian neutrality may be diminished. Although no direct evidence has yet been presented to support this claim, it is commonplace for analysts to argue that closer ties between aid agencies and military forces places the former at greater risk by undermining the protection afforded to them by neutrality.[110] Finally, there is potential for incoherence between agents who might be encouraging or discouraging flight. We noted earlier that when peacekeepers are deployed they tend to create explicit or de facto 'safe zones,' which encourage flight. This might undermine the efforts of local communities and aid agencies to remain *in situ*.

This brings us to a fourth problem: the tensions between *self-protection activities and external agendas*. Because, to date, relatively little attention has been paid to the steps that communities take to protect themselves, not only are external efforts not calibrated to complement local efforts but certain types of activities might actually impede local protection efforts. On the one hand, it is important to recognise that external agents alter the calculations of local actors. For example, the establishment of military camps, feeding depots and medical centers might encourage displacement and undermine local coping strategies. Promises of protection might encourage local actors to engage in risky behavior, be it resistance, flight, or refusing to flee imminent danger because of the promise of external protection. Arms embargoes designed to protect civilians might have a disproportionate impact on the ability of self-defense groups to acquire arms whilst support for rebel groups may be

[109] Mohammed Ali Saeed, 'UN Envoy accused of Waging War in Sudan', *Mail & Guardian* (Johannesburg), 20 October 2006.

[110] See Sarah Kenyon Lischer, 'Military Intervention and the Humanitarian "Force Multiplier"', *Global Governance*, 13/1: 99-118 (2007).

counter-productive to protection. Also, failure to satisfy needs and replenish assets may lead communities into taking more desperate measures.

Finally, there is a tension between the *primary responsibility of the state and the way protection is commonly conceived and pursued.* It is widely acknowledged that the consent and cooperation of the host state is a vital determinant of protection. Indeed, even when peacekeepers are deployed with a Chapter VII mandate to protect civilians, the host state can make protection much easier by cooperating or much harder by not doing so. It is also worth recalling that the vast majority of UN peace operations with civilian protection mandates are deployed to *support* the host state.[111] Yet, one of the least well understood elements of the RtoP principle is the question of what states need to do to exercise their responsibility to protect their populations. Beyond the study of sanctions – which evidence suggests can often be counterproductive – we have little idea about the strategies needed to persuade states to fulfill their responsibility to protect civilians.[112] More research is needed to understand which agents should be responsible for this effort, how it might impact on humanitarian neutrality, the potential effect of ICC investigations and indictments, and which tactics have proven effective in persuading states to cooperate when external assistance is needed.

Together, these problems have left the protection agenda somewhat limited and contradictory in certain respects. In the final section we identify some areas which need much greater research and attention if these problems are to be overcome.

Advancing the Civilian Protection Agenda

Our suggested protection agenda rests on the three pillars of physical protection from immediate harm; the provision of vital needs; and the freedom to exercise fundamental human rights. Implementing such a broad agenda clearly requires a multidimensional approach involving a wide range of actors, many of whom have very different goals, interests and worldviews. While a subject as politically sensitive as civilian protection is unlikely to produce anything approaching universal consensus – and it is certainly not our intention to argue that any single actor should assume responsibility for the totality of the

[111] Holt and Smith, *Halting Attacks on Civilians.*

[112] See Ban Ki-moon, 'Implementing the Responsibility to Protect', Report of the UN Secretary-General, A/63/677, 12 January 2009.

agenda – it is important to address some of the major deficiencies of current thinking and practice. Instead of a conclusion, we propose four areas that require much greater attention if civilian protection is to be made more effective.

Enhance State Capacity

Fundamentally, the long-term solution to the protection problem revolves in large part around the conundrum of how to build political communities (probably states) that are both willing and able to protect all their citizens from atrocity. After war, this agenda inevitably raises several difficult dilemmas relating to legitimacy, security, political economy, autonomy and coordination.[113] At other times, the trick will be to incentivise governments to protect their populations. In general, we suggest that it is crucial to enhance state capacities in three broad areas. First, the country's security forces (military, police, and intelligence) need to be professionalised and brought under civilian control.[114] Of course, once a crisis has broken, security sector reform programmes will not provide instant solutions to the problems of predatory soldiers and dysfunctional security organisations. In the longer-term, however, such programmes are a necessary part of the protection agenda. Second, policies need to strengthen the rule of law by building effective policing and judicial systems. Where appropriate, national efforts can draw support from international institutions such as Interpol or the ICC to help end the culture of impunity for perpetrators of atrocities. The third area concerns systems of state governance and the questions of who rules and how? In the long-term, incentives need to be created to encourage systems of governance 'by and for the people,' and which establish checks and balances upon executive power in order to promote respect for the rights of individuals and minorities. A reasonable place to start is to engineer structures of governance that stress republicanism's emphasis on deliberation, representation and constitutionalism.[115]

Enhance the Resilience of Local Communities

Until states prove both willing and able to protect their civilians, more action needs to be taken to strengthen the resilience of local communities at risk of

[113] For an excellent discussion of the central challenges and dilemmas involved see Paris and Sisk (eds.), *The Dilemmas of Statebuilding.*

[114] See Howe, *Ambiguous Order.*

[115] See Michael Barnett, 'Building a Republican Peace', *International Security*, 30/4: 87-112 (2006).

severe harm. As an initial step, this will require investigation into what factors are most associated with episodes of severe political instability and what factors can stabilise region's on the brink of crises.[116] Naturally, the enduring strength of sovereignty and the non-interference norm will make it particularly difficult to take action in precisely those communities most at risk from their own governments. But such difficulties do not warrant abandoning the objective of enhancing community resilience. In order for this to happen, outsiders need a better understanding of local coping strategies and how communities manage various kinds of crises from famine to physical assaults. Then these activities need to be supported. Ideally, understanding can be built through dialogue and protracted engagement with communities and mapping techniques can be used to build a clear picture of the sources of protection in given regions. In the midst of an emergency, however, there is neither the time nor capacity to conduct these types of activities to the extent needed. In the immediate onset of crises, greater emphasis must go towards limiting displacement not least through attempts to keep local coping economies functioning and ensuring humanitarian access to as much of the at-risk population as possible. In dire circumstances where atrocities are already being committed, external actors may need to think more carefully about how to collaborate with local armed resistance groups, as well as trying to prevent these groups transforming from 'protectors' into 'predators'.[117] Of course, knowing which armed groups to support and which to undermine will always be incredibly difficult and subject to contestation but future collaborative choices will be made easier if more research can shed light on why certain armed groups engage in predatory behaviour.

Strengthen Peace Operations[118]

When states and various local community groups fail to protect civilians, external parties should assume a greater burden of the responsibility. As the most significant form of such external engagement, peace operations need to

---

[116] For relevant discussions see UK Prime Minister's Strategy Unit, *Investing in Prevention: An International Strategy to Manage Risks of Instability and Improve Crisis Response* (London: TSO, 2005); Jack A. Goldstone et al, 'A Global Forecasting Model of Political Instability', unpublished paper (2005) at http://globalpolicy.gmu.edu/pitf/PITFglobal.pdf

[117] See William Reno, 'Patronage Politics and the Behavior of Armed Groups', *Civil Wars*, 9/4: 324-42 (2007).

[118] By peace operations we are referring to all those missions, UN or otherwise, involving foreign uniformed personnel that are deployed to a conflict zone with the consent of the host government.

be better prepared to carry out or facilitate protection activities across the three pillars discussed above. In general terms, this will mean enhancing the level of (human, financial, and material) resources available to peacekeepers. This brings us to the question of how to encourage troop contributing countries to commit the necessary resources to peace operations in an era of declining commitment on the part of the West.[119] One key to recalibrating national interests may be stress the link between strategic interests, the protection of civilians, and the effectiveness of peace operations. Other components of strengthening peace operations include developing relevant doctrine for the military and policing tasks associated with civilian protection, and preparing peacekeepers for the considerable challenges ahead by investing in rigorous training programs both well before and after their deployment.[120] On the other hand, as peace operations will increasingly be judged on how they perform with regard to civilian protection, peacekeepers who abuse their position and inflict harm upon locals must be publicly punished.

Develop Capabilities to Conduct Humanitarian Interventions[121]

In cases of 'supreme humanitarian emergency' where outsiders provide the only hope of protecting civilians from immediate harm it will be necessary to use military force to coerce or defeat perpetrators of atrocities.[122] This means that there must be armed forces capable of performing the necessary tasks. While five international organisations (AU/ECOWAS/EU/NATO/UN) have explicitly expressed an interest in conducting such operations, only NATO has conducted what it claims was a humanitarian intervention in Kosovo/Serbia (1999). Since most organisations find it difficult to project force over long distances, the greatest expectations for action will fall on states that border the crisis zone in question as well as those that can project military power around the globe at relatively short notice. Currently, it is only NATO states that fall into the latter category. The major problems, of course, are that even if such forces could be mustered and trained, humanitarian intervention goes against the grain of most international legal opinion, there are no guarantees that it will 'do no *net* harm,' it is a concept that is easily open to abuse;

[119] See Bellamy and Williams, 'The West and Contemporary Peace Operations'.
[120] See Holt and Berman, *The Impossible Mandate?*; GPTF, *Preventing Genocide*, chapter 5.
[121] By humanitarian intervention we mean military operations to protect endangered populations conducted without the consent of the host government.
[122] See Wheeler, *Saving Strangers*.

and it will not *per se* address the root causes of the atrocities in question. Nevertheless, it is exceedingly difficult to see alternative ways of stopping the types of atrocities witnessed in Rwanda, Srebrenica and Darfur.

When thinking about how to protect civilians in uncivil wars it would therefore make more sense for political leaders to stop repeating the discredited cliché of 'never again' and instead start investing serious resources into figuring out 'who's next?' and how they might be protected.

Chapter Seven

A Responsibility to Protect Persons in the Event of Natural Disasters?

Sara E. Davies

Between 1900 and 2005, there was a significant increase in the number of natural disasters of a biological, geological and hydrometeorological nature.[1] Between 1991 and 2005, Asia experienced the greatest number of natural disasters and suffered the greatest loss of human life and economic damage.[2] Earthquakes, tsunamis, drought, floods and wind storms have been the primary cause of this destruction to economies and human life.[3] If scientific predictions are correct, climate change will increase the number of natural disasters that the world will face in the coming century. The Intergovernmental Panel on Climate Change (IPCC) argues that we are already experiencing the effects of climate change with increased tropical cyclonic activity in the North Atlantic, unusually prolonged drought across the Southern hemisphere and changes in infectious disease vectors.[4] The question of whether governments are prepared to mitigate the effects of natural disasters upon their civilian population has become a key concern to the international community. Recent events where these concerns have come into play include the aftermath of Cyclone Nargis in the Ayeyawady delta, Myanmar in May 2008, when the

---

[1] International Strategy for Disaster Reduction, 'Distribution of natural disasters by origin', *Disaster Statistics, Occurrence: trends-century*, Centre for Research on the Epidemiology of Disasters, 2006. http://www.unisdr.org/disaster-statistics/pdf/isdr-disaster-statistics-occurrence.pdf accessed: 9 November 2009.

[2] International Strategy for Disaster Reduction, 'Average number of people reported killed, per million inhabitants by continent and disaster origin: 1991-2005' and 'Total amount of reported economic damages by continent and disaster origin', *Disaster Statistics, Impact: killed*, Centre for Research on the Epidemiology of Disasters, 2006. http://www.unisdr.org/disaster-statistics/pdf/isdr-disaster-statistics-impact.pdf accessed: 9 November 2009.

[3] Ibid.

[4] Intergovernmental Panel on Climate Change (IPCC), *Climate Change 2007: Synthesis Report*, Summary for Policy Makers, 2007, p. 2-3. http://www.ipcc.ch/pdf/assessment-report/ar4/syr/ar4_syr_spm.pdf accessed: 9 November 2009.

junta initially refused international humanitarian assistance in spite of its failure to meet the needs of the affected population,[5] and the Indian Ocean Tsunami on 26 December 2004, which revealed problems associated with coordinating international responses to large scale disasters and focusing on the protection needs of vulnerable persons.[6]

These, and other cases, give rise to two particular problems. First, there have been instances where states have refused international humanitarian assistance despite being unable to meet the needs of those affected by disasters. Second, there have been occasions where the affected state has been unable or unwilling to ensure that aid from donor states and international organisations is distributed quickly, effectively and equitably.[7] These factors have prompted some governments and international institutions to call for the development of clearer guidelines to direct states in their response to natural disasters, based on the idea that people possess a fundamental right to humanitarian assistance. To date, the main outcome was the 2005 World Conference on Disaster Reduction which led to the Hyogo Framework for Action 2005-2010. The Framework for Action includes a process for evaluating the role of the state in alleviating the economic, health and social vulnerabilities that affect their populations in the aftermath of a disaster.

Echoing the work done in relation to internally displaced persons (IDPs),[8] the focus for attention has been the question of what existing legal protection is available to states, regional and international organisations and, most importantly, affected persons, in the event of a disaster (and its aftermath). This led to the commission of a study by the International Law Commission (ILC) on the protection of persons in the event of a disaster (hereafter referred to as 'protection of persons') in 2006. The purpose of the study (which runs until 2011) is to examine what existing instruments and texts are applicable to the 'main aspects of disaster prevention and relief assistance (including disaster response), as well as to the protection of persons in the event of disasters'.[9]

---

[5] Jurgen Haacke, 'Myanmar: the Responsibility to Protect, and the Need for Practical Assistance', *Global Responsibility to Protect*, vol. 1, no. 2 (2009), pp. 156-184.

[6] Erica Harper, *International Law and Standards Applicable in Natural Disaster Situations*, International Development Law Organisation (Rome: International Development Law Organisation, 2009), p. 15-16; Walter Kalin, 'Foreword' in Harper et al, p. 9.

[7] General Assembly, *Strengthening of the coordination of emergency humanitarian assistance of the United Nations Report of the Secretary General*, Fifty-Fifth Session (30 May 2000), A/55/82-E/2000/61 p. 13.

[8] See Chapters by Roberta Cohen and Erin Mooney in this volume.

[9] General Assembly, *Protection of Persons in the event of disasters, Memorandum by the Secretariat*, Sixtieth Session (11 December 2007), A/CN.4/590, p. 13.

The study also seeks to clarify whether there is, or should be, an equivalent legal 'right' to humanitarian assistance in the event of a natural disaster, that is similar to the right that civilians have under international humanitarian law during 'complex emergencies' brought about by armed conflict (i.e. rights to food, shelter, medical aid). Not surprisingly, the responsibility to protect (hereafter referred to as R2P)[10] persons affected by natural disasters was first mentioned in the proposal for ILC's long-term programme of work in 2006. After the unanimous adoption of R2P by 192 countries at the 2005 World Summit, the Secretariat argued in the 2006 proposal on the protection of persons that this topic was also,

> [L]ocated within contemporary reflection on an emerging principle entailing the responsibility to protect, which, although couched primarily in the context of conflict, may also be of relevance to that of disasters...While recognizing the importance of involving all stakeholders, including regional and international organizations and financial institutions, civil society, including non-governmental organizations and volunteers, the private sector and the scientific community, the declaration affirms the primary responsibility of States to protect the people and property on their territory from hazards, whether natural or induced by human processes.[11]

The first report by Special Rapporteur for the protection of persons, Eduardo Valencia-Ospina, noted that there was relevance in the R2P to the study of the protection of persons, as both seek to highlight the sovereign's responsibility to protect individuals from harm. Referring to the 2006 ILC proposal that linked R2P and protection of persons, Valencia-Ospina argued that,

> [T]he traditional State system is currently witnessing the emergence of various concepts related to the responsibility of States. As the Secretariat noted in its proposal for the topic, the protection of persons may be located within contemporary reflection on an emerging principle entailing the responsibility to protect. The latter concept entails the responsibility to prevent, react and rebuild, corresponding, respectively, to the three phases of a disaster situation.[12]

---

[10] Responsibility to protect is a principle unanimously adopted by heads of state and government at the 2005 United Nations World Summit. In the World Summit Document, paragraphs 138, 139 and 140, detail the obligation of individual States to protect its populations from genocide, war crimes, ethnic cleansing and crimes against humanity. The international community also has a responsibility to assist States in the prevention of these crimes, and should the State be failing to do so, the international community must be prepared to take collective action, in accordance with the UN Charter, to restore protection of civilians. United Nations General Assembly, *2005 World Summit Outcome*, A/RES/60/1, 24 October 2005, paras. 138-40.

[11] Quoted in General Assembly, *Report of the International Law Commission*, Sixty-Fourth Session (4 May-5 June/6 July-7 August 2006), A/64/10, p. 468.

[12] General Assembly, *Preliminary report on the protection of persons in the event of disasters by Mr Eduardo Valencia-Ospina, Special Rapporteur*, Sixtieth Session (5 May 2008), A/CN.4/598, p. 19.

However, recent reports and discussions within the ILC and with member states in the sixth committee of the General Assembly, has led Valencia-Ospina and the Secretariat prepared Memorandum to retract the initial link between R2P and the protection of persons. In 2008, both the Memorandum and Valencia-Ospina noted that as the R2P is primarily concerned with genocide and mass atrocities, there is little in its scope that connects the principle to the protection of persons in the event of a natural disaster.[13] Nonetheless, attempts to link the protection obligations entailed in the R2P to the protection of persons in the event of disasters such as Cyclone Nargis have persisted.[14] Many argue that despite the recent clarification by the Secretary-General that R2P does not apply to disasters (whether natural or man-made),[15] the R2P should be broadened to include situations when sovereigns are manifestly failing to satisfy the essential needs of their population in the aftermath of a disaster.[16] In his second report in 2009, Valencia-Ospina followed the lead of the UN Secretary-General's report on implementing the R2P and concluded that the concept of R2P would not be applicable.[17] Following the report, however, some ILC members disputed this finding suggesting that the ILC is not unanimous in thinking that there is no potential relationship between the two concepts.[18]

In this chapter, I examine the ILC's decision to not link their programme of work on the protection of persons to the R2P.[19] In exploring how the ILC's work has developed thus far, I argue that the exclusion of R2P from the

[13] A/CN.4/598, p. 20; A/CN.4/590, p. 148.

[14] Rebecca Barber, 'The Responsibility to Protect the Survivors of Natural Disaster: Cyclone Nargis, a Case Study', *Journal of Conflict and Security Law*, vol.14, no.1 (2009), pp. 3-34; Mely Caballero-Anthony and Belinda Chng, 'Cyclones and Humanitarian Crises: Pushing the Limits of R2P in Southeast Asia', *Global Responsibility to Protect*, vol.1, no.2 (2009), pp. 135-155; Roberta Cohen, 'The Burma Cyclone and the Responsibility to Protect', *Global Responsibility to Protect*, vol.1, no.2 (2009), pp. 253-257.

[15] United Nations General Assembly, *Implementing the responsibility to protect*, Report of the Secretary-General, Sixty-Third Session (12 January 2009), A/63/677, p. 8.

[16] For example, Lloyd Axworthy and Allan Rock argued that '[I]f R2P does not apply to situations where a government is actively working to deprive large numbers of people of lifesaving assistance, then we must ask how far the international community has come in saying that it will never again sit idly by in the face of mass human catastrophe'. Lloyd Axworthy and Allan Rock, 'R2P: An Unfinished Agenda', *Global Responsibility to Protect*, vol. 1, no. 1 (2009), p. 56.

[17] A/63/677, p. 8.

[18] General Assembly, *Second Report on the protection of persons in the event of disasters by Eduardo Valencia-Ospina, Special Rapporteur*, Sixty-First Session (7 May 2009), A/CN.4/615, pp. 2, 5.

[19] Quoted in General Assembly, *Report of the International Law Commission*, Sixty-Fourth Session (4 May-5 June/6 July-7 August 2006), A/64/10, pp. 329, 332.

mandate was the correct decision for the sake of advancing both principles. In the first section, I briefly examine the historical development of sovereignty as responsibility and how it came to be encapsulated in protection efforts such as the Guiding Principles on IDPs and the R2P principle, first introduced by the Canadian government led International Commission on Intervention and State Sovereignty (ICISS) in 2001. This section argues that the protection of persons – whether from genocide and mass atrocities, internal displacement or natural disasters – share normative roots in sovereignty as responsibility. Hence, it is not surprising that there have been efforts to conflate R2P and the protection of persons. In the second section, I explore the ILC's study on protection of persons. I examine the reports presented on the topic thus far and reveal that despite there being no legal requirement for states to allow international humanitarian access to their populations, there has been an emerging convention over the last decade that states have a *duty* to grant such assistance if they are unable to meet their population's needs. This, I argue, closely reflects the normative roots that underpin the R2P principle – the notion of sovereignty as responsibility. From this history it would appear at first glance that there is reason to link the legal the protection of persons in the event of disasters to the R2P. Nevertheless, I conclude by arguing that while the protection of persons in the event of a disaster is closely linked to the normative agenda of sovereignty as responsibility, the Special Rapporteur has been right not to include R2P in the draft articles being framed on the protection of persons. Both agendas are best served by being kept separate from one another.

State Responsibility for the Protection of Civilians

The notion of the responsible sovereign is long established, if not always adhered to in practice. Hobbes' *Leviathan* established that the state's authority depended on its capacity to protect individuals from the brutishness of the state of nature. As Peter Berkovitz explains: 'Only an agreed-upon sovereign with absolute and indivisible powers, argues Hobbes, can protect subjects from each other and from threats. But in the end, the subject's obligation to obey runs no further than the sovereign's capacity to protect'.[20] The idea that sovereigns should assist other sovereigns in the event of a disaster also has deep historical roots. In the eighteenth century, Emerich de Vattel argued that:

---

[20] Peter Berkowitz, 'Leviathan Then and Now,' *Policy Review*, Iss. 151 (October/November 2008), p. 18. I thank Edward Luck for this reference.

> [W]hen the occasion arises, every Nation should give its aid to further the advancement of other Nations and save them from disaster and ruin...To give assistance in such dire straits is so instinctive an act of humanity that hardly any civilized Nation is to be found which would absolutely refuse to do so...Whatever be the calamity affecting a Nation, the same help is due to it.[21]

Neither of these examples should give the impression that sovereignty as responsibility extended beyond these positions put forward by legal and political scholars. In international law, there was no obligation of the state to its citizens or to other sovereigns to relieve humanitarian distress until the 1949 Geneva Conventions, which applied only in situations of armed conflict.[22] In the event of disasters,[23] man-made or natural, the emphasis has been on the right of the sovereign to determine whether assistance is required, as opposed to the right of the persons affected to receive assistance or the duty of other sovereigns to assist.[24]

The absence of a right to assistance does not mean that there has been no concept of protection for persons, but it is declarative and thus not legally binding. The evolution of sovereignty has 'almost always entailed responsibilities', but what has undergone change is the 'scope of the relevant responsibilities, the identity of those to whom sovereigns are responsible and the effect of that relationship'.[25] We can see this development of sovereignty as responsibility when the Universal Declaration of Human Rights in 1948 declared the 'equal and inalienable rights of all members of the human family is the foundation of freedom, justice and peace in the world'.[26] The International Covenant on Economic, Social and Cultural Rights (ICESCR) clearly refers to multiple rights that an individual has the right to claim from their sovereign in times of peace, disaster and conflict – which include the right to life, food, shelter and health.[27] Since then, the General Assembly has passed numerous

---

21 Quoted in General Assembly, *Report of the International Law Commission*, Fifty-Eighth Session (1 May-9 June/3 July-11 August 2006), A/61/10, p. 469.

22 A/CN.4/590, p. 9.

23 For the purposes of this paper, 'disaster' is defined as 'a serious disruption of the functioning of society, excluding armed conflict, causing significant, widespread human, material or environmental loss', presently the definition used in Draft article 2, United Nations General Assembly, *Second Report on the protection of persons in the event of disasters by Eduardo Valencia-Ospina, Special Rapporteur*, Sixty-First Session (7 May 2009), A/CN.4/615, p. 15.

24 A/CN.4/598, p. 5, 19.

25 Alex J. Bellamy, *Responsibility to Protect: The Global Effort to End Mass Atrocities* (Cambridge: Polity Press, 2009), p. 33.

26 General Assembly, Universal Declaration of Human Rights, A/RES/217 (III) (1948) http://www.un.org/en/documents/udhr/ accessed: 9 November 2009.

27 General Assembly, International Covenant on Economic, Social and Cultural Rights, A/RES/2200 (XXI) (1966) http://www.un.org/Docs/asp/ws.asp?m=A/RES/2200 (XXI) accessed: 9 November 2009.

resolutions that declare the need for persons to be protected and rendered assistance in times of disaster: '[A]bandonment of the victims of natural disasters and similar emergency situations without humanitarian assistance constitutes a threat to human life and an offence to human dignity';[28] And: '[E]ach state has the responsibility first and foremost to take care of the victims of natural disasters and other emergencies occurring on its territory'.[29]

Attempts to articulate the specific responsibilities of sovereigns started to grow by the 1990s. The catalyst, Bellamy argues,[30] was the end of the Cold War and the United Nations Secretary General Boutros Boutros-Ghali's appointment of Francis Deng in 1992 to explore the urgent humanitarian need of displaced persons that had dramatically increased during and in the immediate aftermath of the Cold War period. It was the growing humanitarian crisis of internal displacement (there were 30 million displaced people by 1996), which led Deng to argue that it was one thing for sovereigns to claim territorial integrity as justification for non-intervention, but it should be another thing altogether to use it to deny humanitarian assistance.[31] Francis Deng and Roberta Cohen, both Senior Fellows at the Brookings Institution, conducted an in-depth study into the problem of IDPs. Prior to this, Deng and others had called for a 'pragmatic attempt at reconciling state sovereignty with responsibility' in the case of mass internal displacement in Africa.[32] They argued that by 'effectively discharging its responsibilities for good governance, a state can legitimately claim protection for its national sovereignty'.[33]

Deng continued this theme of sovereignty as responsibility in his UN study on IDPs with Roberta Cohen.[34] In 1998, he presented to the UN Human Rights Commission a 'Compilation and Analysis of the Legal Norms'

---

[28] General Assembly, *Humanitarian assistance to victims of natural disasters and similar emergency situations*, Forty-Fifth Session, A/RES/45/100 (14 December 1990).

[29] General Assembly, *Strengthening of the coordination of humanitarian emergency assistance of the United Nations, Forty-Seventh Session*, A/RES/46/182 (19 December 1991).

[30] Bellamy, *Responsibility to Protect*, p. 21.

[31] Francis M. Deng, Sadikiel Kimaro, Terrence Lyons, Donald Rothchild and I. William Zartman, *Sovereignty as Responsibility: Conflict Management in Africa* (Washington: Brookings Institution, 1996), pp. xi-xiv.

[32] The first phase, after the Peace of Westphalia, was when the sovereign 'reigned supreme domestically and in its relations with the outside world'. The second phase, after WWII, marked the erosion of sovereignty with the 'development of democratic values and institutions internally and with international accountability on the basis of human rights and humanitarian standards'. The end of the Cold War allowed the third phase – reactive assertion of sovereignty – to be ushered in. Deng et al, *Sovereignty as Responsibility*, p. 2.

[33] Ibid, p. 1.

[34] Roberta Cohen and Francis M. Deng, *Masses in Flight: the Global Crisis of International Displacement* and *Forsaken People: Case Studies of the Internally Displaced* (Washington: Brookings Institution, 1998).

of IDPs, which led to the Commission recommending that he draft Guiding Principles on Internal Displacement. The Guiding Principles were then adopted by the Commission in 1999. What was significant about the Guiding Principles was that they did not try to create 'new rights' but articulated the rights that states had already committed to and that individuals could claim from in situations where:

> [I]nternally displaced persons...who have been forced or obliged to flee or to leave their homes or places of habitual residence, in particular as a result of or in order to avoid the effects of armed conflict, situations of generalized violence, violations of human rights or natural or human-made disasters, and who have not crossed an internationally recognized State border.

Though the Guiding Principles are not legally binding, they have been adopted by the Human Rights Commission, the Executive Committee of the Office of the United Nations High Commissioner for Refugees (UNHCR) and reaffirmed by the General Assembly in the 2005 World Summit Outcome Document.[35] The Guiding Principles were based on the premise that both international humanitarian law and international human rights law articulate the responsibilities of governments for which they must be held accountable. What was important about the Guiding Principles was Deng's argument that sovereignty as responsibility meant that if a government was unwilling to provide protection and assistance (in this case to displaced populations), it '*must* accept aid from the international community'.[36]

It was after the affirmation of the Guiding Principles in 1999 that similar language was evoked by the UN Secretary-General Kofi Annan. In 2001, Annan argued while sovereignty offered vital protection it should 'not be a shield for crimes against humanity'.[37] Furthermore, in the same year, he suggested to the General Assembly that a framework outlining the responsibilities of states for receiving and providing assistance in the *event of a natural disaster* should be considered.[38] Neither point was received well by the General Assembly. However, as Bellamy notes, Annan's efforts 'helped to re-focus the debate. The question was now not whether sovereigns had responsibilities but

---

[35] 'We [Heads of State and Government] recognize the Guiding Principles on Internal Displacement as an important international framework for the protection of internally displaced persons and resolve to take effective measures to increase the protection of internally displaced persons', A/RES/60/1, paragraph 132.

[36] Emphasis added, Roberta Cohen, Developing an International System for Internally Displaced Persons, *International Studies Perspectives*, vol. 2, no. 2 (2006), p. 91.

[37] Quoted in Cohen, Developing an International System for Internally Displaced Persons, p. 91.

[38] A/55/82-E/2000/61, p. 23.

what those responsibilities were, how they were best realised and what role international society should play'.[39]

The question of sovereignty as responsibility was further expanded when the Canadian government established an International Commission on Intervention and State Sovereignty (ICISS) in 2000 – chaired by Gareth Evans and Mohammed Sahnoun – with the endorsement of Secretary-General Annan. Though the ICISS Report, which issued its findings in 2001 after extensive consultations via regional roundtables and national consultations, focused rather narrowly on the question of intervention, it drew almost unanimous agreement that there was indeed a sovereign responsibility to protect vulnerable populations (including in the event of a natural disaster).[40] The sovereignty as responsibility concept was subsequently outlined in the 2004 Report of the Secretary-General's High Level Panel on Threats, Challenges and Change, which argued that sovereignty 'clearly carries with it the obligation of a State to protect the welfare of its own peoples and meet its obligations to the wider international community'.[41] Furthermore, picking up on Deng's argument from 1999, it held that if a state remained unwilling to meet its obligations then 'the principles of collective security mean that some portion of those responsibilities should be taken up by the international community, acting in accordance with the Charter of the United Nations and the Universal Declaration of Human Rights, to help build the necessary capacity or supply the necessary protection'.[42] Finally, before the 2005 UN World Summit, Annan again argued that 'if national authorities are unable or unwilling to protect their citizens, then the responsibility shifts to the international community to use diplomatic, humanitarian and other methods to help protect the human rights and well being of civilian populations'.[43]

In 2005, states unanimously endorsed the R2P at the World Summit.[44] It is important to note that the scope of the 2005 World Summit is limited to only four specific crimes. Some have argued that the 2005 World Summit Outcome Document is only the start of a sweeping change to the practice and integrity

---

[39] Bellamy, *Responsibility to Protect*, p. 32.

[40] International Commission on Intervention and State Sovereignty (ICISS), *The Responsibility to Protect: Report of the International Commission on Intervention and State Sovereignty* (Ottawa: International Development Research Centre, 2001).

[41] General Assembly, *A More Secure World – Our Shared Responsibility*, Report of the Secretary-General's High Level Panel on Threats, Challenges and Change, A/59/565 (2 December 2004), p. 22.

[42] Ibid.

[43] Cohen, Developing an International System for Internally Displaced Persons, p. 91.

[44] See note 10.

of sovereignty[45] - to the point where the sovereign's claim of exclusive jurisdiction will increasingly fail to be a permissible excuse for inaction when populations are at risk. The call for intervention to assist populations devastated by Cyclone Nargis in Burma on 2 May 2008, when the Junta failed to allow humanitarian agencies access to the affected Ayeyawady Delta, has been offered as a case in point.[46] However, not only was it pointed out that there was no international legal justification for intervening to assist the Burmese population, but any attempt to provide humanitarian assistance through non-consensual intervention effort would have, in all likelihood, worsened the situation. Furthermore, as grave as the situation was in the Ayeyawady Delta, it did not amount to one of the four crimes under the responsibility to protect.[47]

As will be discussed in the next section, the protection of persons in the event of a disaster calls for different obligations to the responsibility to protect principle. While the ILC's programme of work on the protection of persons in the event of a disaster does share normative roots with the responsibility to protect, we need to be careful about trying to group together principles that have shared normative principles, but different political and legal parameters and practical applications.

Protection of Persons in the Event of a Disaster

In 2004, the same year as the UN Secretary-General's High Level Panel published its report endorsing R2P and three years after Secretary-General Kofi Annan had suggested to the General Assembly that a framework outlining the responsibilities of states for receiving and providing assistance in the onset of a natural disaster should be considered,[48] the ILC considered a submission from the Working Group on the Long-Term Programme of Work to study the protection of persons in critical situations. This was not the first time that some within UN Headquarters had raised the need for a codification of existing rules pertaining to responses to disasters by states, international organisations, and non-governmental organisations. In 1984, the then UN

45 Axworthy and Rock, R2P: An Unfinished Agenda, pp. 54-69.

46 Roberta Cohen, 'The Burma Cyclone and the Responsibility to Protect', *Global Responsibility to Protect*, vol.1, no.2 (2009), pp. 253-257.

47 Asia-Pacific Centre for the Responsibility to Protect, *Cyclone Nargis and the Responsibility to Protect*, 16 May 2008.

48 A/55/82-E/2000/61.

Secretary-General Javier Perez de Cuellar had attempted to introduce a convention on the provision of humanitarian assistance in the case of natural disasters, which failed to gain the support of the General Assembly. In 1994, Monaco proposed a convention on the establishment of safety zones in armed conflict and humanitarian disasters, which was also unsuccessful.[49] By 2004, the UN Secretariat had adopted a different strategy. Rather than seek immediate General Assembly support for a new instrument, it decided that it would first be useful to identify the degree of existing responsibility that states have already agreed to in the area of disaster response, then through the ILC programme highlight the protection and rights gaps that both states and the international community need to 'fill' to ensure the protection of vulnerable persons.[50]

In addition, calls for a study into existing legal rules surrounding protection of persons were generated by the Indian Ocean tsunami on 26 December 2004, which devastated coastal populations in Aceh (Indonesia), Thailand, Sri Lanka, India and Maldives, killing an estimated 227,000 people.[51] The humanitarian response to this immense disaster was generally effective, but some within the United Nations described it as a 'chaotic shoe-string operation in which small groups of overworked and exhausted people in the field and at headquarters constantly improvise to meet the unexpected problems and challenges of an extreme intercontinental catastrophe', not to mention the difficulties involved in convincing UN agencies to work under a new joint operation.[52] The scale of the disaster prompted a large number of non-governmental organisations to deploy to the region in a way that was generally 'unregulated or regulated [but] in a disparate manner'.[53] In 2006, after much discussion within Sixth Committee of the General Assembly and the Working Group itself, the convergence of the Tsunami event and the long standing push within the UN for codification of the protection of persons, led to the ILC accepting into its programme of work the 'protection of persons in the event of a disaster'. The intent was for the focus to be broad enough to include the existing legal norms surrounding the protection and humanitarian assistance needs of persons, but also narrow in that the focus would be on natural

---

[49] A/CN.4/590, p. 20, 156.

[50] Email correspondence with Arnold Pinto, UN Office of Legal Affairs Codification Division, April 2009. Correspondence held on file with author.

[51] Jan Egeland, *A Billion Lives: An Eyewitness Report from the Frontlines of Humanity* (New York: Simon & Schuster, 2008), p. 124.

[52] Ibid, p. 123, 127.

[53] Email correspondence with Arnold Pinto.

disasters and how to reconcile the sovereign right of the state to refuse assistance with the right of persons to receive assistance.

Some forums, such as the UN Inter-Agency Task Force for the International Strategy for Disaster Reduction (ISDR), tasked with assisting states to implement disaster reduction strategies and the 2005 Hyogo Framework for Action[54] – address both man-made and natural disasters as the 'distinction between natural and man-made is somewhat artificial'.[55] As will be discussed below, the Special Rapporteur Eduardo Valencia-Ospena has also argued that the study should explore both man-made and natural disasters, but this has not been met with unanimous support amongst states in the Sixth Committee. One proposed solution was for the study to address 'disasters that emerge from a natural cause (including those natural disasters that may occur in the theatre of an armed conflict)' in the first instance, to allow investigation into the rights surrounding persons affected by a natural diaster.[56]

In line with this rationale, the UN's Office of Legal Affairs suggested that the original focus of the study be on natural disasters, or natural disaster components of broader, complex emergencies. Two reports, one confidential and one available in the 2006 ILC report, explored how the protection of persons topic could be developed. The openly available report defined the protection of persons topic as including natural hazards such as 'earthquakes, floods, volcanic eruptions, landslides, hurricanes (typhoons and cyclones), tornadoes, tsunamis (tidal waves), droughts and plagues'.[57] The Secretariat acknowledged that the inclusion of international principles on disasters broader than the natural category could apply, but that the immediate focus should remain on natural disasters. As noted above, the main finding of the Secretariat's 2006 exploration of the topic was that there should be a 'set of provisions which would serve as a legal framework for the conduct of international disaster relief activities; clarifying the core legal principles and concepts and thereby creating a "legal" space in which such disaster relief work could take place on a secure footing'.[58]

With acceptance of the 'protection of persons' as part of the Commission's programme of work in 2006, the ILC appointed Eduardo Valencia-Ospina as Special Rapporteur. In the same year, the Secretariat was invited by the ILC to

[54] United Nations General Assembly, *International Strategy for Disaster Reduction*, A/RES/62/192, 11 February 2008.
[55] Email correspondence with Arnold Pinto.
[56] Email correspondence with Arnold Pinto.
[57] A/61/10, p. 465.
[58] Ibid. p. 475.

prepare a Memorandum detailing the existing legal instruments and texts that apply to disaster prevention, relief assistance and the protection of persons. The Secretariat's key finding was that the law on the right to humanitarian assistance in disasters remained inconclusive.[59] Furthermore, it found no general convention that governs all aspects of disaster relief, which was notable when compared to the comprehensive international humanitarian law that seeks to protect civilians and their humanitarian needs during armed conflicts, such as the Fourth 1949 Geneva Convention, and Protocols I and II (1977).[60]

The Memorandum found that on the question of access, international law tended to privilege the protection of sovereignty and territorial integrity over the protection of civilians. The 'principles of sovereignty and non-intervention contain two important corollaries: that disaster relief carried out by assisting actors is subject to the consent of the receiving State and that the receiving State has the primary responsibility for the protection of persons on its territory and subject to its jurisdiction or control during a disaster'.[61] The Memorandum went on to argue that states have remained reluctant to cede sovereign control because they remained suspicious that external actors will use the guise of 'humanitarian assistance' to promote their own political agendas. Even the 2005 World Summit Outcome document – despite at least four references to disaster preparedness and response – did not affirm the right of individuals to assistance in the event of a natural or man-made disaster.[62]

However, the Memorandum also revealed that while legal convention yielded to sovereignty for humanitarian actors seeking to gain access to disaster victims, there has been, over the last couple of decades, a growing corresponding duty of sovereigns (though not legally proscribed) to *not deny* assistance. Especially in situations where the state proved unable to effectively meet the needs of disaster victims. One important development in this area was a finding by the International Court of Justice (ICJ) on the Nicaragua-US Contra affair in the early 1980s. The US government had claimed that its military assistance to the rebel Contras was humanitarian.[63] In *Nicaragua vs. US*, finding against the US, the ICJ judged that while states could refuse assistance, the 'provision of strictly humanitarian aid to persons or forces in another

[59] A/CN.4/590, p. 3.
[60] A/CN.4/590, p. 9, 153.
[61] Ibid, p. 2.
[62] A/RES/60/1.
[63] A/CN.4/590, p. 21.

country, whatever their political affiliation or objectives, cannot be regarded as *unlawful intervention*, or as in any other way contrary to international law'.[64] In sum, the ICJ found that although the provision of military assistance by the US was unlawful, the provision of genuine humanitarian aid without the consent of the host state would not have been an unlawful act. As the Memorandum notes, this was a landmark decision for it revealed that the sovereign right to refuse humanitarian aid does not prevail in situations where the aid is necessary, nor does the provision of humanitarian aid without government consent breach sovereignty. Thus, the ICJ found that humanitarian aid in response to disasters was significantly different to other forms of intervention in legal terms.

The Memorandum found that the duty to accept assistance had been further supported by two General Assembly Resolutions - 45/100 (1990) and 46/182 (1991).[65] The first resolution (45/100) specified the responsibility of the state to take care of victims of natural disasters, and the primary role of the sovereign to coordinate humanitarian assistance within its territory. General Assembly Resolution 46/182, which was passed in 1991, goes on to detail the responsibility to accept assistance. The fourth paragraph set out in very clear terms the right of the sovereign to decide whether to request and accept humanitarian assistance, but paragraph 6 qualified this, stating: 'states whose populations are in need of humanitarian assistance are called upon to facilitate the work of these [humanitarian] organizations in implementing humanitarian assistance, in particular the supply of food, medicines, shelter and health care, for which access to victims is essential'.[66] We see this corresponding duty of sovereigns to accept assistance aimed at protecting persons in the event of a disaster emerge again in the 1998 Guiding Principles on IDPs. The Guiding Principles stated bluntly that 'national authorities have the primary duty and responsibility to provide protection and humanitarian assistance to internally displaced persons within their jurisdiction'. This obligation, as noted earlier, extends to persons displaced by natural diasters.[67]

Of greater legal importance than these declarations, principles and judgements are the number of bilateral and multilateral arrangements involving ASEAN (2005), EU (1987, 2001, 2007) and OAS (2007),[68] through which

---

[64] Ibid, p. 23.

[65] A/RES/45/100; A/RES/46/182.

[66] A/RES/46/182, paragraph 6.

[67] UN Commission on Human Rights, *Guiding Principles on Internal Displacement*, E/CN.4/1998/53/Add.2, 11 February 1998.

[68] Reference originals.

states have recognised a sovereign duty to address disasters by, among other things, agreeing to monitor their vulnerability to disasters and setting in place response strategies to deal with a disaster's aftermath, including in some texts a responsibility to reduce the 'spillover' effects of a disaster that might affect neighbouring states (e.g. water contamination after floods).[69] For example, the 2005 ASEAN Agreement on Disaster Management and Emergency Response is particularly noteworthy for advancing the notion of a sovereign's duty to respond to disasters. It is important to note that this Agreement came after the Indian Ocean Tsunami disaster, which no doubt provided the impetus. The Agreement also recalled General Assembly Resolutions 46/182 (1991)[70] and 57/758 (2002)[71] to highlight pre-existing responsibilities to integrate disaster management 'in all its aspects', adopt a culture of prevention and, strengthen cooperation amongst States in the field of diaster preparedness and response.[72] Furthermore, the Agreement's definition of 'disaster' was quite broad – defining disasters as a 'serious disruption of the functioning of a community or a society causing widespread human, material, economic or environmental losses'.[73] The Agreement thus made no effort to delineate between 'man-made' and 'natural' disasters and in Article 5(a) identified both 'natural and human-induced hazards' as requiring state responses.[74] There are two further important points about the ASEAN Agreement. First, it states that Member States have a general obligation to 'immediately respond to a disaster occurring within their territory'. Furthermore, 'when the said disaster is likely to cause possible impacts on other Member States, [the affected state shall] respond promptly to a request for relevant information sought by a Member State or States that are or may be affected by such disasters, with a view to minimising the consequences'.[75] Second, each state is to set up a National Focal Point who can communicate their response to the ASEAN Co-ordinating Centre for Humanitarian Assistance (AHA Centre) on disaster management to indicate what action they are taking to identify and monitor disaster risk. Moreover, the AHA Centre can request data from National Focal Points on disaster risk

[69] A/C.4/590, p. 30-36.
[70] A/RES/46/182.
[71] A/RES/57/758.
[72] ASEAN, *ASEAN Agreement on Disaster Management and Emergency Response*, Vientiane, 26 July 2005, p. 2.
[73] Ibid, Article 1.3.
[74] Ibid, Article 5.1.a.
[75] Ibid, Article 4.b.

management and response, and provide data identifying their response to disasters management and provide regional-risk level analysis.[76]

In the ASEAN Agreement, we see a regional organisation, renowned for its emphasis on national sovereignty and non-interference, adopting measures that call upon states to respond to natural or man-made disasters, to prepare for disasters, and to accept regional efforts to respond and mitigate the effects of the disaster from reaching them. Sovereignty as responsibility is a corollary of the Agreement – that when sovereigns fail to adequately respond to a disaster, ASEAN can approach the state to request that it accepts assistance. To some extent, we saw this in practice with the role played by ASEAN Secretary-General Surin Pitsuwan in the aftermath of Cyclone Nargis in Myanmar in May 2008.

The ASEAN Agreement also refers to the 2005 Hyogo Declaration and the 2005-2015 Hyogo Framework for Action. 168 states were present at the adoption of the Hyogo Framework for Disaster Reduction, which stated that:

> Taking into account the importance of international cooperation and partnerships, each State has the primary responsibility for its own sustainable development and for taking effective measures to reduce disaster risk, including for the protection of people on its territory, infrastructure and other national assets from the impact of disasters. At the same time, in the context of increasing global interdependence, concerted international cooperation and an enabling international environment are required to stimulate and contribute to developing the knowledge, capacities and motivation needed for disaster risk reduction at all levels.[77]

Within both the Framework above, and the Declaration below, states acknowledged their responsibility to protect their populations in the event of a disaster, and to mitigate the effect of a disaster through risk reduction:

> We affirm that States have the primary responsibility to protect the people and property on their territory from hazards, and thus, it is vital to give high priority to disaster risk reduction in national policy, consistent with their capacities and the resources available to them. We concur that strengthening community level capacities to reduce disaster risk at the local level is especially needed, considering that appropriate disaster reduction measures at that level enable the communities and individuals to reduce significantly their vulnerability to hazards. Disasters remain a major threat to the survival, dignity, livelihood and security of peoples and communities, in particular the poor. Therefore there is an urgent need to enhance the capacity of disaster- prone developing countries in particular, the

[76] Ibid, Article 5.4.

[77] International Strategy for Disaster Reduction (ISDR), *Hyogo Framework for Action 2005-2015: Building the Resilience of Nations and Communities to Disasters*, World Conference on Disaster Reduction 18-22 January 2005, Kobe, Hyogo, Japan, p. 4.

> least developed countries and small island developing States, to reduce the impact of disasters, through strengthened national efforts and enhanced bilateral, regional and international cooperation, including through technical and financial assistance.[78]

Though not legally binding, 168 states recognised their responsibility to protect people from hazards that significantly increase their risk of harm. Though there remain gaps in this Framework – in particular the resistance of industrialised countries to providing financial assistance to low-income, disaster-prone countries – this far-reaching declaration linking the 'responsibility' of states to the protection of their population in the event of a disaster was a significant breakthrough for the sovereignty as responsibility concept.

Another example of this concept being incorporated into international law was the reformulation of state obligations to respond to health emergencies that constitute 'a public health risk to other States through the international spread of disease' into the International Health Regulation (IHR) revisions in 2005.[79] The World Health Assembly (WHA) agreed unanimously in 2005 to revise the infectious disease notification protocols under the IHR. The revised IHR calls upon a signatory state to notify WHO and neighbouring states of a suspected disease outbreak that could constitute a 'public health emergency of international concern' and, if the affected state failed to notify WHO, then neighbouring states and non-state actors under the revised IHR have the right to notify WHO of the suspected disease outbreak.[80] In contrast to the Hyogo Declaration, the revised IHR is legally binding (and all 192 WHA members have signed on to the revised IHR between 2005 and 2007). Again, this represents an important shift in thinking about what sovereigns are responsible for in relation to containing and responding to domestic events.[81] However, it is important to note that in the case of the IHR, WHO still requires the state to verify the report of an outbreak before it can send fieldwork response teams to assist in containing the outbreak, and the obligation to report only exists if the domestic event could pose an international threat.

These developments represent a shift from the 'reactive reassertion of sovereignty' that Francis Deng noted in the early 1990s, to a more nuanced,

---

[78] ISDR, *Hyogo Declaration*, World Conference on Disaster Reduction 18-22 January 2005, Kobe, Hyogo, Japan, p. 2.

[79] WHO, *International Health Regulations* (2005), 1st Edn. (Geneva: World Health Organisation, 2005). Accessed online: http://www.who.int/csr/ihr/IHR_2005_en.pdf Date accessed: 20 July 2007.

[80] WHO, *International Health Regulations.*

[81] A/C.4/590: 38-40.

negotiated understanding of 'reconciling state sovereignty with responsibility'.[82] While none of the frameworks or agreements indicate an international legal shift in relation to the role of the state, humanitarian assistance and the protection of persons, they reflect a growing recognition that sovereigns have responsibilities to protect persons within the state and contain the risk of disaster hazards spreading beyond territorial borders. Therefore, there is an emerging sovereign duty to request assistance, if not yet an individual right to receive assistance. Importantly, the duty of the sovereign increases if the disaster is deemed to have implications for neighbouring states and the broader international community. As indicated in some of the multilateral agreements noted above, these developments contribute to an already evolving positive duty on the part of affected states to request assistance - especially if domestic capacity is overwhelmed or if the disaster has the potential to become a 'transboundary hazard'.

But what recourse do civilians have in the event of a disaster if their host state is incapable of providing basic aid and is unwilling to request international assistance? Valencia-Ospina concluded that the right to humanitarian assistance is directly related to the protection of persons because 'it is presently uncertain whether existing international law takes into account all of the legitimate needs of persons affected by disaster'.[83] Likewise, the ILC Memorandum argued that 'the unique situation that disasters present leads to yet another specialized conceptualisation of protection, including, for example, access to the victims, securing safe zones, the provision of adequate and prompt relief and ensuring respect for human rights'.[84] Existing human rights obligations already provide people with rights in these situations but fulfilment of these obligations is dependent upon states recognising that they have a duty to respect, protect and fulfil such rights.[85] It was therefore clear that work was needed to translate these general rights and principles into something more concrete in terms of protection to vulnerable populations.

One possible solution was to base the protection of persons on the R2P principle, agreed by states at the UN World Summit in 2005. As noted above, Valencia-Ospina mentioned this as a possibility in his first report. He observed that R2P was relevant to the protection of persons, as both focus on the sovereign's responsibility to protect individuals from harm. He argued that:

---

[82] Deng et al, *Sovereignty as Responsibility*, p. 2.
[83] A/CN.4/598, p. 19.
[84] A/C.4/590, p. 149.
[85] UN Committee on Social, Economic and Cultural Rights, The right to the highest attainable standard of health, E/C.12/2000/4 (General Comments), 11 August 2000.

> [T]he traditional State system is currently witnessing the emergence of various concepts related to the responsibility of States. As the Secretariat noted in its proposal for the topic, the protection of persons may be located within contemporary reflection on an emerging principle entailing the responsibility to protect. The latter concept entails the responsibility to prevent, react and rebuild, corresponding, respectively, to the three phases of a disaster situation.[86]

After the presentation of the Special Rapporteur's preliminary report, the Sixth Committee of the General Assembly met in 2008 to hear the views of states. China, India, Malaysia and Sri Lanka suggested that the study should lead only to the construction of guidelines that focused exclusively on the responses of humanitarian actors in the immediate event of a natural disaster. They insisted that it was essential that the study recognise the sovereign right to determine whether international assistance was necessary. A rights based approach would not do this and was therefore unacceptable to these states. In addition, they argued that the ILC should consider only the topic of natural disasters, as originally suggested by the Secretariat, and consider man-made disasters only at a later date and in a separate programme of work. Special Rapporteur Valencia-Ospina found lukewarm support for exploring the right to assistance from France, New Zealand, Netherlands, Italy, and the International Federation of the Red Cross (ICRC) – who framed the non-binding IDRL Guidelines in 2006. However, Germany and New Zealand supported a broad definition of disaster and humanitarian assistance (prevention, response and mitigation) but both agreed with China, India, Malaysia and Sri Lanka that the best way of achieving protection may not be through an international 'right' of protection. From these discussions it can be surmised that the arguments presented for this case were threefold. First, the granting of humanitarian access was the exclusive privilege of sovereigns and claiming that individuals have a right to protection in the event of a disaster would not abrogate or limit this sovereign right. Second, it was argued that sovereigns are responsible for establishing the capacity to respond to disasters and that international law cannot compel states do this through the use of 'rights' language. Third, and partly as a result of the first two points, it was argued that the focus for efforts to strengthen the protection of persons should be on assistance responses through bilateral and regional multilateral arrangements framed by an international framework rather than on binding global norms.

There was little enthusiasm for aligning the protection of persons study to the responsibility to protect. The arguments ranged from opposition to the

[86] A/CN.4/598, p. 19.

concept of R2P itself, to the less extreme argument that R2P simply does not apply to natural disasters. Sri Lanka and India, for example, sought to challenge the principle itself. Sri Lanka argued that the Special Rapporteur should be 'cautious in invoking concepts [such as R2P] which are essentially political in nature, the precise legal contours of which are yet to be developed and established and which could drag the work of the Commission into an avoidable mire of political controversy'.[87] India also argued that R2P did not apply 'in the context of persons affected by a disaster [and] is not appropriate for inclusion within the scope of the topic, as the primary responsibility for the protection of persons in its territory of within its jurisdiction lies on the State concerned'.[88] Both, in essence, rejected the notion of sovereignty as responsibility. China also opposed any link between R2P and protection of persons – arguing that the R2P is a 'new concept'. It continued, 'there are still controversies as to its connotation and applicability, resulting in great uncertainty over this concept. To introduce this concept into the area of disaster relief will not be helpful to achieving international consensus on this concept; rather, it will only lead to further confusion'.[89] Sri Lanka agreed, noting that the World Summit Outcome document itself stated that R2P applied only to 'very specific and extreme situations of gross violations of human rights'.[90]

In contrast, others noted that while the link between sovereignty and protection was not unwarranted, the application of R2P was technically misplaced. Malaysia noted that in accordance with the World Summit Outcome document, the responsibility to protect populations only arose in the case of the four crimes – genocide, war crimes, ethnic cleansing and crimes against humanity. A larger debate, Malaysia argued, would be 'required [as to] whether

---

[87] Permanent Mission of Sri Lanka Mission to United Nations, Protection of Persons in the event of disasters – Statement by Dr Rohan Perera P. C. Member ILC, 60th Session of ILC, Geneva, 18 July 2008. http:///www.lankamission.org/index2.php?opition=com_content&task=view&id=579&p accessed 9 April 2009.

[88] Permanent Mission of India to United Nations, Statement by Mr Rajeev Shukla, Member of Parliament and Member of the Indian Delegation, on Agenda Item 75 – Report of the International Law Commission on the Work of its 60th Session – Chapter VII – Responsibility of International Organisations, Chapter VIII – Expulsion of Aliens, Chapter IX – Protection of Persons in the Event of Disasters, and Chapter X – Immunity of State Officials from Foreign Criminal Jurisdiction at the Sixth Committee of the 63rd Session of the United Nations General Assembly on November 03 2008.

[89] Permanent Mission of the People's Republic of China to the UN, Statement by H.E. Ambassador Liu Zhenmin, Deputy Permanent Representative of China to the UN, at the Sixth Committee of the 63rd Session of the UN General Assembly, on Item 75: Report of the International Law Commission on the Work of its 60th Session – Part Three, 3 November 2008. http://www.china-un.org/eng/hyyfy/t520980.htm accessed: 9 April 2009.

[90] Ibid.

the Security Council's Chapter VII powers for the maintenance of international peace and security can be invoked to authorise "humanitarian intervention"'.[91] It is clear therefore that since the 2005 World Summit, most states agree that R2P should be carefully contained to the four crimes defined in Paragraph 138.[92] Any attempt to expand this concept would therefore provoke sharp political resistance, hindering implementation. Therefore, to ensure the advancement of the protection of persons it is important to separate the relationship between R2P and protection of persons. However, this does not mean that the concept of sovereignty as responsibility has no link to the protection of persons – just as the R2P principle has derived from a broader normative position on sovereignty, so too has the principle of the protection persons in the event of a natural or man-made disaster. This brings us to the questions of whether, and how, the broader concept of sovereignty as responsibility relates to the provision of assistance to persons in the event of a disaster.

Conclusion

Aligning the R2P with the protection of persons study would damage both principles. The protection of persons in the event of disasters is being developed with the hope of eliciting a legal obligation on states to ensure that affected persons have access to disaster relief; the R2P is a political principle that aims to mobilise states to implement existing legal obligations in relation to genocide, war crimes, ethnic cleansing, and crimes against humanity.[93] Though both principles evoke the concept of sovereignty as responsibility, there is an important difference in their purpose. R2P is about preventing and halting crimes that are clearly prohibited by international law; at present, protection of persons is about trying to create norms that will improve the provision of disaster relief by states (whether man-made or not). Therefore, aligning the protection of persons agenda to R2P would do little to advance the existing legal protections enjoyed by people in the event of a disaster and would in all probability increase international opposition to the establishment of a legal

[91] Permanent Mission of Malaysia to United Nations, Statement by Ms Baizure Kamal, Representative of Malaysia on Agenda Item 75: Report of the International Law Commission on the Works of its Sixtieth Session at the Sixth Committee of the Sixty Third Session of the United Nations General Assembly, New York, 3 November 2008., p. 4.

[92] See note 15.

[93] Ekkehard Strauss, 'A Bird in the Hand is Worth Two in the Bush – On the Assumed Legal Nature of the Responsbility to Protect', *Global Responsibility to Protect*, vol. 1, no. 3 (2009), p. 320.

framework. For R2P, alignment with protection of persons would sidetrack the principle and make it impossible to distinguish R2P situations from any situation warranting humanitarian aid, significantly diluting the principle's purpose and, therefore, its political utility.

One principle, R2P, requires action by the state and the international community to commit to the legal, moral and political imperatives they have already agreed to for preventing and halting mass atrocities and genocide. In the case of protection of persons, while we have seen an emerging norm calling upon states to assist persons in the event of a disaster – as demonstrated most recently in the ASEAN Disaster Preparedness Agreement – the premise for such a duty is to protect neighbouring states from the flow on of an uncontained disaster, rather than the right of individuals to humanitarian relief. Therefore, while the concept of sovereignty as responsibility underpins both the R2P and protection of persons principles, they are at different purposes and stages of implementation. R2P is concerned with deepening the commitment that states have made to protecting individuals against mass atrocities and genocide. The protection of persons agenda is yet to gain acceptance by states and there is no evidence to suggest that this cause would be helped by aligning it with R2P. The decision this year in the ILC to not align R2P with protection of persons should therefore be applauded. The shared normative history of both these principles must not be confused with their important differences and requirements.

Chapter Eight

The International Community's Responsibility to Protect

Luke Glanville[1]

The concept of the 'responsibility to protect' (R2P) holds that not only do sovereign states bear a responsibility to protect their populations, but so too does the international community. The international community is said to be responsible for encouraging and assisting states to protect and also for taking collective action to enforce the protection of populations in instances where states fail to carry out their obligations. The endorsement by member states at the UN World Summit in 2005 of this notion that the international community itself bears an R2P was to some degree ambiguous. However, the idea was clearly promoted by UN Secretary-General Ban Ki-moon in his January 2009 report, 'Implementing the Responsibility to Protect',[2] and has been widely adopted in the discourse of states.

This idea that the international community bears responsibilities is perhaps the most novel aspect of the R2P concept. After all, the idea that sovereigns themselves are responsible for the protection of their populations has been central to justifications for sovereign authority since the sixteenth and seventeenth centuries.[3] While the precise nature of these sovereign responsibilities may have varied and evolved over time, it has been a common refrain since Thomas Hobbes wrote *Leviathan* that the end for which sovereigns are trusted

---

[1] An earlier version of this chapter was presented at the Asia-Pacific Centre for the Responsibility to Protect's seminar series, October 2009. I would like to thank the participants at this seminar for their helpful comments and also Alex Bellamy, Sara Davies, Richard Devetak, Sarah Teitt, and Clare Glanville for useful feedback on drafts. Correspondence should be addressed to l.glanville@griffith.edu.au or lukeglanville@hotmail.com

[2] 'Implementing the Responsibility to Protect: Report of the Secretary-General', A/63/677, 12 January 2009, p. 9.

[3] See Luke Glanville, 'The Antecedents of "Sovereignty as Responsibility"', *European Journal of International Relations* (Forthcoming).

with authority is the safety of the people.[4] Even during the Cold War, when the rights of sovereign states to freedom from outside interference became so firmly entrenched, international society willingly declared that states bore a 'duty...to observe, promote and defend all human rights and fundamental freedoms within their own territories...'[5] And the notion that the international community bears a *right* (as distinct from a responsibility) to enforce the performance of sovereign responsibilities is also an idea with a long history. Early modern jurists such as Jean Bodin and Hugo Grotius had provided for forcible action by neighbouring princes and states in response to tyranny and in defence of oppressed peoples, and the doctrine of 'humanitarian intervention' had been widely accepted in international law in the nineteenth and early twentieth centuries.[6] And during the 1990s, before the development of R2P, the Security Council had repeatedly authorised sanctions and military interventions in response to the failure of governments to protect their own people. The notion that the international community itself bears an R2P, on the other hand, is a concept that does not enjoy such well-established historical roots. And it would seem to have extraordinary implications, not least for the protection of internally displaced persons who, as other contributors to this volume have demonstrated, so often require protection from the international community in accordance with R2P. Yet, this aspect of R2P remains largely under-examined.

To date, while much has been written about the responsibilities of states and the *permissibility* of holding states to account for their actions, there has been little attempt to conceptualise or understand what is implied in the notion that the international community bears a *responsibility* to act to protect populations. A few scholars have sought to examine the international community's R2P from particular perspectives such as international law,[7] morality,[8] and US

[4] Thomas Hobbes, *Leviathan* (Oxford: Oxford University Press, 1996), xxx:1, p. 222.

[5] Declaration on the Inadmissibility of Intervention and Interference in the Internal Affairs of States, UNGA Resolution 36/103, 9 December 1981.

[6] See Jean-Pierre L. Fonteyne, 'The Customary International Law Doctrine of Humanitarian Intervention: Its Current Validity under the U.N. Charter', *California Western International Law Journal* 4 (1974). For a slightly more cautious assessment, see Simon Chesterman, *Just War or Just Peace? Humanitarian Intervention and International Law* (Oxford: Oxford University Press, 2001), pp. 35-42.

[7] Louise Arbour, 'The Responsibility to Protect as a Duty of Care in International Law and Practice', *Review of International Studies* 34 (2008), Sheri P. Rosenberg, 'Responsibility to Protect: A Framework for Prevention', *Global Responsibility to Protect* 1/4 (2009).

[8] Carla Bagnoli, 'Humanitarian Intervention as a Perfect Duty', in Terry Nardin, and Melissa S. Williams (eds.), *Humanitarian Intervention* (New York: New York University Press, 2006), Kok-Chor Tan, 'The Duty to Protect', in Terry Nardin, and Melissa S. Williams (eds.), *Humanitarian Intervention* (New York: New York University Press, 2006).

domestic politics.[9] But little attention has been paid to the broad questions that need to be considered if we are to comprehend what it means for the international community to bear such a responsibility. At first glance, one such question revolves around the application of the term 'responsibility'. Responsibility implies accountability or answerability. Indeed, the term comes from the Latin *respondeo*, meaning 'I answer'.[10] The question arises, therefore: how and to whom can the international community be said to be responsible? Indeed, the seeming unaccountability of the international community, and of particular international institutions such as the UN Security Council, has been the focus of attention by some of R2P's strongest critics.[11]

The purpose of this chapter is to think through issues such as these in order to begin to determine how the notion that the international community bears a responsibility to protect may be fruitfully conceptualised and understood. I suggest that two central questions need to be addressed. The first asks: what kind of responsibility is it – is it moral, legal, or political, or some combination of the three? Over the past two decades, several scholars have usefully divided their examinations of the *right* of the international community to respond to mass atrocities and human suffering into these three categories.[12] It would seem that we can consider the *responsibility* to protect populations using the same framework, though the findings of such an examination would of course be different. The second question asks: who bears the responsibility – is it the international community broadly speaking, or is it particular international institutions, regional organisations, or individual states? This question speaks to concerns about whether the duty is 'perfectible' and whether we can reasonably expect it to be performed.

The chapter proceeds in four sections. First, I will provide a brief overview of the development of the notion that the international community bears a

---

[9] Jon Western, 'Humanitarian Intervention, American Public Opinion, and the Future of R2P', *Global Responsibility to Protect* 1/3 (2009).

[10] J. R. Lucas, *Responsibility* (Oxford: Clarendon Press, 1993), p. 5. *Black's Law Dictionary* defines 'responsibility' as 'the state of being answerable for an obligation', and defines 'responsible' as 'liable, legally accountable or answerable.' Quoted in J. Angelo Corlett, *Responsibility and Punishment* (London: Kluwer, 2001), p. 9.

[11] See, for example, David Chandler, '*The Responsibility to Protect*? Imposing the "Liberal Peace"', *International Peacekeeping* 11/1 (2004), Philip Cunliffe, 'Sovereignty and the Politics of Responsibility', in Christopher J. Bickerton, Philip Cunliffe, and Alexander Gourevitch (eds.), *Politics without Sovereignty: A Critique of Contemporary International Relations* (New York: UCL Press, 2007).

[12] A particularly noteworthy example is J.L. Holzgrefe, and Robert O. Keohane (eds.), *Humanitarian Intervention: Ethical, Legal, and Political Dilemmas* (Cambridge: Cambridge University Press, 2003).

responsibility to protect populations from the adoption of the Genocide Convention (1948) until the present day. In the remaining three sections I will outline some preliminary thoughts regarding how we might think about this idea from a moral, legal, and political perspective. I will weave into these three sections consideration of who in particular might bear the responsibility and whether or not they may pay a cost for failure to carry it out in certain instances. I do not seek to provide a comprehensive study of the international community's R2P in this chapter, and neither would space permit such a study. Rather, I intend merely to offer a framework for conceptualising and understanding the responsibility borne by the international community for the protection of populations from mass atrocities and grave human suffering, and to outline some of the key avenues for further inquiry that are suggested by this framework.

The development of the international community's responsibility to protect

On 9 December 1948, the UN General Assembly adopted the Convention on the Prevention and Punishment of the Crime of Genocide. Contracting parties to the Convention declared genocide to be 'a crime under international law which they undertake to prevent and to punish.'[13] I will consider the Convention in greater detail later in the chapter. For now it suffices to observe that it has been read by some scholars to provide a legal obligation upon states to prevent and punish genocide even when it occurs beyond their borders.[14] While this legal reading is at best controversial, it would seem clear that after the Convention was adopted there did gradually emerge a belief that the international community or particular powerful states bore some kind of obligation – if not legal then moral or political – to intervene in response to the occurrence of genocide. This belief came to the fore in the 1990s, most obviously in the context of the Rwandan genocide. In 1994, the United States in particular consciously avoided characterising the violence in Rwanda as 'genocide' out of fear that such a determination could trigger unwanted

---

[13] Article I, UNGA Resolution 260 A (III).

[14] For overviews of legal readings of the Convention, see Jeffrey S. Morton, and Neil Vijay Singh, 'The International Legal Regime on Genocide', *Journal of Genocide Research* 5/1 (2003), William A. Schabas, *Genocide in International Law: The Crimes of Crimes* (Cambridge: Cambridge University Press, 2000).

social pressures and political obligations to 'do something'.[15] This behaviour can be read as implicit recognition of an international responsibility to prevent genocide.[16] The apologies later offered by US President Bill Clinton, UN Secretary-General Kofi Annan, and others for the 'failure' of the international community to rescue victims of atrocities in Rwanda and also Srebrenica in the 1990s similarly constituted tacit acknowledgement of an obligation borne by the international community to enforce the protection of populations.[17]

Over the next few years, a concept emerged which holds that the international community possesses not merely the right but the responsibility to protect populations from grave violations of human rights when sovereign states fail to do so. This move was signaled by Secretary-General Perez de Cuellar in 1991 when he called for agreement not on 'the right of intervention but the collective obligation of States to bring relief and redress in human rights emergencies.'[18] In articulating the principle of 'sovereignty as responsibility' in the 1990s, Special Representative on Internally Displaced Persons Francis Deng argued that the international community bears not only a right but a responsibility to hold sovereigns to account for their treatment of populations. 'To the extent that the international community is the ultimate guarantor of the universal standards that safeguard the rights of all human beings,' he insisted, 'it has a corresponding responsibility to provide innocent victims of internal conflicts and gross violations of human rights with essential protection and assistance.'[19] This notion was further developed by the International Commission on Intervention and State Sovereignty whose report, *The Responsibility to Protect*, released in December 2001, quickly became a touchstone for debate. While the 'default responsibility' for the

---

[15] See Linda Melvern, *A People Betrayed: The Role of the West in Rwanda's Genocide* (London: Zed Books, 2000), Samantha Power, *'A Problem from Hell': America and the Age of Genocide* (London: Flamingo, 2002), pp. 329-90.

[16] Luke Glanville, 'Is "Genocide" Still a Powerful Word?' *Journal of Genocide Research* 11/4 (2009).

[17] See Kofi A. Annan, 'Statement on Receiving the Report of the Independent Inquiry into the Actions of the United Nations During the 1994 Genocide in Rwanda', 16 December 1999, James Bennet, 'Clinton Declares U.S., with World, Failed Rwandans', *New York Times* 26 March 1998.

[18] Javier Perez de Cuellar, 'Report of the Secretary-General on the Work of the Organization', UN Document A/46/1, 13 September 1991, p. 5.

[19] Francis M. Deng, Sadikel Kimaro, Terrence Lyons, Donald Rothchild and I. William Zartman, *Sovereignty as Responsibility: Conflict Management in Africa* (Washington D.C.: Brookings Institution, 1996), pp. xii-xiii.

protection of populations rests with the host state, the report suggested, the international community bears a 'residual responsibility'.[20] 'Where a population is suffering serious harm, as a result of internal war, insurgency, repression or state failure, and the state in question is unwilling or unable to halt or avert it, the principle of non-intervention yields to the international responsibility to protect.'[21]

This notion that the international community bears an R2P was endorsed only to a degree by member states at the 2005 UN World Summit. In the agreement negotiated at the Summit, member states consensually declared that the international community '*should*, as appropriate, encourage and help states' to carry out their responsibilities and that it bears 'the *responsibility* to use appropriate diplomatic, humanitarian and other peaceful means, in accordance with Chapters VI and VIII of the Charter, to help to protect populations from genocide, war crimes, ethnic cleansing and crimes against humanity.' However, with respect to Chapter VII enforcement of the protection of populations in instances where states had 'manifestly failed' to provide such protection, the society of states only declared that they were '*prepared* to take collective action…on a case-by-case basis', rather than asserting that they were *obliged* to do so.[22]

It was possibly only the intervention of US Ambassador to the UN John Bolton that prevented a firmer declaration in this regard. The US was reluctant to bind itself to respond to particular cases in particular ways. Consequently, it sought to reject any suggestion that it might be obliged to act when states fail to protect their populations.[23] An early draft of the Summit document had stated, 'we recognize our shared responsibility to take collective action…'[24] Upon reading this draft, Bolton insisted that it should be made clear that 'the responsibility of the other countries in the international community is not of the same character as the responsibility of the host…' While states might have a legal obligation to protect their own populations, he argued, the responsibility of the international community to act was a 'moral responsibility' rather than

---

[20] ICISS, *The Responsibility to Protect: Report of the International Commission on Intervention and State Sovereignty* (Ottawa: IDRC, 2001), p. 17.

[21] Ibid., xi.

[22] Emphasis added. UN Document A/60/L.1, 15 September 2005, para. 138-39.

[23] See Edward C. Luck, 'Sovereignty, Choice, and the Responsibility to Protect', *Global Responsibility to Protect* 1/1 (2009).

[24] 'Revised draft outcome document of the High-level Plenary Meeting of the General Assembly of September 2005 submitted by the President of the General Assembly', A/59/HLP/CRP.1/Rev.2, 5 August 2005.

a legal one. 'Accordingly, we should avoid language that focuses on the obligation or responsibility of the international community and instead assert that we are prepared to take action.' The determination of what particular measures to adopt in specific cases, he insisted, 'cannot be predetermined in the abstract but should remain a decision within the purview of the Security Council.'[25] Bolton was successful in having the language watered down in this regard. Consequently, while the 2005 World Summit agreement does point in the direction of the notion that the international community bears an R2P, it does not explicitly delineate this responsibility at least with respect to the use of collective action under Chapter VII in response to the 'manifest failure' of states to protect their own populations.

For a couple of years after the Summit, the US continued to resist the notion that the international community bears an R2P. In Security Council debates on the protection of civilians in armed conflict, the US repeatedly emphasised that primary responsibility for protection lies with the host state and tended to downplay the notion that the international community might be bound by a responsibility of equivalent weight.[26] However, US officials frequently strayed from this position. In 2006, for example, Secretary of State Condoleezza Rice noted in reference to the crisis in Darfur, 'It is our responsibility to protect those who cannot protect themselves. If the idea of an international community means anything, it is this.'[27] The Obama administration appears to have moved away from Bolton's cautious stance and Ambassador to the UN Susan Rice has clearly acknowledged that the 'international community' does bear a

---

[25] John R. Bolton, 'Letter from John R. Bolton, Representative of the USA to the UN, to Jean Ping, President of the UN General Assembly', 30 August 2005, http://www.un.int/usa/reform-un-jrb-ltr-protect-8-05.pdf. Reference to the 'international community's' use of 'diplomatic, humanitarian and other peaceful means, in accordance with Chapters VI and VIII of the Charter' was also adjusted from early drafts so that it was phrased as a 'responsibility' rather than an 'obligation'. Bolton had recommended the supposedly weaker phrase, 'moral responsibility'.

[26] In the first debate, for example, the US representative stressed: 'the primary responsibility for protecting civilians lies with States and their Governments and that international efforts should complement Government efforts rather than assume responsibility for them. Improving the protection of civilians from the devastating effects of armed conflict depends largely not on what we say or do here, but on what Governments do to protect their own people and on how they allow others to assist.' UN Document S/PV.5319 (Resumption 1), 9 December 2005, p. 8. In subsequent debates, the US acknowledged that, 'In situations where a State is unable or unwilling to protect its civilians, the international community has a distinct role', yet it refrained from suggesting that that 'role' amounted to a responsibility. UN Document S/PV.5577, 4 December 2006, p. 8, UN Document S/PV.5703, 22 June 2007, p. 9.

[27] Condoleezza Rice, 'Address to the Africa Society of the National Summit on Africa', (Washington, DC, 27 September 2006).

'responsibility' to take collective action if a state will not carry out its own responsibilities.[28] This idea has repeatedly been endorsed by other member states since the World Summit and also by Secretary-General Ki-moon and his special adviser on matters relating to R2P, Edward Luck. In the Secretary-General's January 2009 report on R2P, the role of the international community in taking collective action in response to the failure of states to carry out their obligations (pillar three of his 'three-pillar strategy') is clearly framed not merely as a right but as a responsibility.[29]

In sum, the idea that the international community bears a responsibility for the protection of populations was endorsed to a degree by member states at the 2005 World Summit,[30] and has been increasingly adopted in the discourse of states and other international actors. Of course, this development has occurred in clear tension with the continued reluctance among some states to agree that the international community possesses a right let alone a responsibility to interfere in the affairs of sovereign states without their consent, even when they have manifestly failed to protect their populations. This reluctance obviously restrains the development of the international community's R2P. Nevertheless, as the remaining sections of this chapter will demonstrate, moral, legal, and political forces have developed which to some degree do place a burden of *responsibility* on the international community to protect populations despite the ongoing objections of some that the society of states does not even possess a *right* to protect. This chapter now outlines each of these three aspects of the international community's R2P – the moral, the legal, and the political – in turn.

A moral responsibility to protect?

To be sure, the moral, legal, and political aspects of the international community's R2P cannot be easily separated and they tend to feed into each other. The morality of a given decision may be in part affected by existing legal

---

[28] Susan E. Rice, 'Remarks by Ambassador Susan E. Rice, U.S. Permanent Representative, on the UN Security Council and the Responsibility to Protect, at the International Peace Institute Vienna Seminar', (15 June 2009).

[29] 'Implementing the Responsibility to Protect: Report of the Secretary-General', p. 9.

[30] And it has arguably been implicitly endorsed in subsequent resolutions adopted by the Security Council and the General Assembly. See UNSC Resolution 1674, 28 April 2006, UNSC Resolution 1706, 31 August 2006, and most recently in UNGA Resolution 63/308, 14 September 2009.

obligations and conceivable political implications. International law is in part a product of moral beliefs and political calculations. And political obligations tend to be felt in part because of the social costs associated with violating prevailing understandings of morality or established legal principles. Nevertheless, I wish to suggest that our understanding of the international community's R2P can be advanced by distinguishing between these three categories. In this section I will briefly lay out some of the arguments both against and for the notion that the international community bears a *moral* responsibility to protect. I will also consider the notion suggested by some that, even if the international community does bear such a responsibility, it is an 'imperfect duty' that does not fall on any actor in particular.

Against the notion that either a particular state or the international community more broadly bears a moral responsibility to protect those beyond borders we find three well rehearsed arguments: pluralist, anti-imperialist, and realist. Pluralist or communitarian arguments suggest that we do not have a *right* to interfere in the affairs of other political communities and, by logical extension, neither do we possess a moral *responsibility* to interfere. Political communities should be allowed to express their own cultural values and pursue their own conception of the good life, free from the imposition of supposedly 'universal' western conceptions of how human rights should be promoted and defended.[31] Such arguments were commonly heard in debates about the rightfulness of humanitarian assistance and intervention the 1990s, but they appear to have been largely abandoned in recent years at least when the focus of discussion has been clearly restricted to instances of mass atrocity crimes such as those delineated in paragraphs 138-139 of the World Summit agreement. A related claim, and one which has been frequently leveled at the concept of R2P in recent years, holds that present day arguments in favour of interference in sovereign affairs for humanitarian purposes are merely updated versions of morally problematic nineteenth century arguments for imperialist and paternalist practices which were grounded in the specious notion that powerful Western states bore a 'burden of civilisation'.[32] The reply to this critique for the purposes of the present study is simply that the protection of populations by international actors is not inevitably an example

---

[31] See, for example, Robert H. Jackson, *The Global Covenant: Human Conduct in a World of States* (Oxford: Oxford University Press, 2000). See also the debate between Michael Walzer and his critics on 'the moral standing of states', discussed in Michael Walzer, 'The Moral Standing of States: A Response to Four Critics', *Philosophy and Public Affairs* 9/3 (1980).

[32] See, for example, statements by Noam Chomsky and General Assembly President Miguel d'Escoto Brockmann in 'Press Conference on General Assembly Dialogue on Responsibility to Protect', 23 July 2009, www.un.org/News/briefings/docs/2009/090723_GA.doc.htm.

of neo-imperialism, and the fact that the concept of R2P may be abused by some actors does not impact on the question about whether there are instances in which there does exist a moral obligation to act.

Potentially more persuasive is the realist or statist argument against the notion that the international community bears an R2P. This argument is promoted particularly by American officials and scholars who oppose the notion that the US may be bound to intervene where it does not wish to.[33] The argument goes that the moral responsibility of states is to pursue their national interests defined in terms of power,[34] and therefore it would be morally irresponsible for states to instead spend blood and treasure protecting those outside the state. This is a powerful moral argument which, as is noted below, cosmopolitan scholars seek to refute.

There is also a realist argument in *favour* of the notion that external actors are morally responsible for the protection of populations which has been frequently articulated, particularly since the terrorist attacks of 11 September 2001.[35] This argument holds that, in a globalising, interdependent world, states have a national interest and therefore a moral responsibility to protect those beyond borders since grave violations of human rights often spawn undesirable flows of refugees, conditions that facilitate arms and drug smuggling, the proliferation of weapons of mass destruction, and the spread of international terrorism which each pose a threat to international order and stability, and therefore the security of the state. This realist argument, however, suffers from a serious limitation in that while it may be persuasive in certain cases like a Kosovo, it will be less persuasive in other cases like a Rwanda in which the material self-interests of powerful states are not so clearly affected.

The stronger moral arguments in favour of the idea that the international community bears an R2P are grounded not in realism but in cosmopolitanism. Cosmopolitan scholars insist that our moral starting point should not be our national or statist allegiances but our common humanity. Martha Nussbaum, for example, argues that state boundaries are 'morally arbitrary' and insists that those in need of help who live beyond one's borders are no less deserving of one's assistance than those who live within them.[36] To the extent

---

[33] See, for example, Steven Groves, 'The U.S. Should Reject the U.N. "Responsibility to Protect" Doctrine', *Backgrounder* paper no. 2130, The Heritage Foundation (1 May 2008).

[34] See Hans J. Morgenthau, *Politics among Nations: The Struggle for Power and Peace*, Brief ed. (New York: Alfred A. Knopf, 1993), pp. 4-16.

[35] See, for example, Michael Wesley, 'Toward a Realist Ethics of Intervention', *Ethics and International Affairs* 19, no. 2 (2005).

[36] See Rajan Menon, 'Pious Words, Puny Deeds: The "International Community" and Mass Atrocities', *Ethics and International Affairs* 23/3 (2009). pp. 240-41.

that they have the capacity to provide protection, therefore, according to cosmopolitan logic, actors can be said to be obliged to protect those beyond borders by virtue of their common humanity. In a recent work, David Miller has laid out a position between realist or statist accounts and cosmopolitan accounts of responsibilities. In contrast to cosmopolitans, he argues that national identity *is* important and that actors bear special duties to co-nationals, but he also insists that, since peoples everywhere have certain basic needs, actors also have a separately derived responsibility to protect the human rights of those beyond the state.[37]

Now, even if we were to accept the notion that the international community bears a moral responsibility to protect, and I have by no means here offered a sufficient argument for why we should, there remains a possible shortcoming in that it may be a duty which falls on the international community in general, but not on any state in particular. As such, it may be what is known as an 'imperfect duty' since no one in particular is bound to act. As Michael Walzer observes:

> The general problem is that intervention, even when it is justified, even when it is necessary to prevent terrible crimes, even when it poses no threat to regional or global stability, is an imperfect duty – a duty that doesn't belong to any particular agent. Somebody ought to intervene but no specific state in the society of states is morally bound to do so.[38]

Kok-Chor Tan, however, has argued that there are two situations in which a responsibility to protect beyond borders may be considered to be perfect rather than imperfect. The first is if 'there is a capable agent who stands in a *special relationship* of some sort to the people needing the protection.'[39] This might include, for example, a former colonial power which is felt to continue to bear responsibilities with respect to the peace and stability of a former colony. The second is if 'there is an agent who is clearly the *most capable* among potential actors of successfully carrying out the protection duty.'[40] This might be a duty which arises due to geographical proximity or military capacity. To these two suggestions it might be added that some states bear a perfect duty to protect, or at least to facilitate protection, by virtue of their special status as great powers or membership of the permanent five. Further, it could be argued that a perfect duty could fall upon a regional organisation to respond to the

---

[37] David Miller, *National Responsibility and Global Justice* (Oxford: Oxford University Press, 2007).

[38] Michael Walzer, *Just and Unjust Wars*, 3rd ed. (New York: Basic Books, 2000), p. xiii.

[39] Tan, 'The Duty to Protect', p. 96.

[40] Ibid.

occurrence of mass atrocities or displacement within its region. Employing such ideas, we may be able to resolve what Tan terms 'the agency problem'. We can 'distinguish one potential agent from others as the proper agent to perform the duty.'[41] By identifying the specific agent or agents of protection, it is possible that the international community's duty to protect in a given situation may be 'perfected'.

Tan suggests that a further and surer way to solve the problem of specifying which agents bear the burden of the international community's R2P is to institutionalise the concept, and he argues that all members of the international community have an obligation to contribute to such institutionalisation.[42] What is needed, he suggests, is the 'institutionalisation of responsibilities through which the different requirements of the duty to protect are specified and assigned to specific states or international agencies, and each then can be morally bound (in other words, have a perfect duty) to carry out its assigned tasks.'[43] It is arguable that such a process of institutionalisation of R2P has begun and, if indeed the international community does bear a moral responsibility to protect, then as states, regional organisations, and international institutions continue to endorse the R2P and incorporate its principles into international charters and conventions, the international community's duty to protect may be increasingly considered to be a perfect duty which falls on particular agents in particular ways.

A legal responsibility to protect?

The legal dimension of the international community's R2P is rather unclear. While the notion that damages could be imposed as a result of a particular actor failing to forcibly intervene in the territory of a sovereign state in response to mass atrocities would seem to be out of the question at the present time, it would appear that particular actors in particular circumstances may bear some kind of legal responsibility to take measures to prevent the occurrence of a crime such as genocide. In this section, I will briefly note some relevant developments in international law and outline ongoing areas of contestation around the idea that the international community bears a legal responsibility to protect.

---

41 Ibid., p. 100.

42 Ibid., p. 104. See also Bagnoli, 'Humanitarian Intervention as a Perfect Duty'.

43 Tan, 'The Duty to Protect', p. 96.

From the outset, it is worth noting that it is doubtful that the 2005 World Summit agreement and the affirmation of this agreement in resolutions subsequently adopted by the Security Council and the General Assembly in themselves constitute new legal norms about the responsibilities of the international community to protect populations from genocide, ethnic cleansing, war crimes, and crimes against humanity. However, they may be rightly read as interpreting and clarifying existing international legal responsibilities and contributing to the gradual development of customary international law.[44] The place to begin when considering such existing legal obligations is the Genocide Convention.

As was noted earlier in this chapter, contracting parties to the Convention undertake in Article I 'to prevent and to punish' genocide. William Schabas suggests that the meaning of the word 'prevent' is 'Perhaps the greatest unresolved question in the Convention'.[45] The extent to which the provision imposes legal obligations upon states to act when genocide is either reasonably expected to occur or is already occurring outside of their territory has long been unclear. Conservative interpretations suggest that the Convention only requires states to enact appropriate domestic legislation and to take other measures to ensure that genocide does not occur *within* its territory. On the other hand, some view the Convention as demanding that states prevent genocide not only within their borders but *beyond* them, and with military force if necessary.[46] The only provision in the Convention which outlines how states might act to prevent genocide is Article VIII which suggests that they 'may call upon the competent organs of the United Nations to take such action under the Charter of the United Nations as they consider appropriate...' Yet, despite the lack of specificity, signatory states do undertake to prevent genocide's occurrence.

In 2007, in its *Bosnia v Serbia* decision, the International Court of Justice (ICJ) offered a nuanced yet wide reading of the obligations of states to prevent genocide outside of their territories under Article I of the Genocide Convention. The Court found that, while Serbia was not itself responsible for committing genocide, it was responsible for failing to prevent the occurrence of genocide in Srebrenica in 1995. The Court established that the duty to prevent extends beyond Article VIII of the Convention, and that 'the obligation of States is...to employ all means reasonably available to them, so as to prevent genocide as far as possible.' And responsibility was said to be

[44] Rosenberg, 'Responsibility to Protect', pp. 445-46.
[45] Schabas, *Genocide in International Law*, p. 545.
[46] Ibid., p. 546.

incurred 'if the State manifestly failed to take all measures to prevent genocide which were within its power, and which might have contributed to preventing the genocide.'[47]

The Court set forth 'various parameters' to assess whether or not a state had performed its responsibilities. One such parameter was whether the state bore the 'capacity to influence effectively the action of persons likely to commit, or already committing, genocide.'[48] This depended upon a range of criteria such as geographical proximity and the strength of political and other links between the state's authorities and the relevant actors.[49] The Court noted the influence wielded by Serbia over Bosnian Serb forces, and 'the strength of the political, military and financial links' between them, and concluded that Serbia's particular responsibility to prevent the genocide in Srebrenica was 'unlike that of any other States parties to the Genocide Convention.'[50] And since Serbia did not exercise 'due diligence' in seeking to prevent the atrocities, it was found to be in violation of Article I of the Convention.[51] Nevertheless, the ICJ did not assess reparations or damages in the case because it could not conclude 'with a sufficient degree of certainty that the genocide at Srebrenica would in fact have been averted if the Respondent had acted in compliance with its legal obligations.'[52]

On one hand, the emphasis placed by the ICJ on the particularly intimate relationship between Serbia and the Bosnian Serb forces that committed genocide might suggest that a high bar was set for a determination that a state could be found guilty of failing to act to prevent genocide. On the other hand, the Court's broad interpretation of the duties of states – 'to employ all means reasonably available to them' – has led some scholars to suggest that the judgment imposes legal responsibilities on *all* parties to the Genocide Convention, and perhaps even to the international community more broadly, to take every available measure to prevent instances of genocide.[53] Schabas, for example, has

[47] International Court of Justice, *Case Concerning the Application of the Convention on the Prevention and Punishment of the Crime of Genocide (Bosnia and Herzegovina v. Serbia and Montenegro)*, 26 February 2007, http://www.icj-cij.org/docket/files/91/13685.pdf, para. 430.

[48] Ibid.

[49] Ibid. A second parameter provided that the capacity of a state to prevent genocide was dependent upon relevant legal criteria, since 'every State may only act within the limits permitted by international law.'

[50] Ibid., para. 434.

[51] Ibid., para. 438.

[52] Ibid., para. 462.

[53] For a range of arguments along these lines, see Arbour, 'The Responsibility to Protect', Rosenberg, 'Responsibility to Protect', William A. Schabas, 'Genocide and the International Court of Justice: Finally, a Duty to Prevent the Crime of Crimes', *Genocide Studies and Prevention* 2/2 (2007).

observed that the Court's conclusion 'seems pregnant with potential for the promotion of human rights and the prevention of atrocities', and has wondered whether it could be rightly applied to the actions of France, Belgium and even the US with respect to the Rwandan genocide in 1994, or to particular states with respect to the atrocities committed more recently in Darfur.[54] Former High Commissioner for Human Rights, Louise Arbour, has considered the implications of the ICJ's judgment and suggested that members of the Security Council, particularly members of the permanent five, may bear a particularly heavy legal responsibility to ensure the prevention of mass atrocities due to the authority granted to them and their 'global reach'. She has even wondered whether the exercise of a veto by a member of the permanent five to block a resolution designed to contribute to the prevention of genocide may in itself constitute a violation of that state's obligations under the Genocide Convention.[55]

However, these kinds of legal arguments run into difficulties as the number of potentially responsible actors quickly multiplies and the already problematic issue of reparations becomes even more conspicuous. Take the Rwandan genocide for example. How might we determine which particular actors bear legal responsibility for the international community's failure to prevent the atrocities in 1994? Might it be the United Nations as a whole or perhaps just the Security Council? Should we treat these institutions collectively or does the responsibility fall on each individual state within them? Perhaps the responsibility is borne only by those states that had the capacity to deploy forces to protect the victims. Or perhaps it falls on the Secretary-General or other UN officials and departments. And do any or all of these actors owe Rwanda compensation for failing to discharge their obligations? Can other actors impose counter-measures on these actors?[56] Jose Alvarez puts the issue of enforcement well:

> If there is such a thing as a responsibility to protect, the legal mind naturally assumes that a failure to exercise such responsibility is an internationally wrongful act entailing the usual panoply of potential remedies, including the legal liability of the wrongful actor and the potential for countermeasures against that actor by others.[57]

[54] Schabas, 'Genocide and the International Court of Justice', p. 115. For similar suggestions, see Rosenberg, 'Responsibility to Protect', pp. 472-73.

[55] Arbour, 'The Responsibility to Protect', pp. 453-54.

[56] These questions are derived from Jose E. Alvarez, 'The Schizophrenias of R2P', in Philip Alston and Euan Macdonald (eds.), *Human Rights, Intervention, and the Use of Force* (Oxford: Oxford University Press, 2008), pp. 282-83.

[57] Ibid., p. 282.

If the ICJ was unable to assess reparations when finding one state to be so clearly in violation of its responsibility to prevent genocide, how much more difficult would it be to determine damages in a case where a multiplicity of actors were considered to be at fault?

Faced with such seemingly intractable issues, Alvarez recommends that we continue to work within the framework of the older principle of 'humanitarian intervention' which seeks to provide for the legality of intervention and the prevention of atrocities when states choose to act, rather than 'the far more slippery (and dangerous) concept of R2P' which seeks 'to require good Samaritans to act lest they be held legally "responsible".'[58]

It would seem that the extent to which the international community bears a legal responsibility to protect is likely to remain at best highly contested at least in the short term. Important developments have occurred in the realm of international law in recent years, but significant questions remain far from resolved, including how to determine who in particular bears the legal responsibility in a given situation and what remedies are available in instances where actors fail to discharge their obligations. Nevertheless, while the customary international legal obligations to protect populations which appear to be gradually developing may be essentially unenforceable at this stage, there are social and political costs to breaching international law, and these costs matter.[59] Here we are moving into the realm of the political aspect of the international community's R2P.

A political responsibility to protect?

In this final section, I wish to briefly consider the political or social dimension of the international community's R2P. This involves assessing the socio-political forces that to some extent persuade or compel states, regional organisations, and international institutions to respond to mass atrocities, mass displacement, and other instances of grave human suffering because to do otherwise would incur ideational costs which matter to these actors: it might weaken their authority in some way or undermine their domestic popularity or international legitimacy. This political aspect of the international

[58] Ibid., p. 283.

[59] Schabas suggests, 'the [ICJ's] refusal to award damages [in 2007] is likely to discourage future recourse based upon this obligation to prevent genocide. Rather, the court's pronouncement strengthens arguments in the political sphere, which is where genocide prevention really belongs.' Schabas, 'Genocide and the International Court of Justice', pp. 115-16.

community's R2P is distinct from the moral and legal aspect, but it is clear that developments in prevailing understandings of morality and accepted principles of international law feed into political arguments and can variously increase or decrease the socio-political pressures felt by actors to respond to atrocities.

This aspect of the international community's R2P has witnessed profound developments since the end of the Cold War. In the decades between the Second World War and 1990, the socio-political pressures felt by states, regional organisations and international institutions to interfere in the territories of sovereigns in response to mass atrocities and humanitarian crises was for the most part negligible because it was believed that they did not even possess the *right* to interfere, much less a *responsibility* to do so, under the UN Charter. Today, however, these actors regularly behave as though they recognise that they do have an obligation to act to assist and, in extreme cases, compel states to protect their populations.

We find evidence for the recognition of such a socio-political responsibility in three different forms. First, actors sometimes frame a crisis in a particular way so as to deny that a threshold for international involvement has yet been reached, thus implying that international involvement would be expected had the threshold been passed. As noted earlier, such behaviour was clearly seen in the response of the US and other actors in 1994 who sought to frame the violence in Rwanda as an intractable civil war about which the international community could do little, rather than a genocide in which hundreds of thousands of civilians were being slaughtered. It is arguable that such behaviour could also be found in the Security Council debates about the crisis in Darfur in 2004. In these debates, while some states argued that the international community bore a responsibility to assist and compel the Sudanese government to protect its population,[60] others opposed international involvement in the crisis on the grounds that the primary responsibility to protect 'still' lay with the Sudanese authorities, implicitly accepting that, if the crisis sufficiently worsened, the burden of responsibility would shift to the international community.[61]

Second, in instances where a threshold for international involvement does appear to have been reached, actors often seem to feel compelled to justify the sufficiency of whatever response they have taken. Individual states who feel particular obligations due to their proximity, material capability, special

---

[60] See statements by the Philippines in UN Document S/PV.5015, 30 July 2004, pp. 10-11, and by Romania in UN Document S/PV.5040, 18 September 2004, p. 12.

[61] See the statement by Russia in UN Document S/PV.5040, p. 4.

relationship, or special status as great powers, often inform their domestic constituents and also the society of states that they are doing all that they can, thus implying that they possess not merely a right but a responsibility to take all possible measures to prevent atrocities. In 2006, for example, US President Bush repeatedly responded to questions about the policy of the US towards the crisis in Darfur by emphasising that the US was the only state to have called the situation 'genocide', thus tacitly acknowledging a responsibility to respond to the crisis and shifting the blame to other states that were yet to recognise the seriousness of the situation.[62] Regional organisations such as the African Union and ASEAN similarly appear to acknowledge that they need to demonstrate that they are undertaking meaningful responses to crises within their region, such as those that have recently occurred in Darfur, Zimbabwe, and Burma, in order to retain a reputation within the international community as able defenders of regional peace, stability, and human rights, and to justify their opposition to involvement in the crisis from the broader international community. Rather than insisting that they have the prerogative to deal with crises as they see fit, as they once did, they seem to increasingly recognise a need to at least appear to perform the role of assisting and pressuring states and even enforcing the protection of populations. Further, it is arguable that the behaviour of international institutions such as the Security Council at times reveals an awareness that they need to demonstrate that they are taking crises seriously, and that their responses to crises that are perceived by some to be inadequate are in fact justifiable, in order to retain their own legitimacy as bodies that represent the will of the international community. Third, in instances where actors do undertake a meaningful response to a humanitarian crisis, they typically justify it in terms of their responsibilities rather than their rights. However, such language is likely for rhetorical effect and probably does not represent clear evidence that the force of such responsibilities persuaded them to act.

Of course, while the social and political responsibilities felt by actors in the international community does seem to have an increasing impact on the way they behave, any claims about the force of these responsibilities must be tempered by the reality that meaningful responses to mass atrocities and humanitarian crises too often simply do not occur. This is partly because the felt international and domestic pressures to act often remain too weak to compel action. And it is also partly because a number of states, including two of the permanent five, continue to oppose even the *right* of non-consensual interfer-

[62] See Glanville, 'Is "Genocide" Still a Powerful Word?'

ence by the international community in the affairs of states in response to such crimes.[63] This ongoing resistance to non-consensual measures aimed at assisting and compelling the protection of populations provides other actors with an excuse for inaction and is at times a very real impediment to action. It limits the extent to which the ideational pressures felt by some are translated into a meaningful response to suffering. Nevertheless, the development in the political aspect of the international community's R2P is significant. Language matters. The justifications that actors offer for their behaviour restrains, enables, and at times compels them to act in certain ways. Perhaps the fact that the scope of available justifications for inaction in the face of mass suffering has seemingly declined points to a gradual entrenchment of the socio-political notion that the international community bears a responsibility to protect which must be performed.

Conclusion

In conclusion, the notion that the international community bears an R2P can be fruitfully conceptualised in terms of its three key aspects – moral, legal, and political. Each of these dimensions of international responsibility bears serious limitations and is the site of ongoing contestation. Yet, understanding each is important if we are to begin to clarify who in particular bears the responsibility and to what extent we can reasonably expect it to be performed. While powerful counter-arguments continue to be advanced, there is a strong argument to be made for the idea that the international community bears a *moral* responsibility to protect populations which can be rightly understood as a perfect duty that falls on particular actors. Further, the ICJ has confirmed that particular actors within the international community may bear a *legal* responsibility to prevent the occurrence of genocide, though serious questions remain about the range of actors upon which this responsibility may fall and the remedies available in those instances where actors fail to discharge their obligations. These moral and legal aspects of the international community's R2P feed into the *political* aspect which has developed in profound ways over the

[63] The two members of the permanent five that continue to oppose non-consensual interference in the affairs of functioning states in response to mass atrocities and humanitarian crises are China and Russia. See, amongst numerous examples, the statement by China in UN Document S/PV.5898 (27 May 2008), p. 9, and the statement by Russia in UN Document S/PV.5577 (Resumption 1) (4 December 2006), p. 8. It is, however, difficult to reconcile Russia's position here with its appeals to R2P principles when seeking justify its invasion of Georgia in 2008.

last twenty years. Individual states, regional organisations, and international institutions have increasingly demonstrated that they recognise that they bear an obligation to either respond in a meaningful way to mass atrocities and humanitarian crises or to provide a reasonable justification for inaction. The international community's response to the problem of grave human suffering continues to be too often inadequate. Yet it would seem that an argument can be made that the international community does bear a moral, legal, and political responsibility to protect which does matter and which merits close study.

Conclusion

Luke Glanville and Sara E. Davies

In his January 2009 report, 'Implementing the Responsibility to Protect', UN Secretary General Ban Ki-moon noted that the protection of refugees and the internally displaced were important goals tied to R2P.[1] The Secretary General has suggested that the time has come for the international community to translate R2P from words to deeds. It would seem that the improvement of the protection of displaced persons ought to be a central component of this task.

How useful a concept is R2P for advancing the protection of refugees and IDPs? What challenges confront attempts to reconcile R2P and the protection of the displaced? How might these challenges be overcome? These are the kinds of questions that have motivated the contributors to this volume. The volume has brought together some of the leading thinkers and practitioners on refugee, IDP and R2P issues in order to examine the relationship between R2P and the protection of the displaced, and to consider the conceptual and practical challenges that confront the international community if R2P is to add value to efforts to protect displaced persons.

In this conclusion, we want to very briefly draw some of the threads together and outline some of the broad themes of discussion in the preceding chapters about the relationship between R2P and the protection of refugees and IDPs.

A number of contributors to this volume considered the conceptual dilemmas involved in linking R2P to IDP and refugee protection. Susan Martin and Roberta Cohen reflected on the history of protection, outlining how the scope of the protection regime has expanded since the end of the Cold War to include not just refugees who have crossed state boundaries but those who are internally displaced. This prompted consideration about how wide the umbrella of protection ought to extend (Roberta Cohen, Sara Davies), what contribution R2P could make in this regard (Erin Mooney), and what this should mean for the responsibilities of both sovereign states and international organisations (Luke Glanville, Emma Haddad, Phil Orchard, Alex Bellamy and Paul Williams).

[1] 'Implementing the Responsibility to Protect', UN Document A/63/677, 12 January 2009, para. 68.

A number of contributors reflected on the intellectual debt owed by R2P to the work done by Francis Deng and others in the 1990s who developed the concept of 'sovereignty as responsibility' when working to persuade both governments and the international community to improve the protection of IDPs. These historical ties between the framework for IDP protection and R2P have led some observers to expect that R2P will enhance efforts to protect IDPs. Erin Mooney has offered a cautious endorsement of this view. Mooney noted that each of the four crimes with which R2P is concerned – genocide, ethnic cleansing, war crimes, and crimes against humanity – invariably create displacement, and thus the implementation of R2P could go a long way to averting displacement and improving the protection of those who are displaced. Further, Mooney observed that the natural compatibility between the R2P and IDP protection frameworks holds the promise of mutually beneficial coordination of protection efforts.

However, key differences between the two frameworks means that R2P can offer 'only a partial response' to addressing the problem of displacement. Mooney outlined differences between the frameworks in terms of their scope and purpose and also the divergent degrees to which they have each achieved political traction and been implemented in practice. In a similar vein, Roberta Cohen argued that it was by no means inevitable that R2P would enhance efforts to protect the displaced. Indeed, Cohen insisted, it is conceivable that there may be situations in which the application of R2P worsens the plight of existing IDPs and also creates more displacement.

Cohen suggested a number of conceptual and practical challenges that have hampered the extent to which R2P has offered a contribution to the protection of IDPs to date, which other authors picked up in their chapters. One such challenge is the fact that the narrowing of the scope of R2P at the 2005 World Summit to four key crimes has meant that R2P speaks to some but not all causes of displacement. In her own chapter, Sara Davies paid particular attention to the question about whether R2P can contribute to the protection of those who are displaced by natural disasters. Davies found that while the concept of sovereignty as responsibility underpins both the R2P and protection of person principles, they are at different purposes and stages of implementation. R2P is concerned with deepening the commitment that states have made to protecting individuals against mass atrocities and genocide. The protection of persons agenda is yet to gain acceptance by states and there is no evidence to suggest that this cause would be helped by aligning it with R2P.

Other challenges suggested by Cohen include the continued equation of R2P with military intervention in some quarters, and also the practical limits to the benefits that such intervention can offer to IDPs. With respect to the question of intervention, Phil Orchard pondered whether we can expect the international community to ever undertake military intervention to protect populations in response to regime induced displacement. He observed that the Security Council has long been reluctant to authorise military intervention in response to such displacement without the consent of the host state. This reluctance poses a profound obstacle to the international enforcement of R2P with respect to displaced persons. In a related vein, Luke Glanville considered how the idea that the international community itself bears not merely a right but a responsibility to act when states fail to perform their R2P might be fruitfully understood. In particular, he contemplated questions about what kind of responsibility this might be and who in particular might bear it. In her contribution, Emma Haddad contemplated another related and pertinent question: what responsibilities do receiving states have for those fleeing R2P situations? Haddad considered EU protection policies in this regard, revealing divergent approaches to both the concept of 'responsibility' and the concept of 'protection'. Finally, Bellamy and Williams noted the conceptual incoherence and poor implementation of existing policies to protect civilians in armed conflict. They outlined a framework for thinking about the many dimensions that need to be addressed if a comprehensive civilian protection agenda is to be developed, and they offered a number of suggestions for further research in this area.

Mooney rightly concluded that the focus on R2P 'must not overshadow the fact that a more extensive set of protection responsibilities exist, which also must be realised and often are equally demanding of attention and response.' Secretary General Ban Ki-moon has concurred, noting that the development of R2P ought not to detract 'from the much broader range of obligations existing under international humanitarian law, international human rights law, refugee law and international criminal law.'[2] It is important to keep this in mind. The concept of R2P by no means exhausts the range of responsibilities that sovereign states and also the international community are required to perform if the suffering of displaced persons is to be alleviated.

Nevertheless, R2P can offer an important contribution to the protection of the displaced, though such a contribution is by no means guaranteed. As Cohen argues, if a goal of R2P is to protect displaced persons, we must continue to strive to ensure that R2P strategies are tailored to suit their needs. To this end, contributors to this volume have offered a range of strategies to overcome the conceptual, political, and practical challenges faced in reconciling R2P with IPD protection. Such strategies include tempering the stretch of R2P to every situation involving displacement and, instead, considering how

---

[2] Ibid., para. 3.

existing international law and principles could guide more directed action to the needs of the vulnerable; a greater focus on what economic, social, and governance measures prevent states from experiencing situations where displacement becomes a precursor or symptom of mass atrocities; and following on from this second point, more investigation on the precise nature of the international community's financial and political responsibility to proactively engage with preventative policies and, when this fails, their responsibility to protect displaced populations. If R2P is to add value to efforts to protect refugees and the internally displaced, it is crucial that such strategies be examined further and, where appropriate, implemented. R2P promises much for the protection of the displaced. But if present challenges are not adequately addressed, there is a risk that it will deliver little.

This volume is offered as an attempt to advance the discussion of the value that R2P offers to the protection of IDPs and refugees, to clarify existing challenges, and to take some steps towards solving them. It is our hope that it can make some contribution, however small, towards the goal of protecting the displaced.

Index

www.ingramcontent.com/pod-product-compliance
Lightning Source LLC
Chambersburg PA
CBHW052044200926
51615CB00031B/22
* 9 7 8 9 0 0 4 1 8 4 0 3 9 *